21世纪商务英语系列教材

国际贸易实务

International Trade Practice

总主编　蒋　磊
主　编　丁静辉　杜国荣
副主编　崔向红　李　凌　邢春丽
编　者　张雪梅　邢　琰　蒋　磊　丁静辉
　　　　杜国荣　崔向红　李　凌　邢春丽

图书在版编目(CIP)数据

国际贸易实务 / 丁静辉,杜国荣主编. —北京:北京大学出版社,2007.12
(21世纪商务英语系列教材)
ISBN 978-7-301-12703-2

Ⅰ. 国…　Ⅱ. ①丁… ②杜…　Ⅲ. 国际贸易-贸易实务-高等学校-教材-英文　Ⅳ. F740.4

中国版本图书馆 CIP 数据核字(2007)第 135276 号

书　　　名:	国际贸易实务
著作责任者:	丁静辉　杜国荣　主编
责 任 编 辑:	李　颖
标 准 书 号:	ISBN 978-7-301-12703-2/H·1832
出 版 发 行:	北京大学出版社
地　　　址:	北京市海淀区成府路 205 号　100871
网　　　址:	http://www.pup.cn
电　　　话:	邮购部 62752015　发行部 62750672　编辑部 62767347　出版部 62754962
电 子 邮 箱:	zbing@pup.pku.edu.cn
印 　刷 　者:	北京大学印刷厂
经 　销 　者:	新华书店
	787 毫米×1092 毫米　16 开本　17 印张　400 千字
	2007 年 12 月第 1 版　2014 年 1 月第 2 次印刷
定　　　价:	30.00 元

未经许可,不得以任何方式复制或抄袭本书之部分或全部内容。
版权所有,侵权必究　举报电话:010-62752024
　　　　　　　　　　　电子邮箱:fd@pup.pku.edu.cn

《21世纪商务英语系列教材》编审委员会

(按姓氏笔画为序)
王立非（对外经济贸易大学 英语学院院长）
王晓红（中央财经大学 外国语学院院长）
王晓群（上海财经大学 外语系主任）
邓　海（西南财经大学 语言文化学院院长）
田海龙（天津商业大学 外国语学院院长）
许德金（对外经济贸易大学 英语学院通用英语系主任）
林　立（首都经济贸易大学 外语系主任）
修月祯（北京第二外国语学院 国际经济贸易学院副院长）
黄振华（中央财经大学 外国语学院副院长）

Acknowledgements

We are indebted, mainly for the reading selections, to many sources. We have put forth the fullest effort to trace each and every source, and their origins and our acknowledgements are indicated within the book. However, a small number of copyright materials remain uncredited because the original copyright holders could not be located, or we were unable to establish communication with them. It may be the case that some unintentional omissions have occurred in the employment of some copyright materials. We are grateful to these authors and sources, and we apologize for not being able to extend our acknowledgements in detail. For any questions concerning copyrights and permissions, please contact

Copyrights Department
Peking University Press
Beijing, 100871
P. R. China
Telephone: +86 10 62752036
Fax: +86 10 62556201
Email: xiena@pup.pku.edu.cn

We are much obliged for any information concerned and will make necessary arrangements for the appropriate settlement of any possible copyright issue.

前言

融入经济全球化大潮中的中国同世界各国的经济合作和贸易往来日益增加。中国已成为世界排名第三的贸易大国,国际贸易在国民经济中正在发挥着越来越大的作用。快速运行的全球经济和日益频繁的对外经济贸易都呼唤既有娴熟的外语语言技能、又有商贸专业知识的复合型人才。这种需求是单纯的语言型外语专业或外语能力水平单一的专业教育所不能满足的。在全球经济互动的形势下,"专业+英语"或"英语+专业"的复合型人才将在未来的竞争中处于优势,商务英语或经贸英语作为以国际商务为语言背景的应用性学科,已成为一门备受人们青睐的热门专业。目前国内许多大学实行了"英语+商务专业"的办学方针和复合型人才培养模式;同样,也有许多大学将其专业教学计划细化为"专业主干课程+英语"的课程体系,实行双语教学。不管是"商务英语"或"经贸英语"还是其他专业课程试行的"双语教学",其根本教学目标是相同的,即增强学生直接使用英语从事国际经贸的涉外能力、适应能力以及国际商务实战能力。商务人员希望通过对"商务英语"这一学科的学习提高英语的实际运用能力;英语专业的学生希望通过对该学科的学习,熟悉和掌握基本的商务专业知识。同样,财经专业的学生渴望通过"双语教学"模式同时提高其专业水平和英语水平,以及直接使用英语从事相关专业。为了满足国际贸易迅猛发展的新形势需要,我们编写了这套英文版《商务英语》系列教材,《国际贸易实务》是这套商务英语系列书中的专业核心教材之一。

《国际贸易实务》是一门主要研究国际商品交换具体过程的学科,也是一门实践性很强的综合性应用学科;它既是国际商务学科体系中的一门基础课程,又是商务英语专业的骨干支撑课程。该课程的主要任务是,针对国际贸易的特点和要求,从实践的角度,分析研究与国际贸易有关的国际惯例和国际商品交换过程的各种实际运作,以便掌握从事国际贸易的"生意经",学会在进出口业务中,既能正确贯彻我国对外贸易的方针政策和经营意图,确保最佳经济效益,又能按国际规范办事。本书以进出口贸易(主要是货物贸易)

的主要业务环节为主线,系统介绍了各环节的操作规程和国际惯例。全书采用英文编写,旨在使学生在国际经贸英语的语言环境中直接、系统地学习国际贸易专业的基本理论和知识,了解不同人文背景下商贸活动的规范以及具体操作实务,并通过对国际经贸知识的学习,强化商务英语这一专门用途英语的技能,掌握商务领域的英语术语、文体和语言特点,从而提高学习者用英语分析和处理商贸业务的能力。基于这种理念,本教材在编写设计时特别注意把握好商贸活动主题的涵盖面、商贸知识的系统性与完整性,以及语言技能与商贸知识的平衡,力求体现语言技能的训练与商贸知识的学习融为一体,以期达到使选用本教材的学生及相关人员在英语应用能力及商贸专业知识方面均获得提高,实现复合型人才的培养目标。

❖ **教材结构安排**:全书共14章,涵盖国际贸易概述、国际贸易形式、国际贸易实务、国际贸易术语、国际销售合同、商品术语(产品的名称、质量和数量、包装和唛头)、进出口单证、国际货物运输、国际货运保险、国际贸易支付、保险、检验、索赔、不可抗力和仲裁、海外营销机构、国际商务、关贸协定与WTO的基本知识等内容,全面系统地介绍了国际贸易的基本环节和操作规范。

❖ **章节体例安排**:

学习要点(Focal Learning):每章开始的学习目标,简明扼要的概括出本章节的知识点,使学习者在开始学习之前对本章节有个全面的概括性了解,明确重点、难点,便于有的放矢地学习。

生词(Lead-in Vocabulary):课文中出现的主要生词,以帮助学习者排除课文学习的困难,学习掌握一些词汇的常用的意义和用法。

课文:以国贸业务环节为主线分别介绍各环节的操作规程和国际惯例,使学生在学习完课文后对专业术语、英语相关表达方式和专业知识有个全面而清楚的了解。此内容均选自较为权威的书籍和刊物。

常用词组、专业术语及注释:针对相关专业词组和术语以及较难句子的翻译和解释,以帮助学生理解各种专业术语的表达方法,使学生在正确理解文章含义的基础上,学习专业知识。

实践练习(Practical Drills):包括问题讨论、案例分析和角色扮演。贸易实务的学习必须有实际案例作分析。结合各章节的知识点,精心挑选了进出口业务中的经典实际案例来进行分析,可以使学生将知识与实际联系起来,更为客观和理性地处理进出口业务中的问题,从而学到了"活"知识。

拓展练习(Extended Activities)：为使学生真正把所学的知识灵活地运用到专业实践中，每章后面都附有针对性的练习，帮助学生巩固基本词汇、专业术语和相关专业基础知识，强化学生对专业知识点的理解和运用。

◆ **本书具有以下特点：**

1. 英语和专业知识融为一体：本教材兼有英语语言能力训练与商务谈判专业知识的介绍双重任务。在内容安排上给学生提供了充足的语言材料和相关情景，同时又以清晰的专业理论讲解为基础，使学生在掌握了理论知识的基础上，学习词汇和句型，力求达到学以致用的目的。

2. 结构合理，体系完整新颖：本教材强调核心技能培养的渗透性，按照教学流程设计编写体例，循序渐进、潜移默化地培养学生的专业核心技能和语言实际运用能力。教学活动设计充分体现讲练结合原则、任务教学原则、师生互动原则和实践性原则。

3. 案例丰富实践性强：本教材突出"案例导向"和"实践导向"的编写思路。各章都有具体的案例分析和实践活动，增强了可读性、实务性和可操作性。全方位、多功能地培养学生综合素质。

4. 针对性强、适用面广：本教材既可作为高等院校"商务英语或经贸英语"专业学生等复合型英语专业英语教材，亦可供国际贸易、国际营销、工商管理、国际商务、国际企业管理、国际金融等专业本、专科生、非英语专业硕士研究生等专业方向的学生作为双语教材使用。本教材对相关专业的成人教育和职业培训的学生以及经贸、金融、国际商务从业人员强化国际商务英语能力具有一定的借鉴价值。

5. 英语表述简明易懂、选材新颖：每章课文后配有相关知识点的强化训练和练习并辅以参考答案。

本册书参编人员具体分工如下

李　凌　第1—2章

张雪梅　第3—4章

蒋　磊　邢春丽　第5—6章

杜国荣　第7—8章

崔向红　第9—10章

邢　琰　第11章及附录

丁静辉　第12—14章及练习答案

本书的出版得到了北京大学出版社的鼎力支持和热情帮助，在此我们表示衷心的谢忱。

在本书编写过程中,我们参考并借鉴了国内外出版的有关书籍和资料,www.moftec.gov.cn,www.cietac.org.cn,www.iccwbo.org,www.unctad.org,www.wto.org 等网站的资料,以及其他商业网站和国际著名跨国公司网站的资料,在此一并致谢。

由于编者水平有限,书中不当之处恐在所难免,敬请国内外专家、学者和广大读者不吝指正。

编　者
2007 年 7 月

Contents

Chapter 1 An Overview of the International Trade ········· 1
  Section I Reasons for the International Trade ················· 2
    1. Resources Reasons ··· 2
    2. Economic Reasons ··· 2
    3. Other Reasons ·· 4
  Section II The International Trade Policy ························ 5
    1. Gains from Free Trade ·· 5
    2. Different Means of Protection ······························ 6
  Section III The History and Role of the Chinese International Trade ········· 9
    1. The Period between 1950—1976 ···························· 9
    2. The Period after 1976 ·· 10
  Practical Drills ··· 12
    ❖ Case Study—Favorable Balance of Trade vs. Unfavorable Balance of Trade ········· 12
    ❖ Role Play—Establishing Business Relations ················ 13
  Extended Activities ·· 14

Chapter 2 The International Trade Forms ···················· 17
  Section I Selling Agent, Distribution, Consignment and International Subcontracting ······ 18
    1. Selling Agent ·· 18
    2. Distribution ·· 18
    3. Consignment ·· 18
    4. International Subcontracting ································· 19
  Section II Tender ··· 19
    1. Invitation for Bids ·· 20
    2. Submission of Bids ·· 21

Section III　International Counter-trade ······ 22
　　1. Barter Trade ······ 23
　　2. Compensation Agreement ······ 23
　　3. Buy Back ······ 24
　　4. Counter-purchase ······ 24

Section IV　International Technology Transfer and International Technology Licensing ······ 25
　　1. International Technology Transfer ······ 25
　　2. International Technology Licensing ······ 25

Practical Drills ······ 27
　　❖ Case Study—Confirming Offer ······ 28
　　❖ Role Play—Tender and Biding ······ 28

Extended Activities ······ 29

Chapter 3　General Introduction to International Trade Practices ······ 32

Section I　The Definition of Export Transaction ······ 33
　　1. Reasons for Exporting ······ 33
　　2. Definition of Exporting ······ 33

Section II　The Conduct of Export Transaction ······ 34
　　1. Preparation for Exporting ······ 34
　　2. Business Negotiation ······ 35
　　3. Implementation of Contract ······ 35
　　4. Settlement of Disputes ······ 36

Section III　The Parties and Means in the Export Transaction ······ 37
　　1. Basic Parties in the Export Transaction ······ 37
　　2. Other Major Parties and Means in the Export Transaction ······ 37

Practical Drills ······ 39
　　❖ Case Study—Compensation Trade ······ 40
　　❖ Role Play—Talking with a Potential Client ······ 40

Extended Activities ······ 41

Chapter 4　International Trade Terms ······ 45

Section I　Brief Explanations of Trade Terms ······ 46
　　1. International Trade Terms ······ 46
　　2. International Rules and Practices on Trade Terms ······ 47

Contents

Section II   Contents of Trade Terms 48
    1. An Overview of the Structure of Incoterms 2000 48
    2. A Brief Explanation of Terms in Incoterms 2000 49
    3. Comparison between FCA/CPT/CIP and the Traditional FOB/CFR/CIF 53

Section III   Expression and Choice of Trade Terms 53
    1. Expression of Trade Terms 54
    2. Choice of Trade Terms 54

Practical Drills 56
    ❖ Case Study 1—FOB (Incoterms 2000) 56
    ❖ Case Study 2—Why to Send Shipping Advice? 56
    ❖ Role Play—Price Negotiation 57

Extended Activities 57

Chapter 5   International Sales Contract 61

Section I   Definition and Contents of International Sales Contracts 62
    1. Definition of International Sales Contracts 62
    2. Contents of a Sales Contract 63
    3. Major Terms of a Sales Contract 64

Section II   Formation of International Sales Contract 66
    1. Inquiry 67
    2. Offer 67
    3. Counter-offer 68
    4. Acceptance 69
    5. Signing of the Contract 69

Section III   Implementation of the Contract 70
    1. Cargo Readiness 71
    2. Examination of L/C and Amendment to L/C 71

Practical Drills 74
    ❖ Case Study 1—Offer 74
    ❖ Case Study 2—Acceptance 75
    ❖ Role Play—On Terms and Conditions of the Contract 75

Extended Activities 77

Chapter 6　Terms of Commodity　81
Section I　Name of Commodity　82
Section II　Quality of Commodity　83
　　1. Sales by Seller's Sample and Sales by Buyer's Sample　83
　　2. Sales by Description　84
Section III　Quantities of Commodity　85
　　1. Units of Measurement　85
　　2. Calculation of Weight　85
Section IV　Packing of Commodity　86
　　1. Outer Packing　86
　　2. Inner Packing　88
Section V　Marking of Commodity　89
　　1. Shipping Marks　89
　　2. Indicative and Warning Marks　90
　　3. Additional Marks　91
Practical Drills　92
　　❖ Case Study—Dealing with Cartons Damaged　92
　　❖ Role Play—Packing　93
Extended Activities　94

Chapter 7　Export and Import Documentations　96
Section I　Role and Requirements of Documentation　97
　　1. Role of Documentation　97
　　2. Requirements for Documentation　97
Section II　Official Documents　98
　　1. Export License　98
　　2. Import License and Foreign Authorization　99
　　3. Certificate of Origin　99
　　4. Certificate of Inspection　99
　　5. Consular Invoice　100
　　6. Customs Invoice　100
Section III　Commercial Documents　100
　　1. Pro Forma Invoice　100
　　2. Commercial Invoice　101
　　3. Quality Certificate　101

Contents

  4. Weight Certificate ……………………………………………………… 102
Section IV   Financial Documents ……………………………………… 102
  1. Application Form for International Money Transfer ………………… 102
  2. Drafts …………………………………………………………………… 103
  3. Application for Documentary Letter of Credit ……………………… 104
  4. Letter of Credit ………………………………………………………… 104
Section V   Transportation Documents ………………………………… 104
  1. Bill of Lading …………………………………………………………… 105
  2. Shipping Note ………………………………………………………… 105
  3. Packing List …………………………………………………………… 105
  4. Rail Consignment Note ……………………………………………… 106
  5. Road Consignment Note ……………………………………………… 106
  6. Air Waybill …………………………………………………………… 107
  7. Combined Transport Document ……………………………………… 107
  8. Arrival Notification …………………………………………………… 107
Section VI   Insurance Documents ……………………………………… 107
  1. Insurance Policy ……………………………………………………… 108
  2. Insurance Certificate ………………………………………………… 108
  3. Open Policy …………………………………………………………… 108
Section VII   Specimens …………………………………………………… 109
  1. Import and Export Licenses ………………………………………… 109
  2. Certificate of Origin …………………………………………………… 110
  3. Certificate of Inspection ……………………………………………… 111
  4. Pro Forma Invoice …………………………………………………… 112
  5. Commercial Invoice …………………………………………………… 113
  6. Draft (Bill of Exchange) ……………………………………………… 114
  7. Bill of Lading …………………………………………………………… 115
  8. Packing List …………………………………………………………… 116
  9. Insurance Policy/Certificate ………………………………………… 117
  10. Customs Declaration Form ………………………………………… 118

Practical Drills ……………………………………………………………………… 121
  ❖ Case Study—The Advising Bank's Refusal ………………………… 121
  ❖ Role Play—Talking about Credit Card ……………………………… 122
Extended Activities ………………………………………………………………… 123

Chapter 8 International Cargo Transportation ... 126
Section I Ocean Freight ... 127
   1. Conference Shipping ... 127
   2. Non-conference Line Vessels ... 128
   3. Tramp Ships ... 128
   4. Chartered Ships ... 129
Section II Air Transport ... 130
   1. Scheduled Airlines ... 130
   2. Chartered Carriers ... 130
   3. Consolidated Consignments ... 131
Section III Other Means of International Cargo Transportation ... 131
   1. Road Transport ... 131
   2. Rail Transport ... 131
   3. Inland Waterway Transport ... 132
   4. Containerization ... 132
   5. Palletization ... 132
   6. Pipelines ... 133
   7. International Multimodal Transport ... 133
Practical Drills ... 135
   ❖ Case Study—What Would the Exporter Do? ... 135
   ❖ Role Play—Late Delivery ... 135
Extended Activities ... 136

Chapter 9 International Cargo Transportation Insurance ... 138
Section I Fundamental Concepts in the International Cargo Insurance ... 139
   1. Parties Involved ... 139
   2. Insured Amount ... 140
   3. Premium ... 140
   4. Insurance Policy ... 140
Section II Marine Transportation Insurance ... 141
   1. Risks Covered by Marine Insurance ... 141
   2. Losses Covered by Marine Insurance ... 141
   3. Expenses Incurred for the Rescue of Insured Cargo ... 142
   4. Major Categories of General Insurance Coverage ... 142
   5. Procedures of Marine Insurance ... 143
Section III Insurance of Land, Air and Postal Transportation ... 145
   1. Insurance Coverage for Land Transportation ... 145
   2. Insurance Coverage for Air Transportation ... 145
   3. Parcel Post Insurance ... 146

Practical Drills 147
- Case Study—Refusal of Compensation 147
- Role Play—An Exporter Discusses Insurance of an Order with a Buyer 148

Extended Activities 149

Chapter 10 International Trade Payment 152

Section I   Payment Instruments of International Trade 153
1. Bill of Exchange 153
2. Promissory Notes 154
3. Cheques 154

Section II   Methods of Payment 155
1. Remittance 155
2. Collection 157
3. Letter of Credit 159
4. Banker's Letter of Guarantee 161

Section III   Terms of Payment in the Sales Contract 161
1. Payment by Remittance 161
2. Payment by Collection 162
3. Payment by the Letter of Credit 162

Practical Drills 163
- Case Study 1—A FOB Contract 164
- Case Study 2—Letter of Credit 164
- Role Play—Decision on Mode of Payment 166

Extended Activities 166

Chapter 11 Inspection, Force Majeure, Claim and Arbitration 170

Section I   Commodity Inspection 171
1. Necessity of Commodity Inspection 171
2. Time and Place of Inspection 171
3. Inspection Agency and Certificate 173

Section II   Force Majeure 173
1. Concept of Force Majeure 173
2. Consequences of Force Majeure 174

Section III   Claim 174
1. The Definition of Claim 174
2. Settlement of Claim 175

Section IV   Arbitration 175
1. Procedures of Arbitration 175
2. Cost of Arbitration 176

Practical Drills 178
    ❖ Case Study—Arbitration of Dispute 178
    ❖ Role Play—Damage 179
Extended Activities 179

Chapter 12 Marketing Organizations Abroad 182

Section I Agency Arrangements 183
    1. Self-employed Agents Abroad 183
    2. The Nature of the Contract of Agency 183
    3. The Agent's Authority 184
    4. Rights and Obligations of the Agent and the Principal 185
    5. Special Types of the Agents 186

Section II Branch Offices and Subsidiaries Abroad 188
    1. General Understanding of Branch Offices and Subsidiaries Abroad 188
    2. Dealings between Branch Offices Abroad 189
    3. Subsidiary Companies Abroad 189

Section III Sole Distribution Agreements, Licensing Agreements and Franchising 190
    1. Sole Distribution Agreements 191
    2. Licensing Agreements 193
    3. Franchising 193

Practical Drills 195
    ❖ Case Study—Sole Agency Agreement 195
    ❖ Role Play—Joint Venture 197
Extended Activities 197

Chapter 13 E-commerce 200

Section I E-commerce and Its Historical Development 201
    1. E-commerce 201
    2. Historical Development of E-commerce 201

Section II Major Categories of E-commerce 202
    1. Business-to-business (B2B) E-commerce 202
    2. Business-to-consumer E-commerce 202
    3. Consumer-to-consumer E-commerce 202
    4. Consumer-to-business E-commerce 203
    5. Government-to-citizen E-commerce 203
    6. Government-to-business E-commerce 203

Section III Business Process and Models of E-commerce 203

Contents

    1. Business Process of E-commerce ⋯⋯ 203
    2. Business Models of E-commerce ⋯⋯ 204

Section IV   Advantages of E-commerce ⋯⋯ **205**
    1. Low Operating Cost ⋯⋯ 205
    2. Large Purchase Per Transaction ⋯⋯ 206
    3. Integration of Business Procedures ⋯⋯ 206
    4. Flexibility and Availability of Information ⋯⋯ 206
    5. Improved Interactions ⋯⋯ 206

Section V   Limitations of E-commerce ⋯⋯ **207**
    1. Technical Limitations ⋯⋯ 207
    2. Non-technical Limitations ⋯⋯ 207

Practical Drills ⋯⋯ **210**
    ❖ Case Study—Dell Computer: E-commerce in Action ⋯⋯ 210
    ❖ Role Play—Talking about Order On-line ⋯⋯ 211

Extended Activities ⋯⋯ **211**

Chapter 14 Fundamentals of GATT and WTO ⋯⋯ 214

Section I   A Brief Introduction to GATT ⋯⋯ **214**

Section II   A Brief Introduction to WTO ⋯⋯ **216**
    1. Objectives, Functions and Basic Principles of WTO ⋯⋯ 216
    2. WTO Structure ⋯⋯ 218
    3. An Outline of the WTO Agreements ⋯⋯ 221

Practical Drills ⋯⋯ **223**
    ❖ Case Study—China and WTO ⋯⋯ 223
    ❖ Role Play—At the Trade Show ⋯⋯ 224

Extended Activities ⋯⋯ **225**

Keys ⋯⋯ **228**

Appendix ⋯⋯ **244**
    Appendix 1-1   Sales Contract ⋯⋯ 244
    Appendix 1-2   Purchase Contract ⋯⋯ 245
    Appendix 2-1   Shifeng Double-Star Tire CO., LTD. ⋯⋯ 248
    Appendix 2-2   Commercial Invoice ⋯⋯ 249
    Appendix 3   Proforma Invoice ⋯⋯ 250
    Appendix 4   Bill of Lading ⋯⋯ 251
    Appendix 5   Letter of Credit ⋯⋯ 252

Bibliography ⋯⋯ **253**

Chapter 1

An Overview of the International Trade

Focal Learning

After the completion of this chapter, you are required to know:
- the definition of the international trade;
- why the international trade takes place;
- the international trade policy;
- the history and importance of China's foreign trade.

Lead-in Vocabulary

border	n.	边界,国界,边境
geographical	adj.	地理的
commodity	n.	日用品
distribution	n.	分配,分布
viable	a.	可行的
constituent	n.	选民
unimpeded	a.	无阻的,不受阻的
allocate	v.	分配,分派
accrue	v.	增大
erect	v.	建立,树立
proliferation	n.	激增
specialization	n.	专门化
potential	adj.	潜在的,可能的
autarky	n.	自给自足
		(不依赖进口或经济援助的自给自足的政策)
production gain		生产收益
static gains		静态收益
dynamic gains		动态收益
ad valorem tariff		从价税

non-tariff barriers		非关税壁垒
alleviate	v.	使减轻
retrenchment	n.	紧缩，节省
alacrity	n.	乐意

The international trade refers to the buying and selling of goods and services across national borders. The international trade is the backbone of our modern, commercial world, as producers in various nations try to profit from an expanded market, rather than be limited to selling within their own borders.

The international trade is also known as world trade or global trade, when viewed from the business relationships and outcomes among different countries; and may also be called foreign trade or overseas trade, when viewed from those between a country and the other countries or its externals. Because of the country's geographical characteristics or historical traditions, a country's foreign trade can be called external trade or import and export trade. In this book, we will mainly use the concept of export trade to refer to the international trade.

Section I
Reasons for the International Trade

Why does the international trade take place? There are many reasons, including lower production costs in one region versus another, specialized industries, lack or surplus of natural resources and consumer tastes. However, the main reasons for the international trade can be summarized as follows:

1. Resources Reasons

No nation has all of the commodities it needs. The uneven distribution of resources around the world is one of the most basic reasons why nations trade with each other. For example, the Middle East has rich oil reserves and is the main source of oil supply to the world, taking up over 50% of the world total reserves and about 40% of the world total output. Over 2/3 of the oil in West Europe and Japan need importing from the Middle East and the US oil military consumption in Europe and Asia is largely purchased from that area. Similarly developing countries are not yet able to modernize their industries and economies without advanced machinery, equipment and plant without advanced machinery, equipment and plant. As a result, this has given rise to the need for developing the international trade.

2. Economic Reasons

With the development of manufacturing and technology, there arose another incentive for nations to trade, that is, economic benefits. In addition to getting the products they need, countries also wish to gain economically by trading with each other. For the same commodity, it has various prices around the world, reflecting the differences in the cost of production.

❖ Absolute Advantage

Adam Smith, generally considered Father of Economics, published his famous work *The Wealth of Nations* in 1776 in London. In this book, Smith expressed two main ideas, absolute advantage and the division of labor, which were fundamental to trade theory.

In the theory of absolute advantage, Smith assumed each country might have the same average wage level and could produce one or more commodities at a lower real cost than its trading partners. Smith applied his ideas about economic activity within a country to specialization and exchange between countries. He concluded that a country should specialize in and export those commodities it produced more efficiently to trade those commodities it produced less efficiently because the absolute labor required per unit was less than that of the prospective trading partner, so both countries can benefit from trade.

Table 1

Absolute-Cost Case

Country	Days of Labor Required to Produce	
	Cloth (1 bolt)	Wine (1 barrel)
Scotland	30	120
Portugal	100	20

From Table 1, we can see clearly that Scotland should specialize in the production of clothes on which it has a cost advantage. Instead of spending 120 days of labor to produce a barrel of wine, Scotland should import wine from Portugal. Similarly, Portugal should concentrate on the production of wine and import cloth from Scotland.

Although Smith's ideas were crucial for the early development of classical thought and for altering the view of the potential gains from international trade, it was David Ricardo who expanded upon Smith's concepts and demonstrated that the potential gains from trade were far greater than those Adam Smith had envisioned in his concept of absolute advantage.

❖ Comparative Advantage

David Ricardo, in his 1819 work entitled *On the Principles of Political Economy and Taxation*, sought to take the basic ideas set down by Smith a few steps further. Ricardo noted that even if a country possessed absolute advantage in the production of two products, it still must be relatively more efficient than the other country in the production of one commodity than the other. Ricardo concluded each country would then possess comparative advantage in the production of one of the two products, and both countries would then benefit by specializing completely in one product and trading for the other.

Table 2

Comparative-Cost Case

Country	Wine	Cloth	Price Ratios in Autarky
Portugal	80 hrs./bbl.	90 hrs./yd.	1W: 8/9C
England	120 hrs./bbl.	100 hrs./yd.	1W: 6/5C

(Note: Price Ratios in Autarky refers to the price ratio when the country has no international trade.)
(Note: hrs-hours/bbl-barrel/yd-yard/w-wine/c--cloth)

In Table 2, Portugal has an absolute advantage in the production of both commodities. From Smith's perspective, there is no basis for trade between these countries because Portugal is more efficient in the production of both goods. England has an absolute disadvantage in both goods. Ricardo, however, pointed out that Portugal is relatively more efficient in the production of wine than that of cloth and that England needs relative less hours to produce wine (80 in Portugal, 120 in England, 2/3) than to produce cloth (90 in Portugal, 100 in England, 9/10). Because of these relative cost differences, both countries have an incentive to trade. To see this, consider the autarky (pre-trade) price ratios, in England, 1 barrel of wine should exchange for 6/5 yards of cloth, while in Portugal, 1 barrel would exchange for only 8/9 yard of cloth. Thus Portugal stands to gain if it can specialize in wine and acquire cloth from England at a ratio of 1 barrel:6/5 yards. Similarly, England would benefit by specializing in cloth production and exporting cloth to Portugal, where it could receive 9/8 barrels of wine per yard of cloth instead of 5/6 barrel per yard at home. Even though trade is unrealistically restricted to two goods in this basic analysis, similar potential gains also occur in more comprehensive analyses. The main point is that the basis for and the gains from trade rest on comparative, not absolute, advantage.

There are two ways to illustrate the gains from trade: one is in terms of labor time saved, the other is to state that more goods can be obtained for the same amount of labor time than is possible in autarky.

3. Other Reasons

Foreign trade usually occurs when one nation can sell some items at a lower cost than other countries. Japan has been able to export large quantities of radios and television sets because it can produce them more efficiently than other countries. It is chapter for the United States to buy these from Japan than to produce them domestically. Foreign trade also takes place, as a country often does not have enough of a particular item to meet its needs. Although China is a producer of oil, it consumes more than it can produce internally and thus must import oil. Even though a country can produce enough of an item at reasonable costs to meet its own demand, it may still import some from other countries for innovation or a variety of style. For example, the United States produces more automobiles than any other country, it still imports large quantities of autos from Germany, Japan and so on, primarily because there is a market for these different brands.

Chapter 1

All in all, in today's complex economic world, neither individuals nor nations are self-sufficient. Nations have utilized different economic resources; people have developed different skills. This is the foundation of international trade and economic activities.

Section II
The International Trade Policy

If you ask an economist or even a politician their opinion on trade policy, the standard response is either unabashed support for free trade or a response similar to the following: "I am basically in favor of free trade... but..." or "I believe in free trade but also fair trade". In short, selective protectionism is considered as a viable policy option by some. While selective protectionism has always had support among politicians and their constituents, it is only recently that it has become a legitimate source of debate among economists.

Table 3

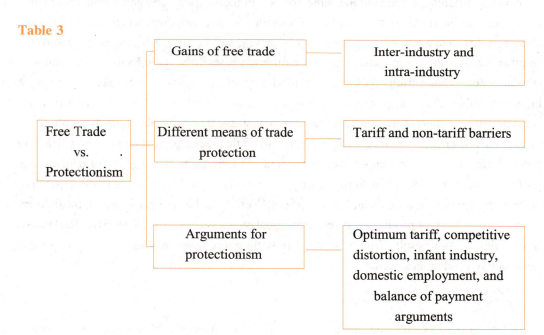

1. Gains from Free Trade

How does free trade benefit countries? It does so by enabling countries to specialize in producing those goods at which they are best. Specialization can take the form of either inter-industry or intra-industry specialization. As the gains from free trade differ from each other according to the type of specialization, it is necessary to consider the following two cases separately.

❖ **Gains from Inter-industry Specialization**

Inter-industry specialization is the specialization of a country in the full range of products of an industry, which has been considered in the classical and neo-classical trade theories. These theories show that when two countries engage in unimpeded trade with each other, each will specialize in the goods in which it has a comparative cost advantage. As a consequence, each country is able to obtain a greater bundle of the two goods exchanged than it was able to produce under autarky. This gain has two elements: a production gain and a consumption gain. The former means that the country can now use its scarce resources more efficiently, that is, they are optimally allocated. Specialization enables the country to employ its resources in those industries in which it is relatively more efficient. The latter holds that consumers are able to buy more of the imported product at a lower price. Such gains are the static gains from inter-industry specialization. They are once-and-for-all improvements in economic welfare that accrue to the countries involved.

❖ **Gains from Intra-industry Specialization**

Intra-industry specialization tends to occur in industries characterized by the existence of imperfect competition. In most cases, intra-industry specialization involved countries exchanging different varieties of the same goods. In these cases, the gains from trade come more from an increase in the number of varieties of a good from which consumers can choose, rather than a reduction in the prices of these goods or more efficient use of resources. In other words, the static welfare gains are different where free trade leads to intra-industry specialization. For various reasons, intra-industry specialization is also likely to result in bigger dynamic gains than inter-industry specialization. One reason is that intra-industry specialization is more common in industries where average costs fall with the volume of output. Trade enables producers to get further down their average cost curve, in which case further gains accrue to the importing country either in the form of lower prices or increased profits. Another reason is that intra industry trade exposes producers to greater competition, compelling firms to cut costs and lower prices. Yet, a further reason is that intra-industry specialization enables producers in research-intensive industries to recover fixed R&D costs more quickly. As a result, firms will be more willing to engage in R&D, leading to a more rapid rate of product innovation.

2. Different Means of Protection

Despite the fact that free trade increases global economic welfare, most governments interfere in trade by erecting either tariff or non-tariff barriers in order to grant protection to a particular industry threatened by foreign competition. Trade may also be distorted by government measures such as subsidies that favor domestic producers over foreign producers. Now let's see how these government-imposed barriers affect trade.

❖ **Tariff Barriers**

Tariffs are taxes on imports or exports and may take the form of a specific duty payable on each unit imported or an ad valorem tariff expressed as a percentage of the unit value of goods imported. Tariffs are the most common forms of trade restrictions. Tariffs generally raise the price of imports although not always by the full amount of the tariff because the incidence of the tariff may be borne both by the consumer in the importing country and the foreign supplier. The reason for imposing tariffs may not always be protectionist. In poorer countries which lack the adequate base for raising sufficient revenues from the taxation of incomes, reliance is often placed on customs duties along with other forms of commodity taxation for the welfare not only of exporting countries, whose access to foreign markets is restricted, but also of the importing country imposing the duty.

Tariff has five different effects. First, the rise in the price of the product reduces consumption—the consumption effect. Second, the increased price leads to increased domestic production of the goods—the production effect. Third, the fall in consumption plus the increase in domestic production results in reduced imports—the balance of trade effect. Fourth, the tariff generates increased fiscal revenues for the importing country—the revenue effect. Finally, the tariff lowers the economic welfare of the importing country—the welfare effect. Tariffs lower economic welfare because they raise prices to consumers and, therefore, reduce their real income. This loss to consumers is measured using the concept of consumers' surplus.

❖ **Non-tariff Barriers**

As tariffs on almost all goods have come down to modest levels, there has been a corresponding rise in non-tariff barriers (NTBs) to trade. They have become more prominent in recent years. Economists have noted that as tariffs have been reduced through multilateral negotiations during the last 35 years, the impact of this reduction may have been largely offset by the proliferation of NTBs. They are generally disliked by economists because, unlike tariffs, they are not "transparent". That is, the effects of these barriers are difficult to estimate.

In the principle all barriers other than tariffs that in some manner impede trade or raise the cost of trading, which includes informal measures, should be included among non-tariff barriers.

The United Nations Conference on Trade and Development (UNCTAD) designed a classification of NTBs during the early 1980s. This system breaks them into seven major categories: a) price control measures, b) finance control measures, c) automatic licensing measures, d) quantity control measures, e) monopolistic measures, f) technical measures, g) miscellaneous measures. Each of these broad groups is further subdivided into particular measures, as shown in Table 4:

Table 4

The UNCTAD Classification System for Non-tariff Barriers

1. Price control measures
    (1) Administrative pricing
    (2) Voluntary export price restraint
    (3) Variable charges
    (4) Antidumping measures

    (5) Countervailing measures

2. Finance control measures
    (1) Advance payment requirements
    (2) Multiple exchange rates
    (3) Restrictive official foreign exchange allocation
    (4) Regulations concerning terms of payment for imports
    (5) Transfer delays

3. Automatic licensing measures
    (1) Automatic license
    (2) Import monitoring
    (3) Surrender requirement

4. Quantity control measures
    (1) Non-automatic license
    (2) Quotas
    (3) Import prohibitions
    (4) Export restraint arrangement
    (5) Enterprise-specific restrictions

5. Monopolistic measures
    (1) Single channel for imports
    (2) Compulsory national services

6. Technical measures
    (1) Technical regulations
    (2) Pre-shipment formalities
    (3) Special customs formalities
    (4) Obligation to return used products

7. Miscellaneous measures for insensitive product categories
    (1) Market permits
    (2) Public procurement
    (3) Voluntary instruments
    (4) Product liability
    (5) Subsidies

Note: used in the UNCTAD TRAINS (1997) database: TRAINS stands for Trade Analysis and information System.

Chapter 1

Section III
The History and Role of the Chinese International Trade

China's foreign trade, inspite of a small component of gross national product, plays an important role in sustaining and modernizing the Chinese economy.

1. The Period between 1950—1976

Foreign trade is the balancing sector in the planning process with imports making up for shortfalls in domestic production and providing goods that cannot be produced in sufficient quantity, or at all, in China. Exports are not viewed as an end in themselves but as a means to pay for imports. Foreign trade policy has been very cautious. Self-reliance has been the guiding principle. Despite its small share and conservative policy, trade has been quite important to China's economic development. Imports aided the rebuilding of China's industrial base in the1950's, alleviated agricultural failures, and have provided industrial supplies and advance technology to spur economic growth and modernization. In addition, foreign trade has often provided a useful entree in China's relations with other countries.

❖ **The 1950's—Leaning to One Side**

Economic and political necessity led to heavy dependence on the U.S.S.R. The need to rebuild the economy amid the Western trade embargo imposed during the Korean War impelled China to pursue a policy of "leaning to one side", by which China based its industrial and technological growth on a rapid buildup of trade with the Socialist countries. As a result of the close economic cooperation with the former U.S.S.R. and Eastern Europe, trade between China and the Socialist world shot from only $ 350 million in 1950 to almost $3 billion in 1959. Trade with the West fell off after 1951. With the relaxation of Western trade restrictions in the second half of the decade, trade with the Western countries rose. However, this trade still represented only about 30 percent of total China's trade in 1959.

❖ **The 1960's—Reorientation to the West**

The rift with the Soviet Union opened wider in the midyear of 1960 when Moscow withdrew its technicians, blueprints, and all. This was an added blow to the Chinese economy, already overstrained by poor agricultural performance and the excesses of the Great Leap. From 1960 to 1962, China's exports fell as industrial production declined, and imports were cut back sharply. Trade with the Socialist countries plummeted form the $3 billion level of 1959 to only $ 1.1 billion in 1964.

❖ **1970—1973, a Rapid Growth**

With the restoration of order to economy and the resumption of regular planning, China embarked on a program of increase emphasis on trade to spur economic development. At the same time rising industrial production in the 1970's created needs for larger imports of industrial supplies such as metal and rubber.

China's trade soared from $4.3 billion in 1970 to $ 10.3 billion in 1973 with most of the growth coming in trade with the Western countries. Trade with the Socialist world roughly doubled over the period, but its share of China's total trade slipped from 20% to 17%.

❖ **1974—1976, Retrenchment**

China's trade strategy unraveled in 1974. Rampant inflation in the West and heavy delivery of machinery and agricultural products pushed import costs to a peak while the slowdown in the Western economies cut demand for Chinese exports.

In 1975 China made substantial progress in correcting its trade imbalance. This year its import bill for agricultural products was slashed by $ 1 billion. An improved grain harvest in 1974 permitted China to cut imports of wheat and corn to 3.3 million tons, less than half the amount taken the year before. Sugar and cotton imports were also reduced and soybean purchases were nearly eliminated.

A combination of lower volumes and lower prices cut China's import by almost $ 1.4 billion in 1976. As for exports, crude oil earnings fell by almost $ 100 million as sales to Japan dropped off. Continued economic recovery in the West plus further price cuts enabled China to boost sales of light manufactures and other consumer goods enough to keep total exports at the 1975 level.

2. The Period after 1976

After 1976, China's foreign trade policies began to change. The first move was to encourage domestic enterprises to buy inputs from abroad rather than to discourage such purchase. Enterprises responded with such alacrity that China by 1978 found itself with a growing trade deficit, despite increasing prices for China's petroleum exports. Imports in nominal dollar terms rose 51% in 1978 and by 44% in 1979. Clearly, new and increasing sources of foreign exchange had to be discovered.

In 1979, reforms were introduced to facilitate exports of manufactures and to allow for foreign investment. Efforts were made to break up the monopoly on foreign trade held by the state corporations, and to transfer this authority to regional corporations. Special economic zones were set up to free foreign investors and other exporters from red tape. Various export subsidies were introduced and China's currency was devalued from 1.7 Yuan to the U.S. dollar in 1981 to 2.9 Yuan to the dollar in 1985 to 4.8 Yuan to the dollar in 1990 and to 8.7 Yuan to the dollar in 1994.

Foreign trade responded to these incentives in dramatic fashion. Total volume of foreign trade has expanded from $ 20 billion in 1978 to more than $ 600 billion in 2002. During the past 23 years, foreign trade volume has, on average, outgrown both national production and the world trade. And China has experienced remarkable export growth, averaging 26.46% per year from 1981 to 2000, far higher than the world average of 5.9% over the same period. China's share in total world exports grew from 0.96% to 4.7% in 2002, making China the fifth largest international exporter in 2002. Foreign trade has played a central role in moving China toward a market economy and contributed to the development of industrial and agricultural production, science and technology, and increased national financial revenues and income of foreign exchanges. The national markets are broadened. A variety of products are available for consumers. And a lot of jobs are offered.

Useful Phrases & Technical Terms

overseas trade	海外贸易
external trade	对外贸易
absolute advantage	绝对优势
cost advantage	成本优势
comparative advantage	比较优势
inter-industry specialization	行业间的专业化分工
intra-industry specialization	行业内的专业化分工
U.S.S.R. (USSR)	Union of Soviet Socialist Republics 的缩写，苏联*
plurilateral agreement	多边贸易协议

Notes

1. **Adam Smith:** 亚当·斯密(1723—1790)苏格兰籍经济学家和哲学家。他的巨著,1776年3月9日出版的《国富论》(The Wealth of Nation)，奠定了经济学的基础。这部书代表了亚当·斯密的哲学和经济学理论，即国家财富来源于劳动。该书今天被认为是古典自由政治经济学的第一部理论著作。

2. **David Ricard:** 戴维·李嘉图(1772—1823)，英国经济学家,资产阶级古典政治经济学的完成者。其主要著作《政治经济与税收原理》(1817年)，正是供求在自由市场的定律。

3. **absolute advantage:** 绝对优势。斯密认为，国际贸易和国际分工的原因及基础是各国间存在的劳动生产率和生产成本的绝对差别。一国如果在某种产品上具有比别国高的劳动生产率，该国在这一产品上就具有绝对优势；相反，就是绝对劣势。各国应该集中生产并出口其具有劳动生产率和生产成本"绝对优势"的产品，进口其不具有"绝对优势"的产品，其结果比自己什么都不生产更有利。

4. **comparative advantages:** 比较优势。源于英国李嘉图(经济学家)的比较成本学说：国际贸易的基础是生产技术的相对差别(而非绝对差别)以及由此产生的相对成本。每个国家都应该集中生产并出口其具有"比较优势"的产品，进口其具有"比较劣势"的产品。比较优势原理在更普遍的基础上揭示了贸易产生的基础和贸易所得。

* 指前苏联

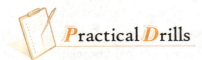

Practical Drills

❖ Questions for Discussion

1. According to David Smith, nations should allow free trade and abolish government intervention. Would you agree with him?
2. Should economic development be the top priority for developing countries in formulating their foreign trade policies?

❖ Case Study

Favorable Balance of Trade vs. Unfavorable Balance of Trade

When nations export more than they import within a certain period (usually one year), they are said to have a favorable balance of trade, or a favorable balance of visible trade. When they import more than they export, an unfavorable balance of trade exists. Nations try to maintain a favorable balance of trade, which assures them of the measure to buy necessary imports.

To obtain an idea of the favorable balance of trade and unfavorable balance of trade, look at the following table 7, which provides information on the balance trade. The table indicates that between 1981—2002, China has either favorable balances of trade or unfavorable balances of trade. However, it has kept favorable balances of trade since 1994.

Balance of trade is one of the most important compositions of current account of a nation's balance of payment. The position of nation's balance of trade has great impact on its balance of payment.

Table 7

China's Total Value of Import and Export from 1981 to 2002

Unit: millions of dollars

Year	Total Value	Export	Import	Balance	Growth Percentage		
					Total Value	Import	Export
1981	44,022	22,007	22,015	-8	—	—	—
1982	41,606	22,321	19,285	3,036	-5.5	1.4	-12.4
1983	43,616	22,226	21,390	836	4.8	-0.4	10.9
1984	53,549	26,139	27,410	-1,271	22.8	17.6	28.1
1985	69,602	27,350	42,252	-14,902	30.0	4.6	54.1
1986	73,846	30,942	42,904	-11,962	6.1	13.1	1.5

(Continued)

1987	82,653	39,437,	43,216	-3,779	11.9	27.5	0.7
1988	102,784	47,516	55,268	-7,752	24.4	20.5	27.9
1989	111,678	52,538	59,140	-6,602	8.7	10.6	7.0
1990	115,437	62,091	53,345	8,746	3.4	18.2	-9.8
1991	135,702	71,910	63,791	8,119	17.6	15.8	19.6
1992	165,525	84,940	80,585	4,355	22.0	18.1	26.3
1993	195,703	91,744	103,959	-12,215	18.2	8.0	29.0
1994	236,621	121,006	115,615	5,391	20.9	31.9	11.2
1995	280,863	148,780	132,084	16,696	18.7	23.0	14.2
1996	289,881	151,048	138,833	12,215	3.2	1.5	5.1
1997	325,162	182,79	142,370	40,422	12.2	21.0	2.5
1998	323,949	183,712	140,237	43,475	-0.4	0.5	-1.5
1999	360,630	194,931	165,699	29,232	11.3	6.1	18.2
2000	474,297	249,203	225,094	24,109	31.5	27.8	35.8
2001	509,768	266,206	243,580	22,626	7.5	6.8	8.2
2002	620,790	325,570	295,220	30,350	21.8	22.3	21.2

Sources: www.moftec.org

❖ *Role Play*

Establishing Business Relations

A: Hello! Welcome to Guangzhou Fair.

B: Thank you. I'm from America. Here is my business card.

A: Glad to meet you, Mr. Smith. My family name is Wang and here is my name card.

B: Great! This is my first visit to the Fair. Everything is new to me. Would you please give me some information?

A: Glad to. The Fair is a big gathering taking place twice a year. Thousands of businessmen from more than a hundred and fifty countries and regions are here to trade with China.

B: What about your company?

A: Ours is a company specialized in exporting leather products. And what about yours?

B: My firm has a high standing in my country. My bank is the City Bank, New York. You may refer to it for my status. Would you please show me some samples and price lists?

A: Certainly. Here are some samples and price lists for you. After studying them, I'm sure you will be satisfied.

B: Thank you very much. I'd like to have a talk in more detail, say, tomorrow morning, will that be suitable?

A: Yes, surely. See you tomorrow morning.

B: See you tomorrow morning.

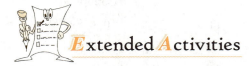

Extended Activities

I. Answer the following questions.

1. What are the differences between international trade and domestic trade?
2. Why is international trade necessary?
3. What is the "comparative advantage"? Do you think comparative advantage is still workable in China?
5. What are the gains from the inter-specialization?
6. What are non-tariff barriers? Please name at least 8 types of non-tariff barriers.

II. Look at the terms in the left-hand column and find the correct definitions in the right-hand column. Write the corresponding letters in the blanks.

1. _____	free trade	a. to provide certain products or services, relying on exchange with others to provide the other goods and services they require
2. _____	specialization	b. the exchange of goods and services between different countries
3. _____	productivity	c. trade among countries that occurs without barriers such as tariffs or quotas
4. _____	international trade	d. the ability to produce a good at a lower cost, relative to other goods, compared with another country
5. _____	average cost	e. a policy of protecting domestic industries from foreign competition
6. _____	comparative advantage	f. a relatively consistent course of conduct pursued by one country in its relationship with another country
7. _____	protectionism	g. the total cost of production divided by the total quantity produced
8. _____	foreign policy	h. efficiency with which goods and services are produced, as measured by the quantity produced per person per hour

III. Decide whether the following statements are true or false by writing "T" for true and "F" for false in the bracket besides each statement.

1. (   ) Foreign exchange control is also a tariff barrier that can restrict imports effectively.
2. (   ) Non-tariff barriers are extremely effective restrictions, though they are more visible than tariffs.

3. (　) When nations export more than they import, they have a favorable balance of trade. When they import more than they export, an unfavorable balance of trade exists.
4. (　) Import trade is virtually the foundation of a country's foreign trade.
5. (　) Generally speaking, the distribution of natural resources in the world is uneven.
6. (　) According to absolute model, each country should specialize in and supply the products where it has an absolute advantage.
7. (　) Ricardo developed the comparative cost model which also advocated free trade.

IV. Complete the following diagram according to what you have read in the text.

Types of Trade Restrictions

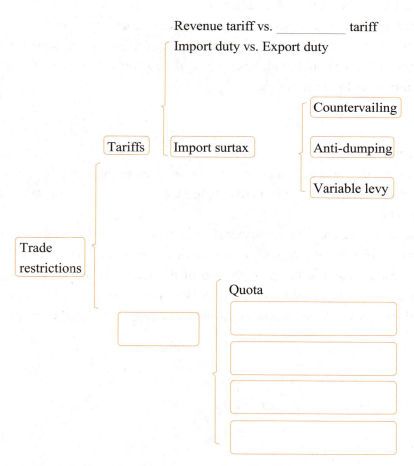

V. Translate the following sentences into English.
(1) 通过国际贸易,可以使消费者和贸易国获取本国没有的商品和服务。
(2) 通过国际贸易,富裕国家可以更高效地使用其劳动力、技术或资本等资源。
(3) 与当地企业不同,跨国企业都是在全球范围内从事经营活动。

(4) 近年来,中国的对外贸易呈现高速、稳定的增长。

(5) 发达的工业化国家仍居国际贸易的主导地位,其贸易额占世界贸易总量的一半以上。

VI. Translate the following passage into Chinese.

  Economic "globalization" is a historical process, the result of human innovation and technological progress. It refers to the increasing integration of economies around the world, particularly through trade and financial flows. The term sometimes also refers to the movement of people and knowledge across international borders. There are also broader cultural, political and environmental dimensions of globalization that are not covered here.

  At its most basic, there is nothing mysterious about globalization. The term has come into common usage since the 1980s, reflecting technological advances that have made it easier and quicker to complete international transactions—both trade and financial flows. It refers to an extension beyond national borders of the same market forces that have operated for centuries at all levels of human economic activity—village markets, urban industries, or financial centers.

VII. Speaking activities.

Oral presentation

  Form groups of three or four and prepare jointly for the oral presentation topic below. Then vote for a representative in a group to make a 5—15 minute presentation before the whole class.

  There are a variety of goals of international trade policies (national security, stable employment, balance of payments considerations, economic development, etc.), and these goals could not be all on the top of the agenda at the same time when international trade policies are formulated. How would government make their choices among these goals? What suggestions would you make for China's foreign trade policy?

Chapter 2

The International Trade Forms

Focal Learning

After the completion of this chapter, you are required to know:

- the definition of selling agent, distribution, consignment and international subcontracting;
- the definition of tender;
- the definition of the counter trade;
- the definition of the ITT and franchising.

Lead-in Vocabulary

unilateral	a.	单边的
consignment	n.	代销
auction	n.	拍卖
del credere	n.	保证收取货款
selling agency		销售代理
distribution	n.	经销
consignor	n.	代销商
subcontract	n.	转包合同,分包合同
reciprocate	n.	互给,互换
buy back		回购
outsourcing	n.	外部采购
contract manufacturing		合同生产

Section I
Selling Agent, Distribution, Consignment and International Subcontracting

International trade forms refer to the common practices and channels between countries for the flow of commodities or services. It includes the specific forms of import and export transaction or various ways of transaction. Unilateral import and export are the commonly used business methods. In the current international trade there are various ways of trade forms such as exclusive sales, sales agency, consignment, tendering, counter-trade, barter-trade, compensation-trade, plus some forms such as the technological transfer, technology licensing, international franchising, and Joint ventures etc.

1. Selling Agent

According to the power the principal has delegated to a selling agent, the agent may just introduce the potential customer to the principal or actually negotiate and conclude the contract between the two parties. They have the following characteristics:

(1) An agent can only operate within the marketing territory authorized by the principal;
(2) An agent does not carry stock. The goods are carried only as consignment inventory; Payment is based on delivery to the ultimate buyer;
(3) The principal sets the retail price, retains title and controls the goods;
(4) The profit and risk of loss remains with the principal, unless the agent is a del credere one;
(5) Agents are usually paid with commission.

2. Distribution

Unlike agents, distributors buy goods from the principals on their own account and take title to them and resell them to their customers in their territory. Thus, there is no contractual relationship between the principal and the ultimate customers. Instead there are separate sets of contracts: those between the principal and the distributor, and those between the distributor and the ultimate customers. The distributor takes his remuneration from the margin between the customers. Since the distributor is an independent contractor, he assumes far more risks and obligations than an agent does, bad debts, advertising expenditure, warranty claims and maintenance, etc., therefore distributors generally enjoy more freedom and higher remuneration.

3. Consignment

Under consignment, the consignor sends the goods to a foreign consignee who will sell the goods for the consignor according to the agreed terms. The essence of consignment trading is that goods exported on the consignment remain the property to the exporter. Therefore, consignment exports are not really exports because the exporter retains title to the goods until the importer sells the goods to final customers or third parties. So, the exporter is not paid until the goods are sold over the overseas marketplace.

4. International Subcontracting

International subcontracting is a cross between licensing and investment, and is also known as outsourcing or contract manufacturing. In subcontracting, a company gets the technology of a product from an independent manufacturer in a foreign target country and subsequently markets that product in the target country or elsewhere. These contracts may be long term as part of a buyer-supplier relationship, or they may be temporary arrangements that terminate when the relevant contracts' activities come to an end. Subcontracting encompasses agreements ranging from the purchase of components made overseas for assembly at the home base of the company to the complete production of specific products by foreign manufacturers. To acquire a product manufactured to its specifications the company is usually involved in the transfer of technology and technical assistance to the foreign manufacturer when it is eventually able to develop some new features related to the product. There are basically five major modes of technology transfer via subcontracting.

Section II
Tender

A tender is an offer or proposal to purchase a specified quantity of a commodity for a specified price. The international plant-engineering contract is a comprehensive international cooperation in economy and technology, including machines and equipment, technology, capital and service, under which one party shall undertake the responsibility for fulfilling the building of a certain project item, and the other party shall offer necessary working conditions and give the acceptance to the project, and pay the agreed amount of the price value and the service of tenders, bid opening, tender discussion and tender decision, establishment of contract, and execution of contract.

Bidding, as one special trade form, is widely used in international trade nowadays, especially for government construction projects and purchase of goods in large quantity. In bidding, the price of goods or service is not quoted by the seller, but decided by choosing the most advantageous one from the offers of bidders. For bidders, it is always a difficult task to offer a low price to win the bid and still earn a profit. Invitation for bids and submission of bids are the two different aspects of the process. International bids can generally be divided into two kinds: one is open bids or unlimited competitive bid; another is selected bids or limited competitive bids.

1. Invitation for Bids

Generally speaking, big or complicated technical items, financed by international banking facilities or assisted by the United Nations and international organizations are often contracted out by invitation for bids.

To call for bids, the promoter will have to organize a special committee on invitation of bidding to be in charge of the invitation to bid, at the same time a supervisory organ is also set up to supervise the work.

❖ **Bid Documents**

Namely, inquiry documents, should be carefully prepared for invitation to bid. They are regarded as the foundations for calling, for bids and mainly consist of:

(1) Invitation for tender

(2) Information for or instructions to tenderers

(3) Formation of application for tenders and attachments

(4) Terms of contract

(5) Formation of contract

(6) General description

(7) Form of general engineering operation capacity or general bill of work quantities

(8) Drawings and attachments

(9) Basic data

(10) Additional data list

(11) Summary of bid documents

❖ **Terms of Contract**

Terms of contract constitute the chief contents in the contract document of international plant—engineering, which prescribe the legal relations among the employer, the contractor and the supervisory engineer, and their rights and duties respectively.

The following fundamental clauses are usually included in the terms of contract:

(1) Rights and duties of supervisory engineer and his representatives

(2) Clause of assignment or subcontract

(3) General duties of the contractor

(4) Clause of special natural conditions and artificially imposed obstacles

(5) Clause of the contractor's supervision

(6) Clause of engineering protection

(7) Clause of insurance

(8) Clause of tests

(9) Clause of shutdown

(10) Clause of delay in completion

(11) Penalty of late completion

(12) Loss of working time

(13) Clause of maintenance

(14) Working charges and modifications of plant-engineering
(15) Claim for supplementary fees by the contractor
(16) Clause of payment
(17) Breach of contract by the contractor
(18) Breach of contract by client
(19) Arbitration
(20) Clause of special risks

2. Submission of Bids

If the tender offering is open to the public, the organs in charge of invitation of bidding should make use of every possible means to publish the notice inviting for bidding so as to attract contractors to bid. After the contractors have got the information, they must make application for bidding if they are interested in the plant-engineering contract. But only those who have passed through pre-qualification may buy bid documents, prepare tender documents and compete with other contractors for winning the bid.

❖ **Tender Documents**

Tender documents must usually include the following contents:
(1) Form of tender and attachments
(2) Tender guarantee
(3) Price and expenses list
(4) Job schedule of plant-engineering
(5) Time and method of payment
(6) Construction scheme
(7) Construction organization and biographical records of the major managerial personnel to be appointed
(8) Labor arrangement program
(9) All relative data, such as agreement, terms of contract, drawings of plant—engineering, description and other lists and materials

Tender documents usually consist of all the instruments for tender mentioned in the bid documents except the summary of bid documents, but having already been filled by the bidders: an amending bid document, a question sheet and written answers, a letter of guarantee for tender or tender bond, a letter on submission of tender.

❖ **Tender Documentation**

First of all, an all-round hydrological and geological survey must be made before tender documentation. Only on the basis of the field investigation, a technology appraisal and an economic evaluation of the project item proposed to build can be made for further feasibility study.

According to the items listed in bid documents, bidders must fully calculate, work out and fill in quotation data including the unit price, line-item price, total price and other items needed to be filled out. This is the most important work for bidders to do in the process of preparation for bidding. Since the main part of working out bid documents is to calculate the bid price and fill in the documents with it, it is usually referred to as bid quotation or bidding.

To do it well, the bidders must first of all make themselves acquainted with the bid documents, especially the general description of the plant-engineering, technical specifications, construction drawings, general engineering operation capacity, machines, equipment and raw materials to be needed, labor service, and so on. If they may provide better schemes of design and construction for the plant-engineering. They are required to send to the employer a new detailed drawing and description when the quotation is made.

Two major types of tender are usually adopted in international plant-engineering contract and service cooperation. If the bidder independently enters a bid, it is called exclusive tender; if two or more than two contractors organize a new business entity to submit tender together, then it is called joint tender.

Section III
International Counter-trade

Counter-trade is an "umbrella" (general) term covering all forms of trade whereby a seller or an assignee is required to accept goods or services from the buyer as either full or partial payment. International counter-trade is a practice whereby a supplier commits contractually as a condition of sale to reciprocate and undertake certain specified commercial initiatives that compensate and benefit the buyer. While the manner in which the transaction is structured and the assets are exchanged may vary in different compensatory transactions such as barter, buyback, counter-purchase, and offset, the distinctive feature of these arrangements is the mandatory performance element that is either required by the importer or is made necessary by competitive considerations. It is a peculiar form of transaction allegedly popular in less developed countries and in centrally planned economies. It is then often associated with policy objectives in these economies.

Chapter 2

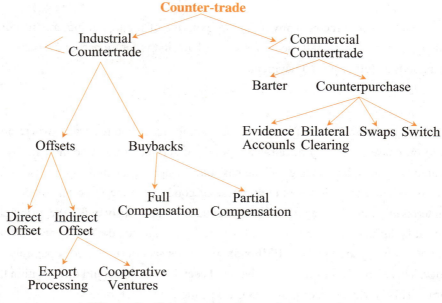

Figure 1   Source: www:barter-house.com/

1. Barter Trade

Barter means the direct exchange of goods and services which is completed in a short period of time, at an agreed rate between two parties. There is no exchange of money, and usually, there are two parties involved in a one-shot transaction.

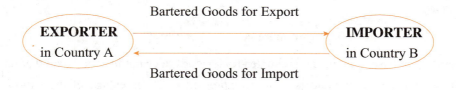

Figure 2   Barter Workflow

2. Compensation Agreement

Compensation agreement is an agreement whereby an exporter will accept a specified amount of products from the importer as a full or partial payment in kind. Full compensation deals are similar to barter. However, a currency of exchange is used, and each party bills for his own shipment. Furthermore, the exporter can assign his commitment to a third party. Partial compensation deals involve partial currency payment, and the rest is in local product.

3. Buy Back

Buy back is an agreement involving an exporter of plant, equipment, machinery and technology, or two or three of these things to take back in the future part of the output produced by these goods as full or partial payment.

4. Counter-purchase

Counter-purchase is one of the most common forms of counter-trade, where an exporter agrees to purchase a quantity of unrelated goods or services from a country in exchange for and in approximate value to the goods he has sold. In signing a counter-purchase contract, the exporter is required to undertake the purchase of goods from the importer's side. Although this undertaking may be negotiated and signed simultaneously with the principal export contract, it is discharged separately. That's to say, separate stand-alone contracts for delivery and counter delivery are signed. Each side of the transaction is settled separately in foreign exchange. Therefore, the timing for discharge of each transaction could differ within the agreed time limit. This is why counter-purchase is also called "parallel trade".

Figure 3 Counter-purchase Workflow

In the counter-purchase, the value of counter-trade goods does not have to equal that of the export. The counter-trade demand is of term expressed as a percentage of the export contract. Separate contracts are signed for each side of the transaction. Usually the counter-purchase is only represented in the first instance by some sort of framework agreement. This merely sets out the conditions of the counter-purchase and may not make detailed reference to the purchase of specific counter-trade goods.

Chapter 2

Section IV
International Technology Transfer and International Technology Licensing

The development of international technology transfer is a simple reality which small, medium-sized and multinational companies experience regularly. Technology, knowledge and know-how Transfers are performed every day, creating international flows of know-how and exchanges which are becoming one of the essential components of international competitiveness.

The flows of technology and knowledge will develop increasingly over the coming years. New technology niches and new forms of cooperation will be created. Technological choice will become more refined. New countries will emerge as producers of technology.

International technology licensing is a business format which is frequently used for business expansion across national boundaries. This chapter offers an intensive briefing on all the key factors about international technology license.

1. International Technology Transfer

International technology transfer studies cover the economic relationship between a transferor and a transferee, as well as a whole series of related issues, such as the relevant national policies and legal framework of the nations in the world. For different environmental and developmental reasons, technological advances in different countries have always been uneven. The uneven nature of technological progress throughout the world provides the very basis for technology transfer. In the past few decades ITT has multiplied by leaps and bounds.

ITT is a complicated aspect of international business which is an organic part of a firm's international strategy, influenced by diverse factors, ranging from firm size, global strategy, cultural and geographical distance to receiving the country's development strategies and investment policies, and the recipient firm's absorptive capabilities. Technology can be transferred through licensing, franchising, foreign direct investment (FDI), sale of turnkey plants, subcontracting, co-production agreements, etc., most of these transfers are difficult to monitor. Only when a technology is transferred via a market mechanism does it have an explicit value, though it may not reflect the "true" value of the technology being transferred.

2. International Technology Licensing

This term is defined broadly, including a variety of contractual arrangements whereby domestic firms (licensors) sell their intangible assets or property rights to foreign firms (licensees) in return for royalties and/or other forms of payment. The transfer of these intangible assets or property rights is the core of a licensing agreement. Under this arrangement the firms typically provide a limited right to produce and market the product in a specified geographical region. The transfer is usually supported by technical services to ensure the appropriate exploitation of the assets. Licensing agreements are normally long-term arrangement that may require significant investment by the licensee. Licensing to foreign companies has long played an important role in business strategies in developed countries. With Japanese companies alone, American firms signed approximately 32,000 licensing agreements between 1952 and 1980. During the late 1980s licensing fees and royalty payments brought to US licensors more than $12 billion a year, roughly twice the rate earned a decade earlier. In the 1990s the pace of international licensing is accelerated, with more recent growth of international licensing led by smaller firms in industries protected by patents, such as biotechnology and pharmaceutical companies. International licensing is often conducted in the form of a cross-licensing agreement or technology swap between firms or as part of a larger, overall strategic partnership between firms.

Useful Phrases & Technical Terms

counter trade	对销贸易
barter trade	易货贸易
compensation trade	补偿贸易
invitation for and submission of bids	招标与投标
selected bids	选择性招标
international technology transfer	国际技术转让
foreign direct investment	国外直接投资
international franchising	国际特许
the multinational corporation	跨国公司
international subcontracting	国际合同转包

Notes

1. The international trade forms refer to the business methods in foreign trade. They include the specific forms of import and export transaction or various ways of transaction. Unilateral import and export are the commonly used business methods. In the current international trade there are various ways of trade forms such as exclusive sales, sales agency, consignment, bidding, calling for tendering, international auction, commodity exchanges, international fair and exhibition of various specialties; counter trade, barter trade, compensation trade, moreover some forms such as the technology transfer,

technology licensing, international franchising, and so on, are frequently used trade forms.

对外贸易方式是指对外贸易经营的方式，包括进出口交易的具体形式或所使用的各种具有不同特点的交易方法，是单边进口和单边出口市场间普遍采用的经营方式。当前在国际贸易中，贸易方式多种多样，如独家经销代理、代销、招标和投标、国际拍卖、商品交易、国际博览会和各种专业性的展销会，还有"对销贸易"、"易货贸易"、"补偿贸易"，此外还有技术转让、技术许可证、国际特许、合资、合作等，也都是经常采用的。

2. Unlike agents, distributors buy goods from the principals on their own account and take title to them and resell them to their customers in their territory. Thus, there is no contractual relationship between the principal and the ultimate customers.

与代理商不同，经销商要先花钱买下货物，拥有它们，然后再卖给他们负责经销区域内的客户。因此最终客户与委托人之间没有直接的契约关系。

3. Barter means the direct exchange of goods and services which is completed in a short period of time, at an agreed rate between two parties. There is no exchange of money, and usually, there are two parties involved in a one-shot transaction.

易货贸易是指按双方协定的价格，在短时期内完成的货物和劳务的直接交换，不涉及货币交换，通常由双方参与只进行一次的交易。

4. Bidding, as one special trade form, is widely used in international trade nowadays, especially for government construction projects and purchase of goods in large quantity. In bidding, the price of goods or service is not quoted by the seller, but decided by choosing the most advantageous one from the offers of bidders.

招标，作为一种特殊的交易形式，如今已在国际贸易中，特别是在政府工程承包和大宗采购中，得到了广泛的使用。在投标中，货物或服务的价格不使用卖方报出的，而是从投标方的报价中选出最有利的价格来决定。

Practical Drills

❖ Questions for Discussion

1. What are the modes available for firms to choose for doing international business?
2. What are the major channels through which a firm engages in export business?
3. What is the tender and what are involved in it?

❖ Case Study

Confirming Offer

Dear Mr. Smith,

Thank you for your inquiry of May 15, against which we have quoted the price as shown in the following firm offer with the e-letter today subject to your reply here by the 15th.

Commodity: Model…—150 full-automatic tube camera equipped with automatic exposure meter & range meter.
Quantity: 500 sets
Quality: Specified in the attached specification sheets
Price: $250.00 CIF Los Angeles in US dollars per unit on Banker's Irrevocable L/C, under which we draw a draft in 30 days.
Shipment: June 30

With the approach of the leisure season, the demand for high quality cameras is increasing. The compact styling and superb quality will certainly present excellent soles as shown by our production ration.

We trust you will take advantage of this seasonal opportunity and favor us with an early reply.

Very truly yours,
Wei Zhiyong
Sales Manager

❖ Role Play

Tender and Biding

A: Mr. James, our government has invited tenders for the Three Gorges Project. Would you like to take part in?

B: Yes. Participation in tenders is in our line of business. But we would like to know what we shall have to do, if we agree to send our bid.

A: As it stands, in addition to the bid you are to submit information on cost, construction time and the volume of work(s) concerning the projects already constructed by you.

B: We'll try to do it without delay, but we would like to know the requirements of the tender committee.

A: Certainly, we shall get a complete set of tender documents for you and you will be able to study the requirements. The expenses involved will be charged to your account, though.

B: Well, no problem. By the way, must we guarantee in any way our participation in the tender?

A: You will have to pay "earnest money" to guarantee your participation till the end of the tender.

B: That's quite fair. What are our chances of success, Mr. Zhang?

A: We know that you have rich experience in this field and that you render technical assistance on favorable terms. I think you may win the tender.

B: I hope so. We must reconsider your offer and we shall give our reply in the near future.

A: Well, we look forward to your reply as soon as possible.

B: Thank you for your information.

A: You're welcome.

B: Thank you. We'll study it. Shall we meet again next Tuesday morning, say at nine, to discuss the details?

A: All right.

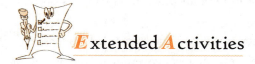

Extended Activities

I. Answer the following questions.

1. What is distribution?
2. What is the difference between "invitation for bids" and "submission of tender"?
3. What is counter trade? And what does it include?
4. What is "ITT"?
5. What are the gains from the inter-specialization?
6. What are non-tariff barriers? Please name at least 8 types of non-tariff barriers.

II. Look at the terms in the left-hand column and find the correct definitions in the right-hand column. Write the corresponding letters in the blanks.

1. _____ counter trade   a. the commercial activity of transporting and selling goods from a producer to a consumer.

2. _____ distribution   b. the sale of goods or services that are paid for in whole or part by the transfer of goods or services from a foreign country

3. _____ trade mark   c. blending of a variety of marketing elements into a marketing program

4. _____ copyright   d. the ability to produce a good at a lower cost, relative to other goods, compared to another country

5. _____ marketing mix   e. a company that is completely controlled by another company

6. _____ subsidiary   f. the sole right, granted by the government, to sell, use, and manufacture an invention or creation

7. _____ patent   g. entering a foreign market by developing foreign-based assembly or manufacturing facilities.

8. _____ direct investment   h. a legal right to exclusive publication

III. Decide whether the following statements are true or false by writing "T" for true and "F" for false in the bracket besides each statement.

1. (　) The host country intermediary plays a small part in a firm's exporting success.
2. (　) The marketing subsidiary can help best exploit the foreign market but it is usually not successful.
3. (　) Licensing could be a satisfactory method of exporting for small firms new to international business.
4. (　) The franchiser usually renders assistance to the franchisee in its business operations.
5. (　) Through licensing, firms can expect higher profits with the help of local licensees.
6. (　) Licensing agreements are usually not subject to the local government's approval.

IV. Fill in the blanks below with the most appropriate terms in appropriate forms from the box.

equivalent	put into practice	be conscious of	otherwise
deal with	prevent from	involve	work on
relate to	nothing more than		

1. The transactions associated with exporting are generally more complicated than those _____ the domestic market.
2. Once a relationship has been established with an overseas customer, representative, or distributor, it is important that the exporter _____ building and maintaining.
3. Licensing _____ granting a license to a foreign firm to produce and market a product for which the foreign firm pays royalties to the parent firm.
4. A licensing agreement must contain clauses concerning jurisdiction, _____ there will be direct competition between the licensor and the licensee.
5. Most multinational firms _____ extremely _____ the licensee's ability to respect the company's reputation for quality and reliability.
6. Several forms of flexible business arrangements including counter trade, export processing, equity joint ventures and contractual ventures have been _____ in China.

V. Explain the following terms in English.

1. international subcontracting
2. tender
3. counter-trade

4. compensation agreement
5. ITT

VI. Translate the following sentences into English.

(1) 如果一个国家没有外汇储备，没有贷款，也不能通过谈判达成其他协定，那么唯一的选择就是易货贸易。

(2) 如有偶发的经济事件发生时，本代理契约可经双方同意，做部分的修改。

(3) 第二次世界大战以后，出现了各种跨国经营活动，比如商品和劳务贸易、对外直接投资和技术转让等。

(4) 在签订许可证协议之前，许可证颁发者应对被许可人国内有关知识产权方面的法规有全面的了解。

(5) 如果本协议的部分被违反，并不意味着整个协议的终止。

(6) 代理人在被指定的地区里担当职务。他的活动仅限于此地区内。

VII. Translate the following passage into Chinese.

There are a number of unique features in technology transfer. First, commercial technology transfer is highly monopolistic. The contemporary patent system has further reinforced such monopoly. In order to maintain the advantage of its technology and products, the owner of a technology does not normally transfer the technology, except in some specific situations. For example, when a transfer is necessary for occupying the market, not threatening its monopoly. In addition, as a result of unequal development of science and technology, developed countries are to impose various restrictions on the transfer of advanced technology in order to maintain their monopolistic position.

VIII. Speaking activities.

Oral presentation

Form groups of three or four and prepare jointly for the oral presentation topic below. Then vote for a representative in a group to make a 5—15 minute presentation before the whole class.

Thanks to the reforms and opening up policy, China has experienced remarkable economic growth for years. And China's firms have grown in their competitive strength the result that an increasing number of Chinese enterprises are going to the international market. However, they may face the problem of choosing an appropriate method of entering foreign markets as they are inexperienced in international marketing, and besides they are to subject themselves to competition of the established multinational companies. Do you have any suggestions as to their choices of their market entry strategy?

Chapter 3

General Introduction to International Trade Practices

Focal Learning

After the completion of this chapter, you are required to know:
- the definition of export transaction;
- the conduct of export transaction;
- the parties and means involved in the export Transaction.

Lead-in Vocabulary

transaction	n.	交易,事务
available	adj.	可用得到的
domestically	adv.	国内的
intensify	v.	加强
boundary	n.	边界
contract	n.	合同,契约
implementation	n.	执行
invitation	n.	邀请,招待
verbally	adv.	口头地
enquiry	n.	询盘
offer	n.	发盘
counter-offer	n.	还盘
delivery	n.	交货
dispute	n.	争议,争端
arbitration	n.	仲裁
litigation	n.	诉讼

Chapter 3

Section I
The Definition of Export Transaction

All governments take an interest in exporting, because exports speed up the economic development and raise the standard of people's living. Its purpose and significances will be discussed in this chapter.

1. Reasons for Exporting

Surprising as it may sound, there is no country in the world that can produce all the things it needs. In order to engage in effective production and reproduction, raw materials, equipment and technology that are not available domestically must be imported from abroad.

However, unless a country exports it will not have the foreign exchange to import the things it badly needs. Therefore, all countries in the world are intensifying their exporting activities in order to capture a large share of the competitive world market.

Exporting is an extension of trading with customers living in one country. This extension of the trader's domain is highly important, since it enables the vendee to make a choice between alternative goods in satisfying his needs. Not only are the goods of his own nation available to him but those of other nations as well. The need to acquire natural resources and capital equipment is vital to the well-being of all nations.

2. Definition of Exporting

Exporting is the process of earning money by providing the right product at the right price at the right time in the right place beyond your home boundary. The ultimate goal is to make sure that the exporter is to be paid for the goods he sells.

This work is concerned only with the contract of overseas sale, which is a contract under which goods leave the county destined for a buyer abroad, whether by land, sea or air, in containers or as ordinary cargo. All other contracts of sale, though they may be preparatory to the export of goods, are domestic sales and therefore outside the scope of this work. It must be noted that in some sale transactions, for example under an ex works contract, the performance takes place entirely within the country of the seller of the goods and therefore the contract exhibits all the characteristics of a domestic sale. In practice there is no difficulty in determining whether the contract of sale has, as its objective, the exportation of goods from the country because of the terms of the transaction, such as the arrangements made for the transport of the goods to destination, and the fact that the buyer resides abroad. A great variety of transactions are export transactions and the rights and duties of the parties will vary according to the arrangements they have made regarding the place of delivery, the transportation of the goods and the method of payment of the purchase price. Mercantile custom has developed a number of trade terms and described methods of performance of export transactions. The examination of those terms in the following pages will attempt to indicate the diversity and the practical use of the chosen means of performance.

Section II
The Conduct of Export Transaction

An export or import transaction is very complicated and it may take quite a long time to complete it. Its operation covers many links that are a constituent part of the transaction. The whole operation usually undergoes four steps: preparation for exporting/importing, business negotiation, implementation of contract, and settlement of disputes. Each step covers some specific links. In this chapter, a broad outline is given just to provide you with a bird's eye view of the whole of the export transaction, since the export and import transaction are two sides of the same coin, and one nation's export is another nation's import.

1. Preparation for Exporting

"A good beginning is half done", that is also the case in the conducting of an export trade. Any exporter who wants to open a new market in a foreign country, he must acquire a good knowledge of that market to which his products are sold. As a new exporter, how does he know where to find an overseas market for his products? Even for an old exporter, there still remains the question of finding new markets for his new products or maybe to expand market share of his old products.

To answer this question is one of the objects of market research, which is so vital to success in overseas markets. To look for a good market, an exporter must consider such factors as political and economic conditions, physical and climate conditions, social conditions, traditions and customs, existing products and structure of trade, geography and communications, legal aspects and so on. For example, if there is a low standard of living with poor wage levels; say, in some parts of Africa, there may be no market at all for automobiles or other luxurious products. In order to build the market picture, the exporter has to gather a great variety of information for his decision making. The question is how to find these details. The exporter certainly can not go to every country to find out every piece of information.

Once the overseas market has been founded, the next step is to look for suitable customers with whom the maker or exporter expects to establish good business relationships. Undoubtedly, he or she wishes to deal with those customers of high credit standing, and that is one of the chief factors to consider at the time of setting up new business connections.

Export promotion stands for activities that communicate the merits of the product and persuade target customers to buy it. The promotion or communication instrument is in many markets the most conspicuous element of the marketing mix. The marketing communication mix consists of four major tools: advertising, personal selling, sales promotion and publicity.

2. Business Negotiation

International business negotiation is an important part of conducting a foreign trade. It is the dealings between supplier and customer in order to reach agreement on the price, quantity, quality, payment and other terms and conditions of a sale. Obviously, the conclusion of sales contract results from the business negotiation to the satisfaction of both sides.

International business negotiations are carried out either by writing or verbally. In the latter case, traders talk about the terms and conditions of a transaction with each other in person or by telephone. The foreign businessman may call on the domestic trader upon invitation, or the exporter will make a visit to an overseas importer on his own account. Business negotiations are also held at international fairs where businessmen all over the world can negotiate with one another over export and import trade. Through verbal negotiations trading transactions between Chinese and foreign businessmen are concluded in large amounts at the China Export Commodities Fair in Guangzhou twice a year.

To reach to an agreement of the various terms mentioned above, the international business negotiation generally needs going through five links: enquiry, offer, counter-offer, acceptance and conclusion of a contract. Of course, it is not necessary to have all the five links taken for every transaction. Sometimes, only offer and acceptance will do. It is stipulated in the laws of some countries that only offer and acceptance are the two required factors, failure of which will make no contract.

3. Implementation of Contract

Nowadays a lot of export/import transactions are concluded under CIF and sight L/C terms. There are six links that should be taken care of while implementing the sales contract.

❖ **Preparing Goods for Shipment**

After a contract is concluded, it is the main task for the exporter to get the goods ready and to check them against the terms stipulated in the contract. If necessary, the exporter should obtain a certificate of inspection from the institutions concerned where the goods are inspected.

❖ **Examination and Modification of the Letter of Credit**

A letter of credit is the most common method of payment in foreign trade. Once two parties agree to adopt it, it is very important for the exporter to examine the details mentioned in the letter of credit received. If there should be any discrepancies, the exporter should contact the importer immediately for amendments so as to get the due payment.

❖ **Chartering and Booking Shipping Space**

When the goods are ready, the exporter has to choose the right mode of transport. He may well try and find the cheapest mode of getting his goods to the export market. In general, the most common and the cheapest method of transport is a ship that often takes several months to compete its voyage. If sea freight is chosen, the exporter has to make an arrangement with a shipping company to have the goods to be shipped on or before the date of shipment agreed to in the contract.

❖ **Customs Formalities**

By booking the shipping space, the exporter knows when and where to load the goods so as to have the goods loaded on board a booked ship. Before the goods are loaded, certain procedures in customs formalities have to be completed. After the goods are loaded, the shipping company issues a bill of lading, which serves as a receipt of the loading of the goods on board the ship.

❖ **Insuring Goods**

Long distance sea freight is subject to many risks. The exporter usually applies to an insurance company for insurance covering the goods to be transported in an attempt to protect the goods in transit against damage or loss. In this way an insurance policy is made out by the insurance company. Both the bill of lading and insurance policy constitute the chief shipping documents which are vital in export trading.

❖ **Bank Negotiation**

In the international trade, it is essential that the exporter delivers the goods and the importer makes the payment of the goods. If the exporter has duly shipped the goods, he is entitled to receipt of the payment. Under a letter of credit term, he draws a bill of exchange, or a draft, and presents the bill accompanied by shipping documents to the bank who pays the documentary bill. As to the shipping documents they include commercial invoice, bill of lading, insurance policy, packing list, weight memo, certificate of inspection, and in some cases, consular invoice, certificate of origin, etc.

4. Settlement of Disputes

Despite the careful performance of a contract by the parties involved, sometimes, complaints or claims may arise. For example, the importer does not receive goods of the kind, quality he anticipates, or the exporter does not receive the due payment. All these will lead to complaints and claims. In accordance with specific conditions, complaints and claims may be made to the exporter, importer, insurance company or shipping company as the case may be.

In case the loss or damage is caused by the perils covered by an insurance policy, a claim is made to the insurance company. When the exporter and importer are involved in trouble, to settle the disputes it is advised that arbitration is better than litigation, and conciliation is better than arbitration. Of course, it is best to prevent the disputes at all by abiding by the sales contract in all respects.

Chapter 3

Section III

The Parties and Means in the Export Transaction

The parties who are involved in an export transaction are numerous and are described variously.

1. Basic Parties in the Export Transaction

The basic parties in the export transaction are as follows:
1) **the buyer who purchases the goods;**
2) **the seller who provides the goods.**

The exporter may sell directly to the importer abroad, but it may sell to an export house or confirming house, which will act either as the agent of the importer or as a principal in its own right. If it acts as an agent it will earn commission from the importer; if it acts as a principal it will earn the profit on the resale abroad. The exporter may also appoint an agent or set up a branch office.

2. Other Major Parties and Means in the Export Transaction

Alternatively the exporter may use other means to conclude export transactions.

❖ **Sole Distribution Agreements**

A sole distribution agreement involves the distributor abroad being granted sole or exclusive rights to represent the exporter. Although the distributor is not an agent as such, he does not have to account to the exporter for profits made in selling the goods in question. What this means ought to be specified clearly by the parties, but the agreement will generally involve the granting of sole trading rights, in a specified territory, of specified goods. The exporter will generally agree not to compete with the distributor or allow others to do so.

❖ **Licensing Agreements**

A licensing agreement involves the granting by an owner in particular territory of a form of intellectual property, such as a patent or a trade mark, to a licensee of a right to a licensee of a right to exploit that property in another territory. The advantage of this type of arrangement is that the licensee provides the capital needed will carry the commercial risk of the transactions. Two matters are to be noted: the issue of quality control must be dealt with in the licensing agreement and indeed the licensor should protect his reputation by insisting on a right to test samples of the goods produced under license.

❖ **Franchising Agreements**

Where the exporter has a strong and recognizable corporate image, the so-called brand, a particular form of licensing—franchising—may be adopted. Under this arrangement the exporter-franchiser will rigidly control the way in which the import-franchisee conducts the business of selling the goods abroad. The strict control is designed to achieve uniformity between outlets so that customers, wherever they may be, cannot distinguish between outlets owned by the franchiser and those run by the franchisee. Quality control is therefore rigidly maintained. The franchisee will own the outlet and raise his own capital and will source, to the extent of the franchise agreement, goods from the franchiser-exporter.

❖ Entering a Joint Venture with a Party Abroad

A joint venture is a common undertaking created by two or more participants for a specific purpose, usually of a commercial nature. The common undertaking may take one of various legal forms and does not necessarily result in the creation of a separate legal entity, as the venture may be purely contractual. Aside from the common project planned, the joint venture partners will pursue their own commercial objects. The joint venture is the preferred vehicle for the conduct of international transacts of certain less industrialized nations who have adopted legislation which encourages foreign investment and the protection of their own essential interests.

❖ Electronic Data Interchange

The accelerating development of technology has afforded exporters the opportunity of dealing in a paperless environment. The means by which electronic data interchange is conducted and its potential application in export transaction is mentioned in the other book.

Useful Phrases & Technical Terms

China Export Commodities Fair	中国出口商品博览会
Customs formalities	报关单
Insuring goods	给货物保险
export house	出口公司, 出口管理局
confirming house	保付行, 保付公司
sole distribution	独家经销协定
exclusive rights	专有权
licensing agreement	特许权协议或许可证协议
intellectual property	知识产权
trade mark	商标
legal entity	法人实体

Notes

1. Exporting is the process of earning money by providing the right product at the right price at the right time in the right place beyond your home boundary. The ultimate goal is to make sure that the exporter is to be paid for the goods he sells.

出口是指在本国之外,以合理的价格,在适当的时间、适当的地点提供合适的产品,来获取利润的过程。其最终目的是确保出口商售出商品后得到支付。

2. International business negotiation is an important part of conducting a foreign trade. It is the dealings between supplier and customer in order to reach agreement on the price, quantity, quality, payment and other terms and conditions of a sale. Obviously, the conclusion of sales contract results from the business negotiation to the satisfaction of both sides.

国际商务谈判是对外贸易的重要组成部分。它是买卖双方为了在价格、数量、质量、支付方式以及其它条款方面达成协议所进行的交易。显然,令双方满意的谈判才能促成合同的达成。

3. license agreement: 许可证协议

是一方准许另一方使用其所有的或拥有的工业产权或专有技术,被许可方依照合同得到该项使用权并支付使用费的合同。许可证合同的客体主要是技术使用权,具体的讲,即专利使用权、商标使用权和专用技术使用权。

4. franchising agreement: 特许协议

是指特许经营权拥有者与被特许经营者之间签订的特许经营合同,特许者以合同约定的形式,允许被特许经营者有偿使用其名称、标志、专有技术、产品及运作管理经验等从事经营活动的商业经营模式。

5. joint venture: 合资企业

合资企业一般指中外合资。中外合资经营企业是由中国投资者和外国投资者共同出资、共同经营、共负盈亏、共担风险的企业。外国合营者可以是企业、其他经济组织或个人。

Questions for Discussion

1. Name the various ways of dealing in export trade in our country?
2. Exporting is not easy, how is export business promoted?

❖ Case Study

Compensation Trade

Dear Sirs,

Our bankers, Bank of England, inform us that you require our Modal AI-S Sewing Machines and wish to pay for them with the window curtains processed under compensation trade arrangements. Subject to satisfactory arrangements as to terms and conditions, we should be pleased to conclude the deal.

We can offer you 50 sets of sewing Machines, Model A1-S, at the price of US$80 per set CIF China Port. The cost of machines will be advanced by us and be repaid by you in installments, plus freight and interest at 10 per annum.

Meanwhile, we would like to receive your quotation for Linen Window Curtains, 1,000 dozen a month. Upon receipt of your firm offer, we will try to package the two deals and work out a draft agreement for you to consider.

We look forward to your quotation and your suggestion as to other terms and conditions.

Yours faithfully,

Letter of Reply

Dear Sirs,

We are pleased to learn from your letter of March 18 that you will consider compensation wade arrangements for the supply of Model A1-S Sewing Machines.

As requested by you, we are making you an offer, subject to your acceptance by March 31, for 10,000 dozen Linen Window Curtains at US$3 per piece CIF EMP, to be delivered monthly in 10 lots two months after the trial operation of the Sewing Machines. The price of these curtains is to pay for the 50 Sewing Machines you supply plus freight and an annual interest of _____ %.

For your information, we enclose a copy of our compensation trade agreement with a Swiss firm, we suggest that we include the same Arbitration Clause in the draft agreement you are to prepare.

We look forward to receiving the formal agreement from you soon.

Yours faithfully,

❖ Role Play

Talking with a Potential Client

A: Hello, Mr. Li.

B: Hello, Mr. Smith, glad to see you again.

A: I'm very interested in your products, and would like to talk something about that.

B: I'm glad to hear that my firm has wide business relations with many corporations in your country. Every year, we export a lot of our products to European countries, but yours seems quite new to us.

A: Well, we work for leather products only for two years, but we are in a position to place large orders with competitive suppliers. This time, we are desirous to see the possibilities of switching our purchase to you.

B: That's fine. Our leather bags have enjoyed a high reputation in the European market. Have you got anything in mind you're interested in?

A: Well, I find article No. 338 rather attractive.

B: It's our newly designed one. Compared with the old ones, it is much better in style. Reports from different markets show that this model is the choice of discriminating buyers.

A: You know, Mr. Li, quality is as much important as the price.

B: Yes. This style is an improvement upon the old styles in many respects. We pay much attention to not only its quality but also its cost. After studying our samples and price list, I'm sure you will be satisfied.

A: That's good.

Extended Activities

I. Answer the following questions.

1. What are the major benefits of exporting?
2. Have you conducted any marketing research?
3. What is the purpose of marketing research?
4. What is the usual way of transporting the goods to the foreign countries?
5. How do you understand free trade?
6. What is anti-dumping?
7. List the basic and major parties involved in an export transaction.
8. If your country does not have enough surplus, should you still import? Why or why not?

II. Match the questions with their corresponding actions required.

Question	Action Required
1. Am I well prepared?	a. Obtain detailed information of market and buyer requirements, be ready with options.
2. Do I know my best markets and buyers?	b. Determine what can be considered to be a sustainable sales agreement; decide ahead of time not to enter into a transaction simply for the sake of exporting; remember that no deal is better than a bad deal.

3. Am I ready to make concessions?

4. Do I know the non-price benefits of my products?

5. Will the buyer listen to me seriously?

6. Will I be in a position to accept the negotiated deal?

c. Undertake thorough research on target markets and buyers.

d. Decide on the maximum concessions that can be made; prepare several negotiating options.

e. Practice projecting confidence maintaining two-way communication.

f. Develop a list of product benefits that could be used to counter price objections.

III. Decide whether the following statements are true or false by writing "T" for true and "F" for false in the bracket besides each statement.

1. (   ) In order to build the market picture, the exporter has to gather a great variety of information for his decision-making.

2. (   ) There are many ways of direct investigation: by visits, personal interviews, telephone contracts with customers, sending questionnaires and so on.

3. (   ) The export promotion consists of four major tools: advertising, personal selling, sales promotion and publicity.

4. (   ) It is said that litigation is better than arbitration, and conciliation is better than arbitration.

5. (   ) The contract which is generally adopted in import and export business is the informal written contract, either a sales contract or a purchase contract.

6. (   ) The information about the credit or financial standing of an overseas trader can be obtained only from banks.

7. (   ) An offer without engagement is made when a seller promises to sell goods at a stated price within a stated period of time.

8. (   ) Countries with different political and economic systems take different attitudes toward foreign trade and their policies related to import and export, foreign exchange control, customs duties may not greatly affect the demand for your products.

IV. Fill in the blanks below with the most appropriate terms from the box.

access to	in terms of	at stake	made strides in
adhere to	in breach of	lead to	at the heart of
come to	left out		

1. For the WTO's procedure to succeed, countries must _____ its decisions, even when they disagree with them.

2. Defining fair practice is _____ many trade disputes, as countries naturally have differing perspectives on what is and is not fair.
3. Less spectacularly, it _____ the more difficult areas of reducing trade barriers in agricultural products and textiles.
4. A country found to be _____ trade rules by a panel may appeal to the Appellate Body.
5. Much has been _____ wider trading relations.
6. Under this legislation a country could lose _____ the entire US market, not merely that of the offending product.
7. Its growth as a trading power suggests it can no longer be _____.
8. Labor standards, including practices such as child labor, have _____ be included in human rights principles generally.
9. Co-operation in pursuing international cartels has progressed and could _____ some form of multilateral antitrust organization in the future.

V. Explain the following terms in English.
1. exporting
2. license agreement
3. franchising agreement
4. joint venture

VI. Translate the following sentences into English.
(1) 本合同由双方代表于1999年12月9日签订。合同签订后，由各方分别向本国政府当局申请批准，以最后一方的批准日期为本合同的生效日期，双方应力争在60天内获得批准，用电传通知对方，并用信件确认。若本合同自签字之日起，6个月仍不能生效，双方有权解除本合同。
(2) 我们愿在平等互利的基础上与贵公司建立业务关系
(3) 我们一直努力设法扩大与中国的合作范围。
(4) 如果你方同意我们进行易货贸易的建议，我们将用纸与你们交换木材
(5) 我们同意与你们进行来料加工贸易。
(6) 成功意味着增加出口量，也意味着使出口多样化——不仅仅就产品而言，而且针对出口市场。
(7) 贸易上这种范围的扩展是很重要的，因为它使得买方在可供选择的商品之间做出选择，以满足自己的需要。

VII. Translate the following passage into Chinese.
A country must achieve a surplus from the export of products that it is good at producing, so that it may import goods for which it has no comparative advantage. The hunter exchanged his surplus with the farmer, and the business was conducted on a barter basis. Most trade is now carried out using money, both within a country and internationally.

Many objectives have been cited for engaging in exporting, particularly at the national level. Ultimately, however, the most important goal is the earning of profit. If it fails, then the other objectives will also fail. The cost outlays must be less than the revenues received from sales; if not, the resources of the companies will be drained away, and it will wither and die. In the long run, the revenues must exceed the costs in order to sustain the company in existence. Exporting may generate great profits, but it involves great risks, too. Above all, the country, the company or the individual will benefit a lot by exporting. This seemingly simple question is not understood by all.

VIII. *Speaking activities.*

Oral presentation

Form groups of three or four and prepare jointly for the oral presentation topic below. Then vote for a representative in a group to make a 8—15 minute presentation before the whole class:

International trade is buying and selling among countries. Nations trade for many reasons. First, they trade because there are differences in natural resources in different countries. The plants that can be grown are different. The mineral resources are also different. The second reason nations trade with one another is that it pays to specialize. Specialization makes the best use of a country's productive resources—natural and human resources, facilities, and technology. It pays a country to specialize even if it can produce everything cheaply. Research and find out the reasons why nations trade with one another, and why there is no loser in international trading.

Chapter 4

International Trade Terms

Focal Learning

After the completion of this chapter, you are required to know:
- the definition and the role of trade terms;
- the six commonly used trade terms;
- the other trade terms;
- Incoterms 2000.

Lead-in Vocabulary

warehouse	*n.*	仓库
	v.	存仓
premise	*n.*	（企业、机构等使用的）房屋连地基
inspection	*n.*	验收，检验
claim	*n. / v.*	索赔
arbitration	*n.*	仲裁，调停
dock	*n.*	码头，船头
jurisdiction	*n.*	司法权，裁判权
within someone's jurisdiction		在……司法管辖范围内
fulfill	*v.*	履行
carrier	*n.*	运输公司（从事运输旅客或货物的人、商业公司或组织）
procure	*v.*	取得
adjoining	*a.*	邻近的
stipulate	*v.*	规定
charter	*v.*	租
premium	*n.*	保险费
mandatory	*a.*	强制的，托管的

cover	n.	保险
	v.	给……保险
marine	a.	海运的，航海的
quay	n.	码头
wharf	n.	码头
stow	v.	理舱
trim	v.	平舱

Section I
Brief Explanations of Trade Terms

We have discussed above international trade is the exchange of commodities or services between different nations. As it is known, doing international business is just like playing games with people from all around the world. To insure the play fair and smooth, a set of rules and laws must be in place. With hundreds of years' development, quite a few rules and laws have come into being to regulate and administer the transactions of international trade.

1. International Trade Terms

International trade terms are a universally recognized set of definitions of some international conventions in trade practices. They define trade contract responsibilities and liabilities between the buyer and the seller. They are an invaluable and cost saving tool. The exporter and the importer need not undergo lengthy negotiations about the conditions of each transaction. Once they have agreed on using a commercial term like FOB, they can sell and buy at FOB without needing to discuss who will be responsible for the freight, cargo insurance, and other costs and risks.

❖ **Definition of International Terms**

When quoting prices to his overseas buyer, an exporter will naturally take into account payment of the various expenses involved in getting the goods from the factory or warehouse in his own country to the buyer's premises. In international trade, terms and conditions of quality, quantity, packing, price, delivery, insurance, terms of payment, inspection, claim and arbitration should be clearly and reasonably stated in the contract so as to clarify the duties and obligations of the Seller and the Buyer. These are the basic terms and conditions of the contract, among which the price term is the most important one. For example, an exporter, in calculating his export price, works out dock charges, clearing and forwarding charges, freight and insurance, and certainly also their profit margin, and adds them to the price paid to the manufacturer to make it, say, USD 2000 per metric ton CIF London including 4% commission. What is "USD 2000 per metric ton CIF London including 4% commission"? It is one of the trade terms, or delivery terms as we usually call them.

Trade terms, also known as price terms or delivery terms, are a set of uniform rules codifying the interpretation of trade terms defining the price composition and the rights and obligations of the buyer and the seller in international transactions.

Trade terms are key elements of international contracts of sale, since they tell the parties what to do with respect to:

Delivery terms—carriage of the goods from the seller to the buyer and division of costs and risks between the parties;

Price terms—stipulating what are included in the price the buyer paid to the seller, e.g. cost, freight, insurance, export and import clearance fees, etc;

Delivery obligations—what documents should the seller provide, e.g. bill of lading insurance policy, etc.

❖ The Role of Trade Terms

Trade terms are standardized terms used in sales contracts that describe the place and manner for the transfer of goods from the seller to the buyer. These trade terms, such as free on board (FOB) and cost, insurance, and the price, the time when the risk of loss shifts from the seller to the buyer, and the costs of freight and insurance. The use of trade terms greatly simplifies the process of negotiation of contract, thus saving time and cost for business.

2. International Rules and Practices on Trade Terms

Trade terms have been developed in practice for many years. However, as different countries might have different interpretations of the terms, misunderstandings occurred frequently. To clear up the confusion, some commercial organizations drew up sets of rules or standard definitions.

❖ *Warsaw-Oxford Rules 1932* (W. O. Rules, 1932)

It was drafted by International Law Association in 1932, which contains 21 clauses, only stipulate the nature of CIF contract.

❖ *Revised American Foreign Trade Definitions 1941*

It was made out by 9 American commercial organizations in 1948, a set of foreign trade terms which are considered obsolete, but still sometimes used in domestic U.S. trade. It contains 6 trade terms: EX, FOB, FAS, C&F, CIF, and EX DOCK.

❖ *International Rule for the Interpretation of Trade Terms, Incoterms*

This rule was developed and issued by the ICC in Paris. It was first published in 1936 and has been periodically revised to account for changing modes of transport and document delivery. The current version is *Incoterms 2000*, which came into force on Jan. 1, 2000.

Incoterms are well known throughout the world, and their use in international sales is encouraged by trade councils, courts and international lawyers. However, since Incoterms are not laws, neither are they implied into contracts for the sale of goods, parties who adopt the Incoterms should make sure they express their desire clearly.

Section II
Contents of Trade Terms

This section, we will mainly study trade terms according to the Incoterms 2000. First of all, let's have a view of the structure of Incoterms 2000. Then, we'll offer a detailed explanation on every term of Incoterms 2000.

1. An Overview of the Structure of Incoterms 2000

The terms in Incoterms 2000 are grouped in four basically different categories: (1) Group E term, (2) Group F terms, (3) Group C terms and (4) Group D terms, with increasing responsibilities, costs and risks for the seller and decreasing responsibilities, costs and risks for the buyer.

Group E has one term only, Ex Works(EXW). It is called a departure term whereby the seller makes the goods available to the buyer at the seller's own premises.

Group F has three terms: FCA, FAS and FOB. These terms call upon the seller to deliver the goods to a carrier appointed and paid by the buyer.

Group C contains four terms: CFR, CIF, CPT and CIP. In these terms the seller has to contract and pay for carriage, but the seller does not assume the risk of loss of or damage to the goods or additional costs due to events occurring after shipment and dispatch.

Group D includes five terms whereby the seller has to bear all costs and risks needed to bring the goods to the country of destination: DAF, DES, DEQ, DDU and DDP.

Incoterms 2000

Group E Departure	EXW—Ex Works (... named place)	All modes of transport including multimodal
Group F Main Carriage Unpaid	FCA—Free Carrier(... named place)	Ditto
	FAS—Free Alongside Ship(...named port of shipment)	Sea and inland waterway transport only
	FOB—Free On Board(...named port of shipment)	Ditto
Group C Main Carriage Paid	CFR—Cost and Freight (...named port of destination)	Ditto
	CIF—Cost, Insurance and Freight (...named port of destination)	Ditto
	CPT—Carriage Paid To (...named place of destination)	All modes of transport including multimodal
	CIP—Carriage and Insurance Paid To (...named place of destination)	Ditto

Group D	DAF—Delivered at Frontier (...named place)	Ditto
	DES—Delivered Ex Ship (...named port of destination)	Ditto
	DEQ—Delivered Ex Quay (...named port of destination)	Ditto
	DDU—Delivered Duty Unpaid (...named place of destination)	Ditto
	DDP—Delivered Duty Paid (...named place of destination)	Ditto

2. A Brief Explanation of Terms in Incoterms 2000

Incoterms 2000 aim at providing such a set of standardized terms which mean exactly the same to both parties to a contract and will be interpreted in exactly the same way by courts in every country. For the purpose of easier reading and understanding, a brief explanation will be given based on the above four groups respectively.

❖ **Explanations of Group E**

EXW

EX WORKS (...named place)

The term means that the seller delivers when he places the goods at the disposal of the buyer at the seller's premises or another named place (i.e. works, factory, warehouse, etc.) not cleared for export and not loaded on any collecting vehicle.

This term thus represents the minimum obligation for the seller, and the buyer has to bear all costs and risks involved in taking the goods from the seller's premises.

This term should not be used when the buyer cannot carry out the export formalities directly or indirectly. In such circumstances, the FCA term should be used.

❖ **Explanations of Group F**

FCA

FREE CARRIER (...named place)

The term FCA means the seller delivers the goods, cleared for export, to the carrier nominated by the buyer at the named place. This means that the buyer bears all risks and any costs occurring after the goods have been delivered. It should be noted that according to Incoterms 2000, the chosen place of delivery has an impact on the obligations of loading and unloading the goods at that place. If delivery occurs at the seller's premises, the seller is responsible for loading. If delivery occurs at any other place, the seller is not responsible for unloading.

FAS

FREE ALONGSIDE SHIP (...named port of shipment)

The term FAS means that the seller delivers goods, when the goods are placed alongside the vessel at the named port of shipment. This means that the buyer has to bear all costs and risks of loss of or damage tot the goods from that moment.

The FAS requires the seller to clear the goods for export.

This is a reversal from previous Incoterms versions which required the buyer to arrange for export clearance.

This term is used for sea or inland waterway transportation.

FOB

FREE ON BOARD (...named port of shipment)

When "free" is used in a trade term, it means that the seller has an obligation to deliver goods to a named place for transfer to a carrier. According to ICC's Incoterms 2000, in Free On Board, the seller delivers when the goods pass the ship's rail at the named port of shipment. This means the buyer has to bear all costs and risks of loss of or damage to the goods from that moment. In FOB the seller is required to deliver goods on board a vessel that is to be designated by the buyer at the particular port. For example, FOB Singapore requires the buyer to name the ship that will accept delivery in Singapore. The seller is also required to clear the goods for export. The FOB term, as its name suggests, is a maritime trade term, is used only for ocean or inland waterway transport.

The essence of an FOB contract is the notion that a seller is responsible for getting goods on board a ship designated by a buyer. What is meant by "on board" has been the issue in many cases and is described in detail in the Incoterms. Traditionally, goods are "on board" a ship the moment they cross its rail.

The seller's responsibilities in detail are:

(1) Obtaining export license or other official documents and carrying out all customs formalities for the export of the goods.

(2) Delivering the goods on board of the vessel designated by the buyer at the port of shipment within the period stipulated in the contract.

(3) Providing the commercial documents or its equivalent electronic message to the buyer.

The buyer's responsibilities are:

(1) Chartering ships or booking liner spaces, paying the freight, informing the seller of the name and the date of arrival of the ship.

(2) Obtaining all kinds of documents required for import clearing and carrying out import formalities.

(3) Taking delivery of the goods, making payment to the seller.

The FREE ON BOARD term is commonly used in the sale of bulk commodity cargo such as oil, grain and ore where passing the ship's rail is important. However, it is also commonly used in shipping container loads of other goods.

❖ Explanations of Group C

CFR

COST AND FREIGHT (...named port of destination)

Under the CFR term, the seller must pay the costs and freight necessary to bring the goods to the named port of destination.

The cost and freight term is the same as the FOB term except that the seller instead of the buyer is responsible for making arrangement of the ship (chartering a ship or booking a space).

CIF

COST, INSURANCE AND FREIGHT (...named port of destination)

Under the CIF term, the seller must pay the costs and freight necessary to bring the goods to a named port of destination, and must also procure marine insurance against the buyer's risk of loss of or damage to the goods during the carriage.

CIF is the same as CFR except that the seller is responsible for effecting insurance, paying the premium. The insurance required under a CIF contract has to cover minimum conditions.

CIF is the most important and commonly used shipping term. The CIF is preferred by buyers because it means that they have little to do with the goods until the goods arrive at a port of destination in their country. A CIF price quotation also allows buyers to compare prices from suppliers around the world without having to take into consideration differing freight rates, since the seller pays the freight and insurance. Export-sellers are often under pressure from their governments to use domestic carriers and insurers, so they too like the term. On the other hand, sellers may not be able to find domestic carriers or insurers; and the buyers, under pressure from governments that are also concerned about employing national carriers and insurers, may settle for an FOB contract.

CPT

CARRIAGE PAID TO (...named place of destination)

This term means that the seller pays the freight for the carriage of the goods to the named destination. The risk of loss of or damage to the goods, as well as any additional costs due to the events occurring after the time the goods have been delivered to the carrier, is transferred from the seller to the buyer when the goods have been delivered into the custody of the carrier.

CPT requires the seller to clear the goods for export.

This term may be used for any mode of transport including multimodal transport.

CIP

CARRIAGE AND INSURANCE PAID (named place of destination)

CIP means that the seller has the same obligations as under CPT but with the addition that the seller has to procure cargo insurance against the buyer's risk of loss of or damage to the goods during the carriage. The seller contracts for insurance and pays the insurance premium.

The buyer should note that under CIP the seller is only required to obtain insurance on a minimum coverage.

This term requires the seller to clear the goods for export. It may be used for any mode of transport including multimodal transport.

❖ Explanations of Group D

DAF

DELIVERED AT FRONTIER (...named place)

This term means that the seller delivers when the goods are placed at the disposal of the buyer at the named point and place at the frontier. From that moment, the buyer must bear all risks and costs. The seller must clear the goods for export. But he is not responsible for the unloading of the goods from the arriving means of transport.

This term is mostly used in the transaction of two adjoining countries.

DES

DELIVERED EX SHIP (...named port of destination)

DES means that the seller fulfils his obligation to deliver when the goods have been made available to the buyer on board the ship uncleared for import at the named port of destination. The seller has to bear all the costs and risks involved in bringing the goods to the named port of destination.

This term can only be used for sea or inland waterway transport.

DEQ

DELIVERED EX QUAY (...named port of destination)

DEQ means that the seller fulfils his obligation to deliver when he has made the goods available to the buyer on the quay at the named port of destination, cleared for import. The seller has to bear all risks and costs including duties, taxes and other charges of delivering the goods thereto.

This term should not be used if the seller is unable directly or indirectly to obtain the import license. When this term is used, the seller must assume any risk of import prohibition and must ascertain that a customs clearance performed by a party not domiciled in the importing country is accepted by the authorities.

This term can only be used for sea or inland waterway transport.

DDU

DELIVERED DUTY UNPAID (...named place of destination)

DDU means that the seller fulfils his obligation to deliver when the goods have been made available at the named place in the country of import. The seller has to bear the costs and risks involved in bringing the goods thereto as well as the costs and risks of carrying out customs formalities for export and transit through another country. The buyer has to pay any additional costs and to bear any risks caused by his failure to clear the goods for important in time.

This term may be used irrespective of the mode of transport.

DDP

DELIVERED DUTY (...named place of destination)

DDP means that the seller fulfils his obligation to deliver when the goods have been made available at the named place in the country of importation. The seller has to bear the risks and costs, including duties, taxes and other charges of delivering the goods thereto, cleared for import. This term represents the maximum obligation.

DDP should not be used if the seller is unable directly or indirectly to obtain the import license.

If the parties wish the buyer to clear the goods for import and to pay the duty, the term DDU should be used.

3. Comparison between FCA/CPT/CIP and the Traditional FOB/CFR/CIF

❖ *Similarities*

(1) All are symbolic delivery, the corresponding sales/purchase contracts are shipment contracts.

(2) The seller is responsible for export clearance, and the buyer is responsible for import clearance.

(3) FCA is somewhat like FOB, CPT like CFR, and CIP like CIP.

❖ *Differences*

(1) Modes of transportation: FCA/CPT/CIP are applicable to all modes of transport, including rail, road, air, sea, inland waterway and multimodal transport. FOB/CFR/CIF can be used only for sea or inland waterway transport.

(2) Different point of risk dividing: in FCA/CPT/CIP, the risks are divided when the goods are delivered to the carrier, while the traditional ones are at the ship's rail.

(3) Charges for loading and unloading the goods: for FCA/CPT/CIP, the carrier is responsible for loading and unloading; therefore no derived terms are used.

Section III
Expression and Choice of Trade Terms

Trade terms are also referred to as "price terms" or "delivery terms". Trade terms are a set of uniform rules codifying the interpretation of trade terms defining the price composition and the rights and obligations of the buyer and the seller in international transactions. Different expression or choice of trade terms can lead to different meanings, as a result we should pay more attention to the expression and choice of trade terms.

1. Expression of Trade Terms

Trade terms are expressed in the unit price for goods.

In an international sales contract, the unit price usually contains unit, amount and a trade term which is followed by a named port or place of shipment or destination.

2. Choice of Trade Terms

Different trade terms mean different obligations to the buyer and the seller. At present, symbolic delivery trade terms are widely used. Chinese foreign trade enterprises are traditionally inclined to arrange shipment and effect insurance by themselves. The purpose is to develop both Chinese ocean transport industry and insurance industry. Therefore, they often adopt FOB or FCA in their import deals and try to adopt CIF or CIP in their export deals. Sometimes they also adopt CFR or CPT in the circumstance when the other party's countries require insurance to be effected by their own insurance companies.

The following factors should be taken into consideration when choosing trade terms.

❖ **Adapting to the Modes of Transportation**

Since FOB/CFR/CIF are used for sea or inland waterway transport, it is necessary to adopt FCA/CPT/CIP when the cargos are transported by rail or air. Even by ocean transport, when containers are used, it is better to adopt FCA/CPT/CIP because the seller will lose the control of the goods when the cargos are delivered to the carrier.

❖ **Avoiding Risks**

When importing bulk cargoes by charter, basically, FOB should be adopted. In this case, we (the buyer) shall charter the ship or book shipping space and effect insurance, thus avoiding the risks of going up of the seller and the carrier. They may take advantage of the charter B/L to deceive the buyer into making payments.

Useful Phrases & Technical Terms

clearing charges	报关费用
forwarding charges	转运费
profit margin	利润率，毛利率
Warsaw-Oxford Rules	《华沙牛津规则》
Revised American Foreign Trade Definition	《美国对外贸易修订本》
Incoterms	International Commercial Terms 的缩写，表示"国际贸易术语"
Incoterms 2000	《2000年国际贸易术语解释通则》
clearing the goods for export	出口清关
customs formalities	报关单
ship's rail	船舷

insurance premium		保费
premium		在外汇业务中表示"升水",在保险业中示"保费"
import clearance		进口清关
import license		进口许可证
price quotation		报价单,估价单
symbolic delivery		象征性交货

Notes

1. 《Incoterms 2000》4 组 13 种贸易术语

E 组	EXW	工厂交货
F 组	FCA	货交承运人
	FAS	装运港船边交货
	FOB	装运港船上交货
C 组	CFR	成本加运费
	CIF	成本加保险费、运费
	CPT	运费付至
	CIP	运费、保险费付至
D 组	DAF	边境交货
	DES	目的港船上交货
	DEQ	目的港码头交货
	DEU	未完税交货
	DDP	完税后交货

2. FOB 的变形

FOB Liner Terms	FOB 班轮条件
FOB Under Tackle	FOB 吊钩下交货
FOB Stowed	FOB 包括理舱
FOB Trimmed	FOB 包括平舱
FOB Stowed and Trimmed	FOB 包括理舱和平舱

3. Trade terms are also referred to as "price terms" or "delivery terms". Trade terms are a set of uniform rules codifying the interpretation of trade terms defining the price composition and the rights and obligations of the buyer and the seller in international transactions.

贸易术语又叫"价格术语"或"交货条件",它是确定国际贸易中买卖双方价格组成、权利和义务的一套统一的规则和有关规则的释义。

4. International Chamber of Commerce: 国际商会。它是1920年在巴黎设立的重要的工商组织，1946年成为经社理事会咨询机构，下设许多机构从事有关金融、贸易、税收、运输、商务仲裁、工业产权等专门研究。
5. Under FOB, we must make it clear as to who shall bear the loading expenses: 在使用FOB术语时，我们必须明确谁将负担装货费用。

Questions for Discussion

1. What are the differences between FOB, CFR and CIF?
2. Why is it very important for the seller to send shipping advice to the buyer under CFR?
3. Why CIF contract is considered shipment contract?
4. What are the differences between FOB/CFR/CIF and FCA/CPT/CIP?

Case Study

1
FOB (Incoterms 2000)

A contract might refer to "FOB (Incoterms 2000)". Courts will otherwise apply the definitions used in their own jurisdictions. Parties should also refrain from casually adopting any particular set of terms. The ICC's Incoterms, which are possibly the most complete of all such rules, are lengthly and deserve careful study. Finally, parties should be wary about making additions or varying the meaning of any particular term, except to the extent that it is allowed by the rules they adopt or by judicial decision.

2
Why to Send Shipping Advice?

A cable reads: "S.CC215 L/C7643 4000DOZEN SHIRTS SHIPPED FENGCHING101 SAILING26". Why to send shipping advice? The purpose is to inform the buyer or its agent to make preparations for taking delivery of goods.

However, under CFR, there is another purpose, i.e. to inform the buyer to effect insurance. If the seller fails to send shipping advice in time, making it impossible for the buyer to effect insurance promptly, the seller will have to bear the risks of loss of or damage to the goods. Therefore, the seller should pay special attention to the issue of sending shipping advice.

Chapter 4

❖ **Role Play**

Price Negotiation

Martin: OK. Let's talk price.

Robert: The best price I can offer you is US$20.50.

Martin: Are you quoting CIF or FOB?

Robert: All our prices are FOB Tianjin, including five percent commission.

Martin: If I want to make it CIF New York, How much will it come to?

Robert: Would you mind waiting a moment? I need a few minutes to calculate the price.

Martin: While you're calculating, may I ask what are your terms of payment?

Robert: It's our company's policy to request that all transactions should be established with L/C terms.

Martin: I see. How soon can the products be delivered?

Robert: We can deliver them within forty days after receipt of your L/C. OK. The CIF New York price is US$24.50. If you were to sign the L/C today, then I could give you a discount of one percent.

Extended Activities

I. Answer the following questions.

1. What is the purpose of incoterms?
2. What are the different right of the seller and buyer under FOB and CIF?
3. What's the major difference between EXW and DDP?
4. Why do they divide the 13 terms into such 4 categories?
5. Which terms are appropriate for sea and inland waterway only?
6. Who is to pay the import duty under EXQ?

II. Choose the best correct answers.

1. Warsaw-Oxford Rules 1932 was made up by the Association of International Law for explaining _____.
   A. CIF contract   B. FAS contract
   C. DES contract   D. CPT contract

2. For trade terms in Group C, after departure, the risks of loss of or damage to the goods are borne by _____.
   A. the seller   B. the buyer
   C. the carrier   D. the ship owner

3. According to Incoterms 2000, in CPT, the buyer is not responsible for _____.
   A. making a contract of carriage   B. making payment
   C. accepting goods   D. clearing goods for import

4. The derived terms of FOB are to illustrate who shall bear _____.
   A. the charges for clearance   B. the charges for loading
   C. the charges for unloading   D. freight

5. In CIF, if the seller is ready to bear the charges for unloading the goods onto the dock of the port of destination, which of the following CIF derived terms is to be adopted?
   A. CIF Landed   B. CIF Ex Tackle
   C. CIF Ex Ship's Hold   D. CIF Trimmed

6. The term CFR should be followed by _____.
   A. point of origin   B. port of shipment
   C. port of destination   D. port to exportation

7. The term DDP should be followed by _____.
   A. point of origin   B. port of shipment
   C. port of buyer's premises   D. port of exportation

8. The term FOB should be followed by _____.
   A. point of origin   B. port of importance
   C. port of discharge   D. port of exportation

9. The term EXQ should be followed by _____.
   A. point of origin   B. port of importance
   C. port of discharge   D. port of exportation

10. the term FAS should be followed by _____.
    A. point of origin   B. port of destination
    C. port of shipment   D. port of exportation

III. Decide whether the following statements are true or false by writing "T" for true and "F" for false in the bracket besides each statement.

1. (   ) EXQ takes the exporter's costs and risks one step forward in comparison with EXS.
2. (   ) Proper or improper price terms may make no difference between profit and loss, between seller and the buyer.
3. (   ) DDP is the best delivery term for the importer.
4. (   ) The terms of delivery are always quoted by the buyer rather than by the seller.
5. (   ) China adopts an independent trading policy and never follows any international practices.
6. (   ) The import duty is to be paid by the seller under EXS.
7. (   ) FAS denotes that an exporter should load the goods onto the ship.
8. (   ) The exporter is required, under CIF to take out marine insurance which covers the total value of the contract plus indefinite percentage of expected profit.
9. (   ) Under FOA, the exporter fulfills his obligations by supplying the goods to the airport authority.
10. (   ) Each term has a "liability point", which means that costs and risks are all moved over to another party from that very point.

Chapter 4

IV. Complete the following diagram according to what you have read in the text.

INCOTERMS 2000

Categories of Terms	Name of Specific Terms
Group E	Ex Works (_____)
Group F	1. Free Carrier (_____) 2. _____ (FAS) 3. Free On Board (_____)
Group C	1. Cost and Freight (CFR) 2. Cost, Insurance and Freight(_____) 3. Carriage paid to (_____) 4. Carriage and Insurance Paid To (_____)
Group D	1. Delivered At Frontier (DAF) 2. _____ (DES) 3. Delivered Ex Quay (DEQ) 4. _____ (DDU) 5. Delivered Duty Paid (DDP)

V. Translate the following sentences into English.

(1) 买方会预测所有成本和风险并安排货物运输事宜,而且必须根据合同条款支付货款。

(2) 如果还有其他运输方式,这些条款就不适用,即使有一部分运输是海运。

(3) 根据CFR合同,卖方的义务和FOB的一般条款相同,而且在装船之后,买方就不承担货物损失的责任。

(4) 当货物装上火车或卡车之后,或海运或空运时货物交付承运人后,卖方就不再对损失承担责任。

(5) 统常买方会安排以后的装运事宜,尽管合同可能规定应该卖方去安排。

VI. Translate the following passage into Chinese.

Those who do business only domestically avoid many of the problems that beset the international trader. In addition to other cultural conflicts, those who trade entirely within their own borders are free from the complications that arise from differing legal systems, languages, and business practices. The international business forum is a fertile place for contractual misunderstandings and an expensive place to resolve them through litigation.

VII. Speaking activities.

Oral presentation

Form groups of three or four and prepare jointly for the oral presentation topic below. Then vote for a representative in a group to make a 8-15 minute presentation before the whole class:

Recognizing a compelling need for universal terminology in international trade contracts, the International Chamber of Commerce, among others, has developed a standard set of terms and abbreviations called Inoc terms. These terms have been carefully defined in all major languages. As a result, the rights and obligations of each party to a contract should be more clearly understood if the contract is expressed in Inoc terms.

What are the advantages of using Incoterms?

Chapter 5

International Sales Contract

Focal Learning

After the completion of this chapter, you are required to know:
- the significance and definition of sale contract;
- the terms of sales contract;
- the formation of sales contract;
- the implementation of the contract.

Lead-in Vocabulary

marine insurance	n.	海事保险
London underwriters	n.	伦敦保险商
Lloyds Coffee House		劳氏咖啡俱乐部
The Lloyds S & G. (Ship & Goods) Policy		劳氏 S&G（航运与货物）保险单
Hague Rules		海牙规则
draft	v.	草拟
placement of risks		风险承担条款
shipment contract		装运港交货合同
destination-type sales contract		目的港交货合同
shipping terms		装船条件
distort	v.	歪曲
force majeure clause		不可抗力条款
irresistible force		不可抗拒的力量
commercial impracticability		贸易不可实现
unforseeability	n.	不可预见性
nullity	n.	无效
choice of law and choice of forum		适用法律和管辖的选择
mandatory	a.	强制的
performance	v.	履行

implied choice		默示规定
breach	v.	违约
remedy	n.	补救方法
enforcement	n.	执行
CISG		《联合国国际货物销售合同公约》(United Nations Convention on Contract for the International Sale of Goods,简称 CISG)
offer	n.	要约
offeree	n.	受盘人
offeror	n.	报盘人
assent	n.	赞成
duly	adv.	适时地
countersign	vt.	副署,确认,承认
retune	v.	重新调整(调节)

Section I
Definition and Contents of International Sales Contracts

Business as we know today would be impossible if there was no agreement or contract to bind the contracting parties. Sales contracts play a key role in the law of international business transactions today, which are legally binding written agreements between two or more parties. They are not only an important part of business, but also useful in providing for a common understanding between buyer and seller, thus minimizing disputes. When a dispute does occur, the sales contract can help provide for a fair settlement. Therefore, the importance of a contract in an international sales transaction cannot be underestimated. Often it is the only document between the parties to which they may refer for clarification of mutual responsibilities, resolution of disputes, in the event of disagreement.

1. Definition of International Sales Contracts

Sales contract is an agreement between a buyer and seller covering the sale and delivery of goods, securities, and personal property other than goods or securities. International sales contracts fall under the United Nations Convention on Contracts for the International Sales of Goods (CISG), also known as the Vienna Sales Convention.

International sales contract is drafted to accommodate traders who deal directly with each other. The bargaining sessions cover such items as prices as affected by market forces, risk factors, and terms relating to security of payment. The final agreements represent the private law of a private transaction. In contrast to the usual domestic transaction, performance of international agreement involves greater distances and longer periods of time before the goods are delivered and payment is required. And, as we have seen, international transactions carry the following unique risks: more than one currency, system of governmental regulation, legal system, language, and set of cultural expectations.

The rights and duties of the buyer and seller in the international transaction vary according to the arrangements they make with respect to the place, time and method of delivery of the goods and the payment of the purchase price. Despite the distance and the time factors and the additional international risks, most of the problems center on performance and the placement of risks. Traders operating in a domestic setting often enter into contingencies that may occur. International contracts are generally drafted quite carefully and with close attention to the risks that are present.

2. Contents of a Sales Contract

In the international trade, a written contract refers to a formal written document endorsed by both parties to the transaction. It is very important, because it is endorsed by both parties to the sales, and the written contract is evidence that the two parties have come to an agreement. According to the United Nations Convention on Contracts for International Sales of Goods, a contract is not restricted to the written form, but according to Chinese commercial law, only the written form of contract can be considered a legal contract. In international trade practice, the contents of an offer should be:

- Complete—usually six trade conditions are included;
- Clear—clearly expressed, the contents shall not result in misunderstanding;
- Without reservation—a communication that contains words like "subject to our final confirmation" shall be considered as with reservation, and therefore it is not an offer.

According to the Law of the People's Republic of China on Economic Contracts Involving Foreign Interest, a contract generally shall contain the following terms:

(1) The corporate or personal names of the contracting parties and their nationalities and principal places of business or domicile;
(2) The date and place of the signing of the contract;
(3) The type of contract and the kind and scope of the object of the contract;
(4) The technical conditions, quality, standard, specifications and quantity of the object of the contract;
(5) The time limit, place and method of performance;
(6) The price, amount and method of payment, and various incidental charges;
(7) Whether the contract is assignable and, if it is, the conditions for its assignment;
(8) Liability to pay compensation and other liabilities for breach of contract;
(9) Methods for settling contract disputes;
(10) The language(s) in which the contract is to be written and its validity.

In trade practice, a contract can take the form of either a sales contract or a sales confirmation. The contract will contain not only the specific terms of the transaction but also clauses concerning commodity inspection, claims, arbitration and force majeure, etc. The confirmation only contains some specific terms. When the contract is drafted by the seller, it is called sales contract. When the contract is drafted by the buyer, it is called a purchase contract. The same is true with a confirmation. When it is drafted by the seller, it is called a sales confirmation; when it is drafted by the buyer, it called a purchase confirmation. Both confirmation and contract are binding on the seller and the buyer.

3. Major Terms of a Sales Contract

A transaction starts from negotiating the terms of the document that will determine the rights and obligations of both the importer and the exporter. Once this agreement is signed, all the terms should be strictly observed. Therefore, it is important that all the terms should be expressly agreed upon by the importer and the exporter. A sales contract normally consists of the following main terms:

❖ **Placement of Risks**

Ordinarily, the risk of loss rests with the buyer as soon as the seller delivers the goods to the carrier. The rules regarding risk of loss assume that the requirements of the contract have been correctly followed by the seller. How the risk of loss rules is interpreted depends upon whether the contract is a shipment contract or a destination-type sales contract. When the contract calls for "shipment by carrier" and is of the "shipment" type, the risk shifts from the seller on delivery to the carrier. When the contract calls for "shipment by carrier" to a particular destination, the risk shifts from the seller to the tender of the goods by the carrier at the destination point. In all cases, the seller must "put and hold conforming goods at the buyer's disposition" and give the buyer such satisfaction as necessary.

❖ **Shipping Terms**

When shipping terms are specified, they determine when the transfer of risks occurs. For example, if an agreement is FOB shipping point, the seller bears the risks of loss or damage until the goods have been delivered to the carrier, if an agreement is FOB destination, the risk is with the seller until the goods reach their destination. The terms of C&F or CIF place an obligation on the buyer to ship the goods, to pay insurance and freight charges, and to forward the shipping documents within a reasonable time. In this instance, the risk of loss is with the buyer during shipment of the goods.

The use of COD tells the carrier not to deliver the goods until the purchase price is paid. Although the seller retains control over the goods under COD terms, the title passes upon delivery to the carrier. In the case of shipments made on a "to arrive" basis or contracts based on "no arrival, no sales," the seller is not responsible for the goods failure to arrive if it has not been negligent, but the buyer may avoid the contract. In an ex ship agreement, the risk of loss does not pass to the buyer until the goods are properly unloaded.

Chapter 5

❖ Price Terms

Since the purpose of foreign trade in the free-market nations is dominated by the theory of comparative advantage, there's a realistic price mechanism in contracts. Market forces, such as the costs of raw materials, transportation, production, and marketing, influence pricing in a free market. In the non-market nations, pricing depends on a variety of social, economic, and political factors. When the economic plan fails, the foreign trade corporations are directed to purchase goods for export from sate factories at domestic wholesale prices and to sell in foreign markets at the best price available. In the case of imports, the directions are the same. The goods are purchased in foreign markets at the best prices and sell domestically at prices determined by the plan. Therefore, price is distorted, and somewhat arbitrary.

❖ Force Majeure Clause

Force Majeure literally means "greater force", also "irresistible force". These clauses excuse a party from liability if some unforeseen event beyond the control of that party prevents it from performing its obligations under the contract. Typically, force majeure clauses cover natural disasters or other "Acts of God", war, or the failure of third parties— such as suppliers and subcontractors—to perform their obligations to the contracting party. It is important to remember that force majeure clauses are intended to excuse a party only if the failure to perform could not be avoided by the exercise of due care by that party.

When negotiating force majeure clauses, make sure that the clause applies equally to all in international trade parties to the agreement—not just the licensor. Also, it is helpful if the clause sets forth some specific examples of acts that will excuse performance under the clause, such as wars, natural disasters, and other major events that are clearly outside a party's control. Inclusion of examples will help to make clear the parties' intent that such clauses are not intended to apply to excuse failures to perform for reasons within the control of the parties.

In a force majeure clause, it is necessary to set a standard, for instance, the length of time or severity of the occurrence, to invoke the clause. It is likewise important to include a provision for recourse in the case of partial performance.

There are differences in interpreting the force majeure clause in various countries. For example, in France the prerequisites for the discharge of contractual obligation are: (1) unforseeability, (2) absolute impossibility of performance, and (3) no fault on the other party's part. These requirements are strictly enforced, and therefore, if relief is granted, the contract is treated as a nullity, whereas English courts have developed the "radically different" test. That is, the performance becomes radically different from the one that was undertaken under the contract. In Germany, the courts adjust the contractual obligation following commercial frustration as opposed to termination of the contract.

❖ Government Approval Clause

Since international contracts involve governmental regulation at various levels, it is important to include a clause dealing with governmental approval, and especially important in non-market economies. This clause should specify responsibility for getting the necessary licenses, permits, or government approval for the transaction.

❖ Choice of Law and Choice of Forum

All international sales contracts are subject to some systems of domestic law. Although many of the basic elements of contract law are the same in all systems, their role and function differ. For example, some mandatory provisions in each domestic system of law will bind the parties and are important in defining such concepts as force majeure or impossibility of performance. In non-market countries, however, there are two potential problems with enforcing force majeure provisions, namely, most non-market nations do not acknowledge an industrial strike as a force majeure event, and most such clauses do not address the problem of nonperformance caused by changes in the economic plan.

In most nations the courts recognize the right of the parties to choose their own applicable law. However, in the absence of an express or implied choice, no one fact or presumption determines applicable law. In non-market systems, where the contract was made in most situations, government governs what system of law usually applies local law.

It should be noted that even though the parties have selected an appropriate system of law to govern their contract, this does not resolve any disputes. The relevant law must be argued in court.

❖ Breach, Remedy and Enforcement

In a trading relationship, breach of contract occurs most frequently through conflicting understandings or interpretation of the terms of the contract. In dealings with a non-market country, breach is always possible through cancellation. The contract will detail the consequences of breach and the remedies available. All legal systems go along with the parties' agreement on these matters, in the absence of any overriding policy influences brought to bear on the forum. If the breach and remedy clause is not included in the contracts or not acceptable to the forum, then the forum applies its own remedies.

Section II
Formation of International Sales Contract

In the international trade, after business negotiation and having reached an agreement, the two parties of a transaction sign a written contract which shall function as the basis for the performance of rights and obligations by the two parties. Once the sales contract is effectively concluded according to the law, the parties concerned should perform the contract strictly according to the time, the quality and the quantity as stipulated in the contract. The forming of a contract includes business negotiation, conclusion and signing of a contract.

Generally speaking, business negotiation involves four steps: inquiry, offer, counter-offer and acceptance, among which, offer and acceptance are two indispensable steps for reaching an agreement and concluding a contract.

1. Inquiry

Invitation to offer is either an inquiry made to get information about the terms and conditions of a commodity trading, or a conditional suggestion about the transaction. Inquiry is a usual form of invitation to offer involving quality, quantity, price, packing, shipment, asking for samples and catalogue etc. Inquiry can be made by the buyer or the seller, and can be made orally or in writing.

Inquiry can be of two types: general inquiry and specific inquiry. In a general inquiry, a businessman states clearly all the information he needs, including general information, catalogue, or price list, a sample or sample book, etc. In a specific inquiry, the businessman points out what products he wants. He may ask for a catalogue, a price list, samples, or ask for an offer.

2. Offer

An offer is a proposal addressed to specific persons indicating an intention by the offer or to be bound to the sale or purchase of particular goods for a price. According to CISG, a proposal for concluding a contract addressed to one or more specific persons constitutes an offer if it is sufficiently definite and indicates the intention of the offer or to be bound in case of acceptance. A proposal is sufficiently definite if it indicates the goods and expressly or implicitly fixes or makes provision for determining the quantity.

❖ The Constitution of an Offer

(1) To one or more specific persons

For a proposal to be an offer, it must be addressed to "one or more specific persons". Proposals made to the public are ordinarily intended to be nothing more than invitations to negotiate. For example, an advertisement in a newspaper for the sale of goods at a particular price might put the advertiser in the awkward position of having to deliver more goods than he has on hand because of an increase in the cost of the goods between the time the advertisement was placed and the time it appeared. CISG, accordingly, adopts the rule that public offers are only invitations to negotiate "unless the contrary is clearly dictated."

(2) Sufficiently Definite

A proposal is sufficiently definite if it indicates the goods and expressly or implicitly fixes or makes provision for determining the quantity and the price. Other terms and conditions, if not definitely stipulated in the contract, should be added either on the basis of usual practices between both sides or on the basis of CISG.

❖ Firm or Non-firm

Offers may either be firm or non-firm. A firm offer, also called offer with engagement, is made when a seller promises to sell goods at a stated price and within a stated period of time known as validity period. While in a non-firm offer, at times called offer without engagement,

the offeror may add some statements on different occasions, such as:
- The offer is subject to change/alteration without notice;
- The offer is subject to the seller's (final) confirmation;
- The offer is subject to import license;
- The offer is subject to prior sale;
- The offer is subject to buyer's inspection or approval;
- The offer is subject to safe arrival of goods at port of shipment;
- The offer is subject to immediate acceptance by telegram;
- The offer is subject to market fluctuation.

❖ **Term of Validity**

There is a term of validity for each offer, a period within which the offeree can make acceptance, and the offeror is only bound. The offeror may clearly define it in the offer, otherwise a reasonable time should be regarded as the term of validity. But it is hard to tell what a reasonable time is. So we'd better state it clearly in the offer. The ways of stipulating term of validity are:

(1) The latest time   **e.g.** REPLY REACHING HERE BEFORE 15TH.
(2) A period of time   **e.g.** The offer is valid for 3 days.

❖ **Withdrawal and revocation of an offer**

(1) Withdraw

An offer becomes effective only after it reaches the offeree. Thus, offers—including offers that promise they are irrevocable—can be withdrawn prior to their reaching the offeree.

(2) Revocation

Article 16 of CISG states that: Until a contract is concluded an offer may be revoked if the revocation reaches the offeree before he has dispatched an acceptance. However, an offer cannot be revoked if it indicates, whether by stating a fixed time for acceptance or otherwise, that it is irrevocable; or if it was reasonable for the offeree to rely on the offer as being irrevocable and the offeree has acted in reliance on the offer.

❖ **Termination**

An offer is terminated when (1) it is over the term of validity; (2) it is rejected or declined; (3) it is legally revoked.

3. Counter-offer

When the buyer finds that the terms and conditions in the offer are acceptable, he may probably place an order promptly. However, if the offeree deems the price is on the high side, some terms and conditions do not agree to what he expected, he may decline the offer, or most probably, make a counter-offer. A reply to an offer which purports to be an acceptance but contains additions, limitations or other modifications is a rejection of the offer and constitutes a counter-offer. Additional or different terms, put forward by the offeree, relating to the price, payment, quality and quantity of the goods, place and time of delivery etc. are considered to alter the terms of offer materially. This means the offeree declines the terms of the offer.

Therefore, a counter-offer is a new offer and at the same time, the original offer lapses. If later, the offeree wants to accept the original offer, because of some favorable changes in the international market prices or in the exchange rate of foreign currencies, the offeror is entitled to decide whether he will accept or not, even if it is within the time of validity of the original offer.

On receiving the counter-offer, the offeror may weigh the advantages and disadvantages and decide to accept or decline it according to the specific situation. He may also make a re-offer to put forward some new terms or conditions. This is called an anti-counter-offer. Like an offer, a counter-offer is either with engagement or without engagement. A counter-offer in the same way is a firm offer.

4. Acceptance

In the international trade, the acceptance or a confirmation is the assent to the terms of an offer, required before a contract can be valid. It is indispensable for the conclusion of a business and the signing of a contract indicating that the buyer and the seller have come to an agreement on the sale, it is binding on both parties. An acceptance must meet the following requirements:

(1) The acceptance must be made by the offeree;
(2) The contents of an acceptance must conform to that of an offer;
(3) The acceptance must reach the offeror within the time of validity of the offer;
(4) The acceptance must be in oral or written form;
(5) The acceptance can contain no addition, modification, or limitations to the offer.

5. Signing of the Contract

In the international trade of business, the acceptance of an offer or order constitutes a contract. But in accordance with relative Chinese practice and laws, Chinese export and import companies arc required to sign a written contract stipulating rights and responsibilities of the parties concerned with foreign counterparts. After being signed by both parties, a contract will become a formal legal document binding upon both parties. So a contract is an agreement enforceable by law, by which both the buyers and the sellers mutually agree to carry out a trade concluded. Once the contract has been signed, both parties must abide by the contract and keep good faith. As a rule, the written contract forms the basis upon which the two parties perform the contract.

❖ **The Functions of the Contract in Written Form**

The written contract is sometimes a necessary condition for the formation of a contract. When one or two parties declare beforehand that the agreement must be in the form of written contract, the written contract becomes a precondition for the formation of the contract. In international trade, written contracts can take two forms: the sales contract and the sales confirmation. The former is a complete form of contract, and the latter is comparatively simplified.

(1) An Evidence of Formation of Contract

Should any conflict between the two sides arise, reference is generally made to the contract in an effort to resolve the misunderstanding.

(2) A Basis for Implementation of Contract

The contract in written form ensures the smooth implementation of the contract. Inconvenience may otherwise arise. So it is very important to stipulate in the contract the rights and obligations of both sides.

(3) Sometimes a Prerequisite for Conclusion of Contract

In international trade, usually a contract is concluded provided an acceptance is effective. But under some special circumstances, written contracts are required by some laws.

❖ **Forms of the Written Contract**

There is no specific requirement about the forms of contract in international trade. The commonly used forms are: Contract, Confirmation, Agreement, Memorandum, etc. The first two are more commonly used in Chinese foreign trade enterprises which generally have their own printed set format of contract or confirmation.

Once a deal is made, traders may sign two copies of contract face to face. Or the seller may send two copies signed by him to the buyer for counter-signature and the buyer should return one copy to the seller for a file.

Section III
Implementation of the Contract

Both parties, in the trade of business, shall hold joint responsibilities for the performance of the contract. The seller shall execute its basic obligations of delivering the goods, handing over any documents relating to them and transferring the goods, handing over any documents relating to them and transferring the property in the goods as required by the contract. The seller must deliver goods which are of quantity, quality and description required by the contract and which are contained or packaged in the manner required by the contract. The seller must deliver goods which are free from any right or claim of the third party, unless the buyer agreed to take the goods subject to that right or claim.

Chapter 5

1. Cargo Readiness

The quality must conform to the stipulations of the contract and the requirements of the related laws.

(1) Conform to the Contract

When the sale is by description, the goods should comply with the description; when the sale is by sample, the goods should be in accordance with the sample in terms of quality; when the sale is by sample as well as by description, the goods will correspond with both the sample and the description.

(2) Conform to the Requirements of the Related Laws

The requirements by laws regarding quality cover two aspects: first the goods are fit for the purpose for which goods of the same description would ordinarily be used, i.e. the goods are merchantable. This is an implied guarantee of quality required by the law. Second, the goods are fit for any particular purpose expressly or impliedly made known to the seller at the time of the conclusion of the contract, except where the circumstances show that the buyer did not rely, or that it was unreasonable for him to rely, on the seller's skill and judgment.

The quantity must conform to the contract.

a. The words "about", "approximately", "circa" or similar expressions used in connection with the amount of the credit or the quantity or the unit price stated in the credit are to be construed as allowing the quantity or the unit price to which they refer.

b. Unless a credit stipulates that the quantity of the goods specified must not be exceeded or reduced, a tolerance of 5% more or 5% less will be permissible, always provided that the amount of the drawings does not exceed the amount of the credit. This tolerance does not apply when the credit stipulates the quantity in terms of a stated number of packing units or individual items.

2. Examination of L/C and Amendment to L/C

❖ **Urging the Opening of L/C**

In the following cases, it is necessary for the seller to urge the buyer to open the L/C:

(1) The buyer failed to issue an L/C within the time stipulated in the contract. In this case, the buyer breached the contract. However, if the seller still does not want to break off the transaction, he may urge the buyer to open the L/C. The seller, though, reserves the right to claim against the buyer;

(2) In case the seller has already got the goods ready and is prepared to advance shipment, he may inquire of the buyer whether advanced shipment is allowed.

❖ **Examining L/C**

After receiving the L/C, the exporter must examine the L/C against the sales contract. The examining points cover the following.

(1) The Political Background and Financial Standing of the Issuing Bank

If the issuing bank is domiciled in a country which has friendly relations with China, but its nationality is not acceptable, this credit is not acceptable. If the issuing bank is a very small bank with a very poor financial standing, this credit is unacceptable too.

(2) The Nature of the Credit and the Liabilities of the Opening Bank

Credit with a word like "revocable" is not acceptable. The undertaking clause of the issuing bank should be included. Sometimes although there is the word "irrevocable" in the L/C, some "limitation clauses" regarding the undertaking of the issuing bank also include such clauses as "This credit is not effective until we receive the notification of import licenses".

The above two points are also the examining focuses of the notifying bank.

(3) The Amount and Currency

The amount and currency in the credit should conform to the contract. If there is a more or less clause in the contract, the amount of the L/C should cover the more or less part. The unit price and the total price should be correct.

(4) The Quality, the Quantity, Packing Clauses

(5) The Date of Shipment, the Date and Place of Validity

There is usually a reasonable interval between the date of shipment and the date of validity. In this way, the seller has sufficient time to prepare documents and make settlement.

(6) The Documents

The types, copes of documents are required as well as the methods of filling them out.

(7) Other Special Clauses

Other special clauses, are also required to designate the shipping company, the nationality, age and class of the ship, etc.

❖ **Amendment to L/C**

Upon receipt of a letter of credit, the beneficiary finds that the terms stipulated in the credit are not in line with those mentioned in the contract, he must immediately notify the applicant in the shortest possible time. But he should also bear in mind that before receipt of the advice of L/C amendment from the opening bank, he had better not start to make shipment, otherwise he is liable to some very unfavorable situation.

To remind, examine and amend the L/C. In practice, the L/C is joint examined by both the bank that will lay the emphasis on the examination of the political backgrounds, credit standing and payment obligations and the exporting company who will focus on the examination of the conformity of the L/C content with contract.

Chapter 5

Useful Phrases & Technical Terms

marine insurance	海事保险
London underwriters	伦敦保险商
Lloyds Coffee House	劳氏咖啡俱乐部
The Lloyds S & G. (Ship & Goods) Policy	劳氏 S&G(航运与货物)保险单
Hague Rules	海牙规则
shipment contract	装运港交货合同
destination-type sales contract	目的港交货合同

Notes

1. CISG:《联合国国际货物销售合同公约》(United Nations Convention on Contract for the International Sale of Goods,简称 CISG).

2. Invitation to offer is either fill inquiry made to get information about the terms and conditions of a commodity trading, or a conditional suggestion about the transaction.
   邀请发盘是指买方或买方就商品的有关交易条件所做的一种询问(讯盘),或就该交易提出带有保留条件的建议。

3. In the case of shipments made on a "to arrive" basis or contracts based on "no arrival, no sale," the seller is not responsible for the goods' failure to arrive if it has not been negligent, but the buyer may avoid the contract.
   在以"抵港"为基础的运输情形中或者"不抵港,无交易"的合同中,卖方不对货物未抵港负责,但买方可以撤销合同。

4. The term force majeure refers to an "irresistible force". A force majeure clause is similar to the concept of impossibility of performance, or of commercial impracticability. It excuses performance under certain circumstances, namely, natural disaster such as floods, storms, earthquakes, or "acts of God". This type of clause may also designate war, riots, police action, or strikes to excuse performance.
   "不可抗力"是指一种"不可抗拒的力量"。不可抗力条款与履行不能或贸易不可实现相似。该条款使得当事人在一定情况下可以免除履行其义务的责任。不可抗力大多指自然灾害,如洪水、风暴、地震。这种条款也可只因战争、暴乱、警察行为、罢工而免除履行义务。

5. When the contract is called for "shipment by carrier" to a particular destination, the risk shifts from the seller to the tender of the goods by the carrier at the destination point.
   当合同规定"承运"到一特定的目的地时,风险就在目的地由卖方转移到买方了。

6. Since international contracts involve governmental regulation at various levels, it is important to include a clause dealing with governmental approval. This is important in non-market economies. This clause should specify responsibility for getting the necessary licenses, permits, or government approval for the transaction.

   由于国际合同涉及各级政府的调控,因此政府许可条款在合同中十分重要,而且在非市场经济国家中尤为重要。在政府批准条款中,具体规定了如何取得特许、许可证以及政府交易批准书。

7. USP500:《跟单信用证统一惯例同行商会第500号出版物》

   The Uniform Customs and Practice for Documentary Credits, 1993 Revision, ICC Publication No. 500, shall apply to all documentary Credits (including to the extent to which they may be applicable, Standby Letter(s) of Credit) where they are incorporated into the text of the Credit. They are binding on all parties thereto, unless otherwise expressly stipulated in the Credit.

8. Generally speaking, business negotiation involves four steps: inquiry, offer, counter-offer and acceptance, among which, offer and, acceptance are two indispensable steps for reaching an agreement and concluding a contract.

   谈判的过程一般包括询价、发盘、还盘和接受四个环节。其中发盘和接受是达成交易、成立合同不可缺少的两个环节。

Practical Drills

❖ Questions for Discussion

1. If an exporter accepts a buyer's counteroffer and subsequently realizes that the terms contained within it are unfavorable, under what circumstances can the exporter amend the agreement?
2. Under what other circumstances might a contract be deemed to be breached?

❖ Case Study

1

Offer

Beijing, August 2, ...

Copenhagen Trading Co., Ltd.
Copenhagen, Denmark,

Dear Sirs:

Thank you for your letter of July 25 inquiring for 3,000 dozen/ sets Ladies' Pyjamas.

We take pleasure in making you an offer, subject to your acceptance reaching here not later than August 18, as follows: 3,000 dozen/sets of Art. No 208 Ladies' Pyjamas in pink, blue and yellow color equally assorted, with the size assortment of S/3, M/6, and L/3 per dozen, packed in cartons, at Stg. £ 26.00 per dozen /set CIFC 2% Odense, for shipment from any Chinese port in October.

Please note that, since there is no direct steamer available for Odense in October, we find it only possible to ship the parcel with transshipment at Copenhagen.

We look forward to your early reply.

Yours faithfully,
CATHAY EXPORT CORPORATION

2
Acceptance

Copenhagen, July 9, ...

Cathay Export Corporation
Beijing, China

Dear Sirs,

Thank you for your letter of August 2 offering us 3.000 dozen / sets of Ladies' Pyjamas at Stg. £ 26.00 per dozen /set CIFC 2% Odense.

We are glad to have been able to prevail upon our clients to accept your price, though they found it a bit on the high side. We are now arranging with our bank for the relative L/C. When making shipment, kindly see to it that insurance is to be effected against All Risks and War Risk as per the China Insurance Clauses of 1 January, 1996 for 110% of the invoice value. As to the shipping mark, we will let you know soon.

Yours faithfully,
CATHAY EXPORT CORPORATION

❖ Role Play

On Terms and Conditions of the Contract

Zhao Wei: Well, Mr. Black. Now that the price is decided on, we can go over other terms and conditions of the transaction to see if we agree on all the particulars.

Mr. Black: OK, Mr, Zhao. Let's go over it from the very beginning: the whole set of equipment, specifications as shown in the technical data, at US$570000 F.O.B. London. Our transaction is closed at this price, isn't it?

Zhao Wei: Yes, and in one shipment, to be more exact.

Mr. Black:	Oh, you see, I've forgot this.
Zhao Wei:	When is the time of shipment?
Mr. Black:	During February and March. OK?
Zhao Wei:	OK. What about packing?
Mr. Black:	To be packed in wooden cases, of course.
Zhao Wei:	You had better have it clearly stated. To be packed in new strong wooden cases suitable for long distance ocean transportation and well protected against dampness, moisture, shock, rust and rough handling. The sellers shall be liable for any damage to the commodity because of improper packing.
Mr. Black:	We'll see to it that all the machines are properly packed and protected. Don't worry about that. Well, next, payment.
Zhao Wei:	Is it possible by Collection?
Mr. Black:	No, Mr. Zhao. By L/C. That's our usual practice.
Zhao Wei:	What kind of L/C, then?
Mr. Black:	Irrevocable L/C payable against the presentation of the draft drawn on the opening bank together with the shipping documents. You should open this L/C 15-20 days prior to the date of delivery and this L/C shall be valid until the 15th day after the shipment.
Zhao Wei:	That can be done. No problem. Then, any questions about the inspection and claims?
Mr. Black:	None whatsoever. Before making delivery, we always make a precise and comprehensive inspection of the goods and see everything is all right. You may be assured that the quality and performance of our machines can stand every possible test.
Zhao Wei:	That's OK. But after the arrival of the goods at our port, we always apply to the China Commodity Inspection Bureau for a preliminary inspection in respects of the quality, specifications and quantity of the goods. If any discrepancies are found by the Bureau, We'll have the right to file a claim.
Mr. Black:	Of course. And we hope disputes be settled amicably.
Zhao Wei:	We hope so, too. But in case there is any dispute unsettled, it should be refered to, we suppose, the Foreign Trade Arbitration Commission of the China Council for the Promotion of International Trade. Do you agree?
Mr. Black:	Sure, but I am certain there will be no occasion for arbitration at all.
Zhao Wei:	Now, all these points have been agreed upon. The deal has come off nicely.
Mr. Black:	It's been a pleasure doing business with you. We hope that more business will be done in future.
Zhao Wei:	Surely. There will be more to come.

Chapter 5

Extended Activities

I. Check the following letter of credit with the given contract terms.

Trust Bank
New York

Date: June 15, 1997
To: China Chemical Co
Gentlemen:

For the account of New York Dye Co., we hereby authorize you to draw on us at 90 days after sight to the extent of USD10,000 (Say US Dollar Ten Thousand Only)

Your drafts must be accompanied by the following documents (complete sets unless otherwise stated) evidencing shipment(s) of :

200 drums of dye at USD 50.00 per drum CFR Shanghai, from Shanghai to New York, details as per your S/C No. 97/54;

Invoice in triplicate;

Insurance policy in duplicate.

Full set of on board bill of lading, dated not later than September 15, 1997, made out to order of Trust Bank, New York (Reference 1002), marked "Notify New York Dye Co." and "Freight Prepaid".

The major terms in Sales contract:

S/C number: 97/51

Seller: China Chemical Co

Buyer: New York Dye Co

Name of commodity: dye

Quantity: 200 drums

Unit price: US$50 per drum FOB Shanghai

Total price US$ 10,000

Time of Delivery: not later than Sep.15th, 1997

Terms of payment: payment is to be made by irrevocable L/C 60days after sight.

II. Fill in the blanks below with the most appropriate terms from the box.

comply with	take place	in question	break down into
in the event of	guilty of	turn down	have no
intention of	in principle	associated with	

1. He is found _____ stealing.
2. The L/C must _____ the terms and conditions in the contract.
3. It seems that the seller _____ fulfilling their obligations.

4. We politely _____ the invitation.
5. _____ rain, the game will be postponed.
6. The buyer is eager to know how often the shipments will _____ in the next month.
7. The problem _____ is payment terms.
8. The buyer has the obligation to bear the cost _____ delivery.
9. The payment is _____ many installments.
10. _____, there are still some parts need discussion, although we have reached an agreement.

III. Look at the terms in the left-hand column and find the correct definitions in the right-hand column. Copy the corresponding letters in the blanks.

1. _____ cash flow
2. _____ brochure
3. _____ indemnity
4. _____ breakdown
5. _____ tender
6. _____ commission
7. _____ clearance
8. _____ fraud
9. _____ defendant
10. _____ court
11. _____ obligation
12. _____ warranty
13. _____ guarantee

a. the completion of customs entry formalities resulting in the release of goods from customs custody to the importer
b. a social, legal, or moral requirement, such as a duty, contract, or promise that compels one to follow or avoid a particular course of action
c. a deception deliberately practiced in order to secure unfair or unlawful gain
d. the pattern of income and expenditures, as of a company or person, and the resulting availability of cash
e. the party against which an action is brought
f. a small booklet or pamphlet, often containing promotional material or product information
g. the amount paid to an agent, which may be all individual, a broker, or a financial institution for consummating a transaction involving sale or purchase of assets or services
h. a written offer to contract goods or services at a specified cost or rate; a bid
i. a similar authorized tribunal having military or ecclesiastical jurisdiction
j. an analysis, an outline, or a summary consisting of itemized data or essentials
k. an assurance by the seller of property that the goods or property are as represented or will be as promised
l. credit extended that is not supported by a note, mortgage, or other formal written evidence of indebtedness
m. an invoice provided by a supplier prior to a sale or shipment of merchandise informing the buyer of the kinds and quantities of goods to be sent, their value, and important specifications

14. _____ expenditure   n. a pledge that something will be performed in a specified manner
15. _____ open account   o. an expense
                         p. compensation for damage, loss, or injury suffered
                         q. the act or an instance of stealing; larceny

IV. Decide whether the following statements are true or false by writing "T" for true and "F" for false in the bracket besides each statement.

1. (　) Offer must be made by the seller and acceptance must be made by the buyer.
2. (　) Both offer and acceptance can be withdrawn and revoked.
3. (　) The two integral links in international trade negotiation are offer and counter offer.
4. (　) This is particularly important for international trade contracts to ensure that they have agreed on the system of law to be used in the event of legal action being taken.
5. (　) The "bottle of the forms" means the two parties negotiate to agree common ground and the exact terms that will constitute the contract.
6. (　) Acceptance of the offer commits both the buyer and the seller to the specific terms of the sale and forms a legally binding contract that cannot be amended unless the two parties agree in writing to make the changes.
7. (　) Silence, or lack of response to the offer, can be considered an acceptance under UK law.

V. Complete the following diagram according to what you have read in the text.

Works that Needs to be Done Before and After Making Offers
(From the Perspective of the Exporter)

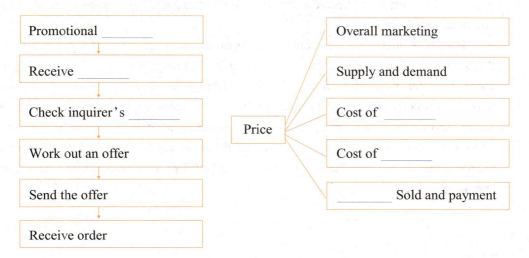

VI. Translate the following sentences into English.

(1) 公司可能更愿意以形式发票的形式报价，因其内容由于订货时可以转成商业发票而更便于管理。

(2) 一旦报价提交给买方，如果买方根据此报价订货，出口商就有责任履行所有报价上的条款。

(3) 可以理解的是买方指出合同已签署，出口方有义务履行其条款。

(4) 当买方公司也在合同中加入自己的条款并试图占上风时就会出现问题。

(5) 除了合同的具体条款之外，出口商还应该准备一些能够写进合同的销售标准条款。

VII. Translate the following passage into Chinese.

Export costing calculations are used to assist exporters in ascertaining how competitive the company's products will be in the target market once all the additional charges and fees have been taken into consideration. Also called "laded costs", they provide the exporter with a breakdown of how the total cost of the product has been reached, which may then identify areas where savings can be made in order to improve competitiveness. Export costing should be seen as a key part of the company's financial planning activities, especially in conjunction with the cash flow forecast, as an accurate costing sheet will allow the company to take all the costs associated with market entry into account.

VIII. Speaking activities.

Oral presentation

Form groups of three or four and prepare jointly for the oral presentation topic below. Then vote for a representative in a group to make a 8—15 minute presentation before the whole class:

History is littered with examples of companies who have entered into contracts on the back of unrealistic quotations and who have subsequently struggled to fulfill their terms. Examine the ramifications of such mistakes, particularly in terms of the long term market entry strategy. Consider also how such mistakes could affect a company's future development into other markets. It cannot be stressed enough that the exporting company must always ensure that it has the capacity and resources to meet the terms and conditions of the contract and must be fully aware of its financial and legal responsibilities.

Chapter 6

Terms of Commodity

Focal Learning

After the completion of this chapter, you are required to know:
- names of commodity and its importance;
- various practices to express the quality and quantity of commodity;
- different approaches to measure quality and quantity of commodity;
- significance of packing and distinctiveness among them;
- classification of marks and their application.

Lead-in Vocabulary

commerce	n.	商业,贸易,商品的买卖
merchandise	n.	商品,货物
initial	adj.	最初的,初始的
negotiation	n.	谈判
interpreted	v.	解释,说明
specify	v.	详细说明
illustration	n.	说明,例证,图解
specification	n.	详述,规格,说明书
machineries	n.	机器,机械
stipulate	v.	规定,保证,说明
prevailing	adj.	占优势的,主要的
bushel		蒲式耳(谷物计量单位;美国 Winchester bushel=35.238 升,英国 Imperial bushel=36.368 升)(英美使用的容积单位,容量等于8加仑)
epitome	n.	梗概
transit	v.	经过,通行,运输

stowage	n.	堆状物
bale	n.	大包，大捆，(指标准量货物，如稻草，麦杆)货物
lotion	n.	洗液,洗剂
cylindrical	adj.	圆柱的 圆筒状的
invoice	n.	发票
specification	n.	规格
prevailing	adj.	最常用的，流行的
sufficiently	adv.	足够的
leakages	n. / v.	泄露
spillage	n. / v.	溢出
strapping	v.	用带捆
pinching	n.	挤压
slings	n.	捆扎绳
crayons	n.	有色的粉笔,蜡笔
likewise	adv.	同样的

A commodity is an article of commerce used for selling of goods, merchandise or produce. It is used to describe any primary product or any raw material marketed internationally, either in its original state or after the initial process which makes it acceptable as an industrial raw material.

In the international trade and contract negotiation, both the buyer and seller must make sure of the commodity intended for transaction and describe the goods in the sales contract exactly. As far as commodity in trade is concerned, it comprises name of commodity, quality of commodity, quantity of commodity, packing of commodity, marking of commodity and commodity inspection.

Section I
Name of Commodity

The name of the commodity is an indispensable section of international trade contract. It is the description of the commodity. Usually, the parties to the contract just specify the name of the product under the subject "Name of Commodity". As the basis of a transaction, it concerns the rights and obligations of the buyer, if the goods delivered do not consist with the named commodity in the contract, the buyer is entitled to lodge a claim for compensation or cancel the contract. Therefore, as a main condition of sale, the name of commodity should be clearly stated. To avoid misunderstanding, both the seller and the buyer should use accepted name agreed by both parties or a name internationally accepted, which can sometimes help to reduce tariff or transportation fees.

Section II
Quality of Commodity

The quality of a commodity is an integration of the intrinsic features and the outer appearance of the commodity and is the most important factor in the sales of goods. Terms indicating qualities are frequently harder to define, as it is a term for defining one particular degree of quality in one country that may have different implication in another. Some quality standards that are in frequent use in some country or specific industry may not be known or may be interpreted differently in other countries or industries. Furthermore, different commodities have different qualities, and even the same commodity has different qualities. Therefore, great care needs to be taken to specify quality terms to avoid any disputes.

In the international trade, the seller and the buyer are usually thousands miles apart. In such a condition, some applicable methods have been developed to help both the buyer and seller to know exactly the quality of the commodity. The table below capitulates some possible international trade practices.

Broader categories	Narrower categories
Sales by sample	Sales by seller's sample
	Sales by buyer's sample
Sales by description	Sales by specification
	Sales by grade
	Sales by standard
	Sales by illustration
	Sales by brand or trade mark
	Sales by place of origin

1. Sales by Seller's Sample and Sales by Buyer's Sample

In the international trade, a sample is the epitome of the quality of the product. It is always selected from a whole or specially designed and processed consignment to encourage potential customers to buy. In terms of sales by sample, the parties agree that the quality and condition of the bulk of the goods will be at least as good as that of the sample. Arts and crafts, garments, light industry products and agricultural native produce are generally sold by sample.

When the seller supplies the sample, it is sales by seller's sample. In case the quality offered is not identical with the sample, the buyer is entitled to claim compensation or reject the contract. When the buyer offers the sample, the transaction held is called sale by buyer's sample. In either case the seller is responsible for delivering goods of equivalent quality.

Quality is an important component of the description of goods. The goods delivered by the seller should have the agreed quality. However, it is always important to add an elastic clause like "quality to be about equal to the sample" or a "quality to be similar to the sample". Furthermore, to avoid disputes upon the quality of goods, the method of Sealed Sample can be applied if necessary. It is also necessary to clarify the buyer's rights if quality of the goods shipped is lower than intended in the sales contract.

2. Sales by Description

In most cases, sales by description is the method to indicate the quality of the commodity. Sales by description may take the form of sale by specification, sale by grade, sale by standard, sale by place of origin, sale by brand or trademark and sale by illustration.

- **Sales by Specification, Grade or Standard**

Specifications are detailed descriptions of the goods to be sold. They include composition, content, strength, purity, size, etc. of the commodity. In case of sales by grade, it is important to state the grades of the commodity such as large, medium small or Grade A, Grade B, Grade C.... While by standard, it refers to those specifications or grades that are laid down and proclaimed in a unified way by government departments or commercial organizations of a country.

It is worthy to note that the standard of a commodity is subject to change or amendment and a new standard often replaces the older one, therefore, in case of sale by standard, it is important to specify the name of the publication, in which the standard of the commodity appears.

In merchandizing the agricultural products, it is a regular practice to use "F.A.Q" (Fair Average Quality) or "G.M.Q" (Good Merchantable Quality) to indicate the quality of the commodity. F.A.Q. denotes a quantity offered not on a particular quality specification but on the basis that is equal to the average quality of the current group, recent shipment, etc. while G.M.Q. refers to the sound quality that is free from defects and is sufficiently good to satisfy the needs of the buyer. However, both terms are too general, therefore when in use, it is better that they are supplemented by some concrete specifications.

- **Sales by Brand or Trademark**

Goods of the same brand or trademark are of the same quality. Their quality remains unified and unchanged. So from the brand or trade mark people can tell what quality the goods possess. It is more convenient to name the brand or trademark of a commodity to indicate its quality than to list so many specifications one by one. Occasionally, the place of origin of the produce is also used for this purpose.

- **Sales by Illustration**

Machineries, instruments, apparatuses and sets of equipment are inclined to sell by illustration, drawing, graphs or diagrams. For those merchandises mentioned, it is extremely difficult to indicate their qualities in details by either specification, brand, or trademark since their structure and function are complicated and the installations, application and maintenance are subject to specified rules. Consequently, related technical booklets, manuals and instruction of directions, pictures and diagrams will serve the purpose.

Section III
Quantities of Commodity

It is obvious that a deal cannot be completed without taking the quantity of the goods sold or bought into consideration. stipulates that the quantity of the goods delivered should be identical to that called for in the contract, and the buyer has the right to reject the goods if their quantity delivered is less than agreed upon. Also he is entitled to reject the whole lot or that portion of the goods excessive in quantity. Therefore due attention should be paid to the quantity terms during business negotiation.

1. Units of Measurement

In international trade, three systems of measurement are commonly used: the metric system, the British system and the U.S. system. In addition, there is another prevailing system—the International Systems of Units, which is commonly applied in China.

The units of measurement extensively used in international business are as follows:
- Numbers: piece, pair, dozen, gross, ream, etc.;
- Weight: kilogram, metric ton, ounce, pound, hundredweight, long ton;
- Length: meter, centimeter, foot, inch, yard, etc.;
- Area: square meter, square inch, square foot, square yard, etc.;
- Volume: cubic centimeter, cubic meter, cubic inch, cubic foot, cubic yard, etc.;
- Capacity: liter, pint, gallon, bushel, etc..

2. Calculation of Weight

There are various ways of measuring the weight of goods: by gross weight, by net weight, by conditional weight and by theoretical weight.
- Gross weight is the total weight of the commodity itself plus the tare.
- Net Weight is the weight of the commodity alone, that is, the tare is excluded.
- Conditioned Weight refers to the weight obtained by deduction of the actual moisture content of the commodity and addition of standardized moisture, both by scientific methods.

Conditioned weight is usually applicable to commodities that have a high unit of value and tend to absorb from the air, such as raw silk, wool and cotton which are of high economic value and with unsteady moisture content.

❖ Theoretical Weight Commodities that have regular specifications and regular size, such as galvanized iron and steel plate, are often subject to use of theoretical weight. So long as the specifications and the size of such commodities are the same, their theoretical weight is construed by the number of the sheets put together.

With respect to the inconvenience caused by the varied systems of measurement, in 1960 the International Measurement Conference adopted international System of Units, which several scores of countries have made known their standpoint ever since then.

The quantity clause in a sales contract is so indispensable that it should always be stated clearly and definitely. The use of such indefinite expression as "about, more or less, etc" will surely give rise to disputes and therefore should be avoided. However, in the trading of agricultural or mineral products, because it is difficult to weigh them accurately, quite often the actual shipment is over-delivered or under-delivered in quantity. Under such circumstances, the clause "5,000 metric tons, 5% more or less at seller's option" is good for this purpose. In this case the quantity delivered can range from 4,750 to 5,250 metric tons, and the payment will be made for the actual quantity delivered at the contracted price or at the market price at the time of shipment.

Section IV
Packing of Commodity

Proper packing can be extremely important depending on the type of product and its destination. Ocean voyages may be most damaging to the goods that are not properly packed. Goods subject to breakage have to be crated, and those subject to moisture should be wrapped in plastic. Others may require some special treatment or coating before shipment, still others have to be refrigerated while in transit. Actually, packing not only serves as a form of protection, but also facilitates loading, unloading and stowage, and prevents pilferage. Furthermore it can promote sales.

Many goods have little or no form of packing and are carried loose. They are nude cargo and cargo in bulk. The former includes iron and steel plates, iron rods, railway sleepers, steel rails, etc., and the latter, oil, ores, grain, coal, etc. Heavy vehicles, locomotives and buses are also carried loose, because of the impracticability and high cost of packing.

1. Outer Packing

The following are types of outer packing usually used in foreign trade.

❖ Bale

Bale is a form of packing consisting of a canvas wrapped often cross-looped by ropes or metal wires. It is most suitable for products shipped in bulk, such as paper, wool, cotton, hay, peat, carpets and rope, etc. Bales have the disadvantage of being easily pilfered, also they are easily damaged by water or hooks, as a matter of fact, water damages can be avoided by wrapping the bale in a waterproof covering ; hook damages can be avoided by fixing ears on the corners of the bale in case of small bales, with ears, small bales with a weight of more than 300 pounds are unlikely to suffer spillage or damage due to the use of hooks. Basically, it is a cheap and effective form of packing which aids handling, However, it offers limited protection to cargo.

❖ Bag

Bags made of paper, cotton, plastic, or jute (fiber from the outer skin of certain plants), are a cheap form of container and are ideal for a wide variety of products such as cement, flour, fertilizer, oil cakes, animal feeding materials, chemicals and many consumer products. Their chief disadvantage is that they are susceptible to the damages caused by water, sweat, leakages, spillage and paper bags tearing and breakage. These damages can be lessened even avoided by using multi-layer bags or strapping a number of bags tighter on a pallet.

❖ Barrel, Drum, Hogshead

This type of containers is usually made of wood, metal or plastic. They are used for the conveyance of liquid or greasy cargoes such as casing for sausage. Acids can also be carried in plastic drums and bottles. The main problems associated with this type of packing, are the likelihood of leakage, if the unit is not properly sealed, and the possibility of the drums becoming rusty in the course of transit, while the advantage is that such a form of packing, particularly drums, can have a resale value in some countries, while others are used continually in various transits, particularly hogsheads.

❖ Box and Case

Boxes, cases and metal-lined cases are also used extensively, particularly in deck tonnage and liner cargo. Basically, this type of packing is wooden in structure and strong enough to withstand the pressure of heavy loads on top of them, and boxes and cases varies in size and capacity. It is an expensive form of packing and has a certain resale value in some countries. Overall, the strength of this type of packing lies in that it provides reliable protection for expensive cargoes such as equipment and car accessories, and it contributes to lessens the risk of pilferage, and makes the handling easier. Moreover, it may be strengthened by the provision on of battens metal binding. Many of them, such as those for tea chests, are lined inside with moisture proof barrier to create airtight packing so as to avoid the troubles arising in passing through zones of variable temperature. However, in recent years, it is becoming less popular as the cost of timber has risen sharply and increasingly use of containerization.

❖ **Carton**

Cartons are now a very common way of packing with the development of containerization and palletization, particularly in international distribution of type of consumer products. They may be constructed cardboard, strawboard or fiberboard. Cartons have various strong points. On one hand, as it is relatively inexpensive, expandable and therefore aids handling and stowage and marketing as some words can be printed on them, then, the use of this form of packing has been on the increase lately. It is especially ideal for containerization and palletized cargo shipment, particularly outstanding in the air freight with the cartons affixed by metal bands to the pallet. The principal disadvantage is its vulnerability to crushing and pilfering. It is a flexible form of packing and, therefore, prevents the breakage which may occur if rigid containers are used.

❖ **Glass container**

Glass containers usually enclosed in metal baskets have a limited use and are primarily employed for the carriage of dangerous liquids cargoes transported in small quantities such as acids. Again, it provides a safeguard to workers and transport vehicles but requires more careful handling.

❖ **Crate or skeleton case**

Crates or skeleton cases are a form of container halfway between a bale and a case. The wooden frame provides protection from the pinching effects of slings. It is often used for heavy weight, bulky goods that may be open or closed, such as machinery, domestic appliances. Items such as refrigerators may be packed in an crate with a transparent plastic covering, which enables the commodity to be seen and will promote careful treatment.

❖ **Container**

Container is a form of packing extensively used in international cargo transportation and logistics. It is the practice of packing cargoes in large metal containers. Though packing by containers is relatively expensive, it has become increasingly popular. The most striking advantages of container are the reduction of water damage, in handling damage and in pilferage. And today most ports and ship are equipped with devices of handling containers.

2. Inner Packing

In contrast to outer packing, there is inner packing (or immediate packing). It is not only designed as protection to reduce the risk of cargoes damaged in transit and prevent pilferage but also to aid marketing. Inner packing is now universally recognized as a decisive selling factor of household consumer goods and goods alike. Marketing, consumer advertising, display, presentation, protection, hygiene, easy handling, and self-service retailing have made sophisticated wrapping an almost universal necessity for small consumer goods. Take shampoo lotion for example, a cylindrical shape of the package makes it convenient to use with one hand while the other hand is scratching the scalp. Nowadays, transparent or window containers are often used. It is convenient for the customers to identify the contents when shopping, thus possibly concluding a transaction.

Section V
Marking of Commodity

When an order is received from abroad, it is essential for the exporter to ensure that goods are not merely suitably packed, but also properly marked on the outer packing with the identifying symbols and numbers in accordance with the instructions or specification of the overseas buyer. In order to enable the customs authorities, the steamship clerks, the buyer to identify the cargoes en route or at the port of destination. It is necessary that the mark (or symbol) and numbers conform to those written in the commercial invoice, the consular invoice, the bill of lading and the other shipping documents used in every respect. Packages should not be marked with crayons, tags or cards. The best method of marking is to stencil the marks on the outer of the package. Some exporters paint the marks with a brush and indelible ink. All in all, marks should be permanent and easily read at a glance. Generally, marks are generally classified into three categories: shipping marks, indicative marks(warning marks) and additional marks.

1. Shipping Marks

Shipping marks are used for the identification of shipment in the same way as ID cards identify a person, the exporter, customs, carriers, and importers rely on them to distinguish one consignment from another; they must comply with the environmental and safety standard. The marks and numbers on the master export pack should be consistent with the marks and numbers on the shipping documents. Shipping marks normally include the following information:

- ❖ Name of exporter and his address
- ❖ Name of importer and his contract number /shipping mark
- ❖ Case or crate number (e.g., 1-25)
- ❖ weight (gross, net)/measurement
- ❖ Name of carrying vessel
- ❖ Ports of shipment and destination
- ❖ Origin of goods

Here symbols with a simple identity code or initials are often used instead of writing out the full name of the consignee in order not to disclose the consignee's name. The package number is often placed under the name of destination. And package may be numbered consecutively or marked only with a total number.

Shipping marks are generally designed by individual business themselves in foreign countries. In China, the Ministry of Foreign Trade and Economic Cooperation requires standard format of shipping marks for Chinese consignees. An example of a Chinese importer's shipping mark might be 05MPTE-47009CJ. In this code

05 is the year of order—2005;

M is the abbreviation of the importer—Machinery I/E Corp;

PT is the abbreviated name of the end user— the Ministry of Post & Telecommunications;

47 is the code of the type of merchandise—electronic instrument;

009 is the contract number—009;

CJ is the abbreviation of the country of export—Japan.

To improve efficiency of cargo handling and to reduce cost, ISO has suggested a shipping mark standard, which has four lines in total with no more than 17 letters in each line and contains no graphs. For example, a standardized shipping mark might look like the following:

CMC(Name of importer)
90MKE-470001CF(Reference number)
SHANGHAI(Port of destination)
1-5 (Serial number)

2. Indicative and Warning Marks

To facilitate handling or to warn the dockers and overcome differing language problems, easily recognizable marking terms and some international pictorial labels or symbols are printed on the exterior, usually written in English or in the language of the country of destination. For the transit of some hazardous materials or cargoes, signs universally adopted by the international Air Transport Association and the International Maritime Organization are extensively used. The following marks are usually found on the exterior of the package during transit to ensure smooth delivery.

Glass	Keep Dry
Top	This Side Up
Perishable	Do Not Crush
Keep Cool	Be Protected from Heat
Lift Here	No Turning Over
Keep on Deck	Stow away from Boiler
Fragile	Keep in Dark Place Open Here Handle with Care
Liquid	To Be Protected from Cold Use No Hooks Bottom
Keep Upright	Keep in Hold
Do Not Drop	Do Not Stack on Top
Keep Flat	Keep in Dry Place

The following are widely used warning marks printed on the outer package.

Oxidizing Material   Compressed Gas   Poison

Chapter 6

Hazardous Article	Material Radioactive	Corrosives
Inflammable	Compressed Gas	Explosives

3. Additional Marks

In international business, sometimes according to the stipulations, articles of the relative regulations, laws of the importing country or upon demand of the importer, it is the practice to supply the supplementary mark giving the dimensions of the package which may be used in customs entry or in assessing the freight. Moreover, it is preferable for the gross and net weights to be likewise shown. The following are the two illustrative examples of this kind of mark:

Dimensions:	1×6.5×0.5 meters	2"511×3"01"×54"
Weight:	Gross weight	165 kilos
	Net weight	150 kilos
	Tare	15 kilos

Useful Phrases & Technical Terms

name of commodity	产品名称
quality of commodity	产品质量
trade mark	商标
outer packing	外包装
glass container	玻璃容器
inner pocking	内包装
marking of cargoes	货物标志
shipping marks	唛头 / 运输标志
comply (with)	(常与介词 with 连用) 遵从,同意,一致
indicative / warning mark	指示性 / 警告标志
additional mark	附加标志

Notes

1. As far as commodity in trade is concerned, it comprises name of commodity, quality of commodity, quantity of commodity, packing of commodity, marking of commodity and commodity inspection.
   就商品贸易而言,它包括商品名称、质量、数量、包装、唛头与检验。

2. The quality of a commodity is an integration of the intrinsic features and the outer appearance of the commodity.
   商品质量是由商品的内在特征与外观组成。
3. It is worthy to note that the standard of a commodity is subject to change or amendment and a new standard often replace the older one, therefore, in case of sale by standard, it is important to specify the name of the publication, in which the standard of the commodity appears.
   值得注意的事,商品的标准受到标准变化与修改的影响,新的标准经常取代旧标准。因此,按标准销售时,规定货物买卖所采用的标准名称十分重要。
4. "Quality to be about equal to the sample" or a "quality to be similar to the sample".
   品质和样品大致相同或品质与样品近似
5. "F.A.Q"(Fair Average Quality) or "G.M.Q"(Good Merchantable Quality)
   中等品质,中等品或良好销售品质(合乎销售标准的良好品质)
6. Sales by specification, grade or standard
   凭商品规格、等级或标准买卖。

❖ Practical Drills

❖ Questions for Discussion

1. What is the power of good packaging? Give an example.
2. Why does packaging involve? What may be the package include?
3. What are the differences between outer packing and inner packing?

❖ Case Study

Dealing with Cartons Damaged

An American food producer exported 2000 cartons to Australia. Both the contract and L/C stipulated that partial shipment was prohibited. When the food was transported to the port for shipment, it was found that 50 cartons were damaged and couldn't be shipped. The consignor decided that according to UCP 5000 % more or less was allowed if the amount didn't exceed the L/C amount. In the end, 1950 cartons were delivered to the importer.

Was it reasonable for the seller to do so?

Chapter 6

❖ *Role Play*

Packing

A: Mr. Zhang, shall we now discuss the packing?

B: Very well. You know, we have definite ways of packing garments. As to blouses, we use a polythene wrapper for each article, all ready for window display.

A: Good. A wrapping that catches the eye will certainly help push the sales. With competition from similar garment producers, the merchandise must not only be of good value but also look attractive.

B: Right you are. We'll see to it that the blouses appeal to the eye as well as to the purse.

A: What about the outer packing?

B: We'll pack them 10 dozen to one carton, gross weight around 25 kilos a carton.

A: Carton?

B: Yes, corrugated cardboard boxes.

A: Could you use wooden cases instead?

B: Why use wooden cases?

A: I'm afraid the cardboard boxes are not strong enough for such a heavy load.

B: The cartons are comparatively light, and therefore easy to handle. They won't be stowed away with the heavy cargo. The stevedores will see to that. Besides, we'll reinforce the cartons with straps. Silk blouses are not fragile goods. They can stand a lot of jolting.

A: Maybe you're right, but the goods are to be transshipped at Hamburg or London. If the boxes are moved about on an open wharf, the dampness or rain may get into them. This would make the blouses spotted or ruined.

B: No need to worry about that. The cartons lined with plastic sheets are water-proof, and as the boxes are made of card-board, they will be handled with care.

A: Well, I don't want to make any chances. Besides, cartons are easy to cut open, and this increases the risk of pilferage.

B. Tampering with cartons is easily detected. I should say that this rather discourages pilferage.

A: Maybe so, but I'm afraid that in case of damage or pilferage, the insurance company will refuse compensation on the ground of improper packing, or packing unsuitable for sea voyage.

B: But cartons are quite seaworthy. They are extensively used in our shipments to continental ports. There are never any complaints from our clients, and such packing has also been approved by our insurance company for WPA and TPND.

A: If you could guarantee compensation in case the insurance company refuses to honor a claim for faulty packing, we would be quite willing to accept cartons.

B: I'm sorry, but we can't take on any responsibility for every kind of mishap.

A: I can understand your position. Perhaps I'm asking too much.

B: We'll use wooden cases if you insist, but the charge for packing will be considerably higher, and it also slows down delivery.

A: Well, I'll cable home immediately for instructions on the matter.

B: Please do. I'll be waiting for your reply.

Extended Activities

I. Answer the following questions.

1. Why should the name of commodity be clearly stated?
2. What are the units of measurement extensively used in the international business?
3. What are the ways of measuring the weight of goods?
4. What are some of the major functions of cargo packing?
5. Why is shipping mark important in the international transportation?

II. Translate the following terms into Chinese.

gross weight	net weight	conditional weight	theoretical weight
metric unit	shipping mark	cargo	sales by specification
sale by seller's sample		sale by illustration	indicative mark
warning mark			

III. Translate the following indicative handling terms into Chinese.

NO.	English	Chinese	NO.	English	Chinese
1	Center of Gravity		7	Keep Frozen	
2	Do Not Drop		8	Keep away from Cold	
3	Maximum Stack		9	Keep Dry	
4	Fragile, Glass		10	Use No Hook	
5	Handle with Care		11	Sling Here	
6	Keep away from Heat		12	This Side Up	

IV. Fill in the following blanks with an appropriate word (the begining Letters of some words are given).

　　The MTS (Marine Transportation System) transports people to work, provides them _____ recreation and vacation opportunities, puts food on their t_____ and brings them many of the items they need in their p_____ and personal lives. The MTS also provides American businesses with ways to suppliers and markets a_____ the world. Within the US, the MTS provides a cost-e_____ means for moving major commodities. F_____, the MTS is an essential element in m_____ national security.

　　The MTS s_____ an extensive range of users, including commercial, recreational, and defense-related activities. For example, in the movement of freight alone, the MTS users include:

❖ Companies that need to ship or receive freight _____ water, including manufacturers, retailers, agricultural concerns, petroleum companies, utilities, and mining operations;

❖ Companies that arrange and physically move the freight to, from and across the water, i_____ ship operation, trucking firms, railroads, third-party logistics operation, freight forwarders, consolidators, customer-house brokers and others.

V. Translate the following Chinese sentences into English.

(1) 青豆可以散装,也可以用麻袋装。
(2) 你已经知道,我们去年订购的那批床单到货时有不少被玷污。希望这次交货时对包装给予必要的注意。
(3) 我们要求工厂用牢固些的纸箱,并用双道箱带捆扎。
(4) 买主把包装和里面的商品看作是一个整体。
(5) 你们的包装必须具有适航性,并能经得起运输中的粗鲁搬运。

VI. Translate the following into Chinese.

1. Virtually all manufactured and processed goods require packaging during some phrase of their production and distribution.
2. The company ought to make decisions that serve society's interests as well as customer and company objectives.
3. Those who reveal the secrets of the company intentionally or unintentionally would be punished severely.
4. We attached a list of our products and we believe that some of these items will be of interest to you.
5. The cost of almost all goods and services soared when price controls were removed.

VII. Complete the following diagram according to what you have read from the text.

A Standardized Format of Shipping Marks for Chinese Consignees

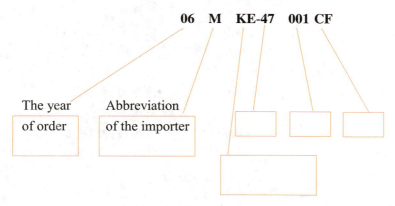

Chapter 7

Export and Import Documentations

Focal Learning

After the completion of this chapter, you are required to know:
- the definition of documentation;
- the major functions of various documentations in international trade;
- the basic characteristics of different documentations;
- the classification of documentation — Official documents, Commercial documents, Financial documents, Transport documents and Insurance documents.

Lead-in Vocabulary

furnishing or authentication	n.	文件或正式文本
confiscate	v.	没收,充公,查抄
ambiguous	adj.	不明确的,模糊的
weed out	v.	剔除,消除
lockup	n.	锁住,被锁住的状态
pro forma invoice		【商】(供进口商据以申请进口证或外汇用的)形式发票,估价发票
notary	n.	公证人
certified	adj.	被鉴定的,合格的
consular	adj.	领事的
commercial Consulate		商业领事馆
preliminary	adj.	预备的,初步的
indemnify	v.	赔偿 补偿
adjunct	adj.	附属的;附件,助手
title	n.	所有权

Chapter 7

Section I
Role and Requirements of Documentation

International trade often comes with various types of documents. According to a study conducted by Organization for Economic Cooperation and Development, an average overseas transaction needs 35 documents with a total of 360 copies. And the study represents that the "paper cost" amounts to 1.4 to 5.7 percent of the total value of international trade.

1. Role of Documentation

Documentation means an act of furnishing or authentication of all or any of the documents relating to a transaction. Domestic business and international trade both need some documents, but in exporting and importing it is necessary for each shipment to be accompanied by a variety of documents, therefore, it can be said that the major difference between domestic and international trade is that there are more documents for every export or import shipment.

The major purpose of documentation is to provide a specific and complete description of the goods so that they can be correctly processed for transport, payment, credit, insurance, import duty, etc.

2. Requirements for Documentation

A good working knowledge of trade documentation can protect traders from unexpected troubles. However, preparing the correct documents to cover an export/import shipment is considered by many to be very demanding. Since there are no international standards for documents, and different countries have their established traditions and practices. The documents actually used in a transaction depend on the requirements imposed by both the importing and the exporting countries. The characteristics of a transaction also determine the complexity of the documentation. As such, failure to complete the forms properly may lead to a fine or unnecessary delay in leaving the goods through foreign customs. If the information given is found to be false, heavy fines may be imposed or the goods confiscated.

In an attempt to reduce the error rate and ensure the timely payment, exporters are recommended to review their documents thoroughly for accuracy and to weed out any errors before the documents are presented. In short, it is important to maintain the consistency between all the documents relating to the same transaction. Usually, documents should have the following characteristics:

❖ Accuracy: The details in documents must be in strict conformity with those in the sales contract. No ambiguous words or expressions should be used.

❖ Completeness: Every necessary detail should be included in each document.

- ❖ Conciseness: No redundant words or expressions should be used, and no correction should be made on the document.
- ❖ Promptness: Make sure the documents are ready when they are needed, so that unnecessary delay or confusion can be avoided.

According to the sources of document, the most commonly used international trade documents can be classified roughly into five categories.

- ❖ Official documents
- ❖ Commercial documents
- ❖ Financial documents
- ❖ Transport documents
- ❖ Insurance documents

Section II
Official Documents

International trade involves complex flows of goods and services between many countries. Therefore, a set of official documents are used by countries to monitor and control these flows. These usually include:

- ❖ Export license;
- ❖ Import license and foreign exchange authorization;
- ❖ Certificate of origin;
- ❖ Inspection certificate;
- ❖ Consular invoice;
- ❖ Customs invoice.

1. Export License

Export license is also called the export permit, which is the first document an exporter must be concerned with. Such a document is normally required for the export of certain key raw material, equipment, machinery or other restricted goods related to national or international security; or works of arts or antiques that are of national, cultural or historic importance. It may be also required to implement a government policy or decisions such as to exercise economic sanctions against some countries. This document is taken by many as the lock-up preventing the exporter from pushing his goods to the foreign market. Processing the export license always experiences several steps as of application, submission, classification, evaluation, issuance or refusal.

2. Import License and Foreign Authorization

Many countries use import license and foreign authorization system to restrict importers to present pro forma invoices to their licensing authorities or to their central banks, or sometimes to both to apply for the license. If the planned importation is legal and meets current requirements, the license will be issued. Therefore, exporters should not ship to importers who need licenses until the licenses are actually in hand. The purpose of such documents is to control the inflow of foreign goods for various purposes such as to protect the domestic industries, or maintain the balance of payments or to implement a political policy, etc.

3. Certificate of Origin

A certificate of origin is the document which states the country or the place of origin of the goods. It is a form to prove that the merchandise in question did come from wherever it is claimed. The certificate is usually prepared by the shipper, signed in the presence of a notary public, and then certified by a non-governmental commercial organ acceptable to the country of destination. The main purpose is to obtain preferred import status for the goods and to get financing easily for the export of goods of certain origin. It is usually required by countries that do not use Customers Invoice or Consular Invoice to set appropriate duties for the import. It contains the nature, quantity, values of goods shipped and their place of manufacture. There is no standard format for certificate of origin and indeed no specific format is required for most nations. The exporter must at all times be ready to obtain a certificate if requested for any export shipment.

In China, this certificate is generally issued by the Import and Export Commodity Inspection Bureau, or China Council for Promotion of International Trade. Nowadays, China enjoys the Generalized System of Preference (GSP) treatment granted by many countries all over the world. GSP documents may be used when exporting to countries like New Zealand, Canada, Japan, and EU members to get preferential import duties.

4. Certificate of Inspection

This document contains many similar kinds of certificate, such as certificate of value, certificate of quality, certificate of quantity, certificate of health, weight memo. The contract may required either the exporter to certify that the quality of the goods meet the contract requirements or for an external inspector to make an independent certification. The contract also stipulates who is to carry out the inspection and who is to pay for it. The General Administration of Quality Supervision, Inspection and Quarantine of the People's Republic of China handles all the inspection for the Chinese exporter and their foreign customers. The purpose is to ensure that the goods meet a certain standard.

5. Consular Invoice

A Consular Invoice is a document certified by the consul of the country for which the merchandise is destined and an exporter must purchase from the importing country's commercial Consulate. The invoice is used by customs officials of the country of entry to verify the value, quantity, and nature of the merchandise imported. Most of the consular invoices are in the language of the country to which the goods are shipped. It is the most difficult document of all and must be filled in with extreme care.

6. Customs Invoice

Customs invoice is required by the importing country in order to clear the customs, to compile statistics, to verify country of origin for import duty and tax purpose, to compare exporting price and domestic price, and to fix anti-dumping duty. It is issued on a special form prescribed by the customs authorities of the importing country.

Section III
Commercial Documents

Commercial document are generally issued by the importer, exporter or some relevant non-governmental business organizations. They aim to ensure smooth transactions and usually include:

- Pro forma invoice;
- Commercial Invoice;
- Quality Certificate;
- Weight Certificate.

1. Pro Forma Invoice

Pro forma invoice is an invoice similar to a commercial invoice and it contains the same information as a commercial invoice but is headed pro forma. It is provided by an exporter prior to a sale or shipment of merchandise, informing the buyer of the kinds and quantities of goods to be supplied, their value, the specifications as weight, size, and similar characteristics. A pro forma invoice is used as a preliminary invoice together with a quotation; it is used for quotations to importer who sometimes need this document to apply for import license and foreign exchange. Specifically, an irrevocable letter of credit is required by the exporter, the importer will use it to substantiate the need for a letter of credit to his banker, or the importer's country requires that an import license be issued for each import and must approve the pro forma invoice before making foreign exchange available for payment by the importer.

Therefore, a pro forma invoice has no legal status. It is only a means to facilitate the buyer to accomplish the corresponding tasks.

2. Commercial Invoice

A commercial invoice is one of the most important documents which identifies the seller and the buyer of goods or services, numbers such as invoice number, date, shipping date, mode of transport, delivery and payment terms, and a complete list and description of the goods or services including prices, discounts and quantities.

It is often used by governments to determine the true value of goods for the assessment of customs duties and also to prepare consular documents. Governments often specify its form, content, numbers of copies, language to be used, and other characteristics to control imports.

Commercial invoice used in international trade serves as a record of the essential details of a transaction. Then great attention should be given to the fact that the commercial invoice must be totally accurate in all respects. If the document received by the importer has mistakes, it may lead to excessive duties or fines and penalties.

A commercial invoice must show the following basic information about the transaction:

(1) The shipper: the full and accurate name of the shipper should be used;

(2) The description: description of the goods in the commercial invoice must be in exact conformity with that spelled out in the letter of credit and other documents;

(3) Net and gross weight: depending on the product, duty may often be applied on the weight of the goods, and if the net and the gross weights are not stated, the customs authorities may just take the gross weight as the weight for duty;

(4) The dimension of the shipment: for handling the goods in transit;

(5) The unit price: the most important information in the invoice; some countries will levy a fine against you if you show a price lower than that agreed upon; and carefully note the "currency" in which the price is listed to make sure that this, too, conforms to that stipulated in the contract;

(6) Freight, insurance, package: be in conformity with whatever is designated in the agreement, but also agree with the actual charges which may be reflected in other documents such as the freight on the bill of lading;

(7) Date: to date the invoice because this could be a determining factor in the date of payment;

(8) Signature: omission of the currency designated is the most common error on the invoice, and a failure to sign the invoice comes a close second.

3. Quality Certificate

A Quality Certificate confirms that the quality/specification of a particular consignment of goods is in agreement with the sales contract at the time of shipment. It may be issued by the exporter or a relevant government department as required under Letter of Credit or Sales Contract terms. It is essential that cargo description in the Quality Certificate conforms to its terms found in other relevant documents, such as the commercial Invoice, L/C, insurance Policy.

4. Weight Certificate

Weight Certificate is usually requested by the importer to confirm that the weight of the goods is in accordance with the sales contract at the time of shipment. It is a supplement to a commercial invoice to show the details of a shipment when specification, quantities, weights or contents of individual units in the shipment vary. Similar to a Quality Certificate, it may be issued by the exporter or a relevant government department as required under Letter of Credit or Sales Contract terms. The purpose of weight certificate is to recognize the goods, to clear the customs and to check the goods.

Section IV
Financial Documents

In international trade, quite a number of financial documents are used to ensure that the exporter receives full and timely payment for the shipment. These documents are usually issued by banks or exporters:

- Application Form for international Money Transfer;
- Drafts;
- Banker's Draft;
- Commercial Draft;
- Sight Draft;
- Time Draft;
- Application for Documentary Letter of Credit;
- Letter of Credit.

1. Application Form for International Money Transfer

When cash in advance or open account is used, payment may be effected by transferring money through banks. Thus, the overseas buyers need to complete the relevant application form for International Money Transfer. This kind of form is essentially a request to a bank to make an international money transfer on the remitter's behalf. In other words, an overseas buyer instructs a bank in the buyer's country to transfer an amount of money to an exporter's bank by M/T, T/T or D/T.

2. Drafts

A draft or bill of exchange is an unconditional order signed by one party (the drawer) requesting a second party (drawee or payer) to make payment in lawful money immediately or at a determinable future time to a third party (payee). In the context of international trade, the drawer and the payee is usually the seller while the drawee and payer is always the buyer. There are banker's draft, commercial draft, sight draft, time draft, clean draft, documentary Draft etc., however, these drafts are not mutually exclusive, that is, one draft can be commercial, documentary, and time draft at the same time.

❖ **Banker's Draft**

A banker's draft is drawn by one bank on another bank. It is used in settling payment obligation between banks.

❖ **Commercial Draft**

A commercial draft is drawn by a firm or an exporter. The drawee can be a firm, an exporter or a bank. A commercial draft is commonly used in international trade in the settlement of payment.

❖ **Sight Draft**

A sight draft is one that is payable on presentation, i.e., the drawee should immediately pay the amount on the draft drawn on him.

❖ **Time Draft**

A time or usance draft is one that is payable in a specified number or days after 1) the date of issue; 2) the date of acceptance, 3) the date of B/L or a fixed future date. The specified number of days is called the "usance period".

❖ **Clean Draft**

A clean draft is one that is paid without the presentation of any other documents attached. A banker's draft is usually clean.

❖ **Documentary Draft**

A documentary draft is one that should be paid only when certain documents have been attached to and presented together with the draft. Commercial drafts are usually documentary. The most important document is bill of lading that represents the title to the goods.

❖ **Promissory Notes**

A promissory note is any written form to pay, it is negotiable instruction that is evidence of a debt contracted by a borrower from a creditor, known as a lender of funds. If the instrument does not have all the qualities of a negotiable instrument, it cannot be legally transferred.

As a promissory note is a promise by the maker instead of drawer to pay to the payee, there are two parties concerned, the maker and the payee. The maker of a promissory note can be more than one person; they are jointly and separately responsible for the payment to the bill.

Promissory notes can be sight promissory notes or time promissory notes. They can also be made by commercial firms or bankers. Promissory notes made by the banker are usually called cashier's check or cashier's order. They are all sight notes. And in international trade, most promissory notes are drawn by bankers that are not negotiable.

In the collection method of payment for goods, a draft is always drawn upon the importer by the exporter to get paid. The exporter through the banking system, get payment against the delivery just by a draft, for the sum agreed as settlement in the export contract. By using a draft with other shipping documents through the banking system, an exporter can ensure greater control of goods, because until the draft is paid or accepted by the overseas buyer, the goods cannot be released.

3. Application for Documentary Letter of Credit

An application for a documentary letter of credit is the form used by the buyer to request his or her bank to open a documentary letter of credit in favor of the seller. It is used to authorize a bank to open a letter of credit.

4. Letter of Credit

As one of the most important finance documents used in international trade, accuracy in the content of a L/C is of vital importance. Usually, an exporter will be advised of the opening of L/C well before the shipment, so that he could have enough time to check the details contained in it. The details listed below are the ones that require special attention when an L/C is opened by the buyer or checked by the seller:

- The method of advice: airmail/cable;
- The type of credit: whether the L/C is irrevocable or revocable;
- The date of expiration;
- Documents required;
- The applicant's name and address;
- The beneficiary's name and address;
- The advising/paying/confirming bank;
- The amount of goods;
- The permission/rejection of partial shipment/transshipment;
- The port of shipment and port of discharge.

Section V
Transportation Documents

A single export shipment can involve a lot of different documents to ensure that the goods reach the final consignee. A few commonly used transportation documents are listed below:

- Bill of lading;
- Shipping note;
- Packing list;
- Rail consignment note;
- Road consignment note;
- Air waybill;
- Combined transport documents;
- Arrival notification.

1. Bill of Lading

A bill of lading is document issued by a carrier to a shipper, signed by the captain, agent, or owner of a vessel, and stating the conditions in which the goods were delivered to (and received by) the ship; and an engagement to deliver goods at the prescribed port of destination to the lawful holder of the bill of lading. A bill of lading is, therefore, both a receipt for merchandise and a contract to deliver it as freight. It is a document of title to the goods, enabling the shipper or owner of the goods to endorse title to other parties, sell goods in transit, and present to banks with other documents in seeking payment under documentary credits. Abbreviated generally as B/L, it is the most important document for sea transport.

2. Shipping Note

A shipping note is a declaration issued by an officer of a vessel in the name of the shipping company stating that certain goods have been received on board his vessel. It serves the shipping company as a delivery or receipt note for particular consignment. That's why it is also called a Mate's Receipt, which is not a title document, but just used as an interim document until the bill of lading is issued. It gives information about a particular export consignment when offered for shipment. The cargo description in a Shipping Note should conform to that found on the commercial invoice.

3. Packing List

This document is really an addendum to the commercial invoice when numerous units of the same product are being shipped or when quantities, weights or contents of individual units in a shipment vary. Occasionally, a separate list is prepared for each package showing the weight and measurements and contents, which helps identify the specific item by the importer and facilitate customs clearance. Upon arrival of the goods, the customs may carry out a partial examination by checking a certain number of the cases. If the packing list proves to be accurate, the rest of the shipment is assumed to be in order.

4. Rail Consignment Note

A consignment note for rail transport serves as the contract of carriage between the railway and consignor, by evidencing the receipt of the goods and the date of acceptance for carriage by the carrier. The consignment note will be delivered with the cargo from the departure station to the consignee at the destination station against payment of the amounts by the consignee. Unlike B/L, it is not a document of title and is not transferable or negotiable. The seller should be responsible for the accuracy of the information in the consignment note. The railway has the right to check if the consignment corresponds with the information in the consignment note.

5. Road Consignment Note

A road consignment note, similar to rail consignment note in form and contents, stands for the contract for the carriage of goods by road in vehicles, completed by the sender and carrier with the appropriate signatures and/or stamp. Like rail consignment note, it evidences the place and date of taking over the goods and the place designated for delivery. It is not a negotiable or transferable document or document of title. The consignment note is made out in three copies signed by sender and carrier. Only the first one is originally kept by the seller, the third copy goes to the carrier and the second copy accompanies the consignment and is finally delivered to the consignee at the destination. In road transport, a separate consignment note sometimes is needed if the goods have to be loaded in different vehicles, or are of different kinds or are divided into different lots. In addition, the seller is liable for all expenses, loss and damage sustained by the carrier by reason of the inaccuracy or inadequacy of certain specified particulars which the consignment note given by him must contain. The consignment note must contain the following particulars:

- The name and address of the sender and the consignee;
- The origination rail station accepting consignment and the station or place designated for delivery;
- The ordinary description of the nature of the goods and method of packing and in the case of dangerous goods, their generally recognized description ;
- The gross weight of the goods or their quantity;
- The charges relating to the carriage;
- The requisite instructions for customs and other formalities.

It should be noted that the sender is responsible for the accuracy and adequacy of information contained in the consignment note. The sender should also provide the necessary information for the purposes of Customs or other formalities which have to be completed before delivery of the goods.

6. Air Waybill

The air waybill (AWB) is one of the most important cargo documents prepared and issued by a carrier or its authorized cargo agents. It is the shipping document when the goods are shipped by air. It is a proof acknowledging receipt of the goods from the shipper by the airline, a contract between the shipper and the airline for moving the goods, a certificate of insurance, a customs declaration, an instruction sheet guiding the carrier's staff in handling the cargo.

The air waybill is an internationally standardized document printed in English or the language of the air carrier. AWB is a straight or non-negotiable bill of lading. Until now, no "to order" or negotiable air waybills are issued by IATA members. Therefore, the word "non-negotiable" must not be crossed out or tampered with in any way.

7. Combined Transport Document

Combined Transport Document proves the contract of carriage of goods by at least two modes of transport, issued by a combined transport operator under a combined transport contract. It is quite similar to "through B/L" and combined transport B/L used for ocean transport, but is broader than them. Through B/L and combined transport B/L are always connected with sea, used for any transport combined with sea, while combined transport document can be applied to any kind of combined transport. Several carriers are involved in through B/L, while the combined transport document is issued by only one carrier, that is, combined transport operator. The combined transport document can be made out either negotiable or non-negotiable.

8. Arrival Notification

An arrival notification is the document furnished to consignee and shipping broker noticing them to the coming-up arrival of freight and availability of freight for pickup. It also requires the consignee to submit appropriate documents, such as original Bill of Lading, for customs clearance. Thus, the carrier can subsequently dispatch the goods to the consignee.

Section VI
Insurance Documents

The cargo insurance document is a contract whereby the insurer (insurance company), on the basis of a premium paid, undertakes to indemnify the insured against loss from certain risks or perils to which the cargo insured may be exposed. It is an indispensable adjunct of international trade. Without adequate insurance and protection of the interests of those with goods in transit, international trade can not be guaranteed. Whether the responsibility for shipment insurance provision is the buyer's or the seller's is decided according to the details of the particular export sales contract. These are the important insurance documents:

- Insurance Policy
- Insurance Certificate
- Open Policy

1. Insurance Policy

Broadly, an insurance policy is the entire written contract of insurance. It provides actionable evidence of an insurance contract. More specifically, it is the basic written or printed document, as well as the coverage forms and endorsement added to it. A typical insurance policy should include the following data:

- Name, address and signature of the insurer
- Name of the insured
- The endorsement of the insured
- A description of the risks covered and the insured time
- description of the consignment
- The sum or sums insured
- Premium

2. Insurance Certificate

An insurance certificate is a document indicating the type and amount of insurance coverage in force on a particular shipment, used to assure the consignee that insurance is provided to cover loss of or damage to the cargo while in transit.

In some cases a shipper may issue a document that certifies that a shipment has been insured under a given open policy, and that the certificate represents and takes the place of such open policy, the provisions of which are controlling. In many countries, it is not actionable.

3. Open Policy

An open policy is recommended for exporters and importers who do a large volume of business. An open policy provides coverage for all goods shipped by the insured while the policy is in effect. The duration of this policy may last indefinitely. China's export by using such policies is automatically covered with pre-agreement of the PICC.

Chapter 7

Section VII
Specimens

1. Import and Export Licenses

中华人民共和国纺织品出口自动许可证

AUTOMATIC TEXTILES EXPORT LICENCE OF THE PEOPLE'S REPUBLIC OF CHINA

No. 5312260

1. 出口商： Exporter 3302704842699 好嘉时装有限公司（深圳）		2. 出口自动许可证号： Automatic export license No. 06AAA01042	
3. 发货人： Consignor 3302704842699 好嘉时装有限公司		4. 出口自动许可证有效截止日期： Automatic export license expiry date: 2006 年 10 月 26 日	
5. 贸易方式： Terms of trade 一般贸易		8. 出口最终目的国（地区） Country/Region of purchase	
6. 合同号： Contract No: JCZ20060822		9. 付款方式： Payment 10% 电汇 + 90% 信用证	
7. 报关口岸： Place of clearance 深圳海关（5300）		10. 运输方式： Mode of transport 海上运输	
11. 商品名称： Description of goods 712 他棉制女士长裤，马裤（指女成人 7016 号女童长裤，马裤）		商品编码： Code of goods 6187005849	

12. 规格，等级 Specification	13. 单位 Unit	14. 数量 Quantity	15. 单价 USD Unit Price	16. 总值(USD) Amount	17. 总值折美元 Amount in USD
A-SH08743	条	5,620.00	4.500	5,620.00	25,190.00
18. 总计 Total	条	5,620.00		5,620.00	5,620.00

19. 备注：
　　Supplement details
供货生产企业名称：天意制衣有限公司
是否转口：　否
转口国（地区）：

20. 发证机关盖章
　　Issuing authority stamp

21. 发证日期：2006 年 5 月 30 日
　　License date

第一联（正本）发货人办理海关手续海关验放签注栏在背面

109

2. Certificate of Origin

1. Exporter	Certificate No.
	CERTIFICATE OF ORIGIN
	OF
2. Consignee	**THE PEOPLE'S REPUBLIC OF CHINA**
3. Means of transport and route	5. For certifying authority use only
4. Country / region of destination	

6. Marks and Numbers	7. Number and kind of packages; description of goods	8. H.S.Code	9. Quantity	10. Number and date of invoices

11. Declaration by the exporter	12. Certification
The undersigned hereby declares that the above details and statements are correct, that all the goods were produced in China and that they comply with the Rules of Origin of the People's	It is hereby certified that the declaration by the exporter is correct.
Place and date, signature and stamp of authorized signatory	Place and date, signature and stamp of certifying authority

3. Certificate of Inspection

中国进出口商品检验广东公司
CHINA NATIONAL IMPORT & EXPORT INSPECTION
(GUANGDONG) CORPORATION

6th Floor Block No. 66 Huangcheng Avenue
Buji Town, Shenzhen, P.R. China.
Tel: (0755) 83160324, 83160326
Fax: (0755) 83160325
Post Code: 518002

No: GDSTR2007028
Date: 2007 年 6 月 20 日

委托人：水韵时装有限公司（深圳）

商品名称："清丽"（Fresh Beauty）女士服装

副本
COPY
0013697

数量：送检样品衣裤各一件

检验结果：

兹证明，本司应委托人的要求，对送检样品进行含量检验，结果如下：

样品名称	项目		
	棉（%）COTTON	羊毛（%）WOOL	氨纶（%）SPANDEX
上衣成分	N/A	90%	10%
裤子成分	95%	N/A	5%

备注：以上检验结果仅对送检之样品负责。

主任检验员：李海天

4. Pro Forma Invoice

ISSUER	形式发票
	PROFORMA INVOICE
TO	
	NO. DATE
TRANSPORT DETAILS	S/C NO. L/C NO.
	TERMS OF PAYMENT

Marks and Numbers	Number and kind of package Description of goods	Quantity	Unit Price	Amount
		Total:		

SAY TOTAL:

PORT TO LOADING:

PORT OF DESTINATION:

TIME OF DELIVERY:

INSURANCE:

VALIDITY:

BENEFICIARY

ADVISING BANK:

NEGOTIATING BANK:

Chapter 7

5. Commercial Invoice

ISSUER	COMMERCIAL INVOICE	
TO		
	NO.	DATE
TRANSPORT DETAILS	S/C NO.	L/C NO.
	TERMS OF PAYMENT	

Marks and Numbers	Number and kind of package Description of goods	Quantity	Unit Price	Amount
			Total:	
SAY TOTAL:				

6. Draft (Bill of Exchange)

凭
Drawn under   BANK OF AMERICA, NEW YORK
信用证   第   号
L/C   No. NYP976574
日期   年   月   日
dated   JULY 15, 2004

按   息   付 款
Payable with interest @ _____ % per annum

号码   汇票金额   中国 . 深圳   年 月 日
No. _____ **Exchange** for USD51, 358.400 Shenzhen, China _____

见票   日后 (本汇票之副本未付)付
At   *** ***   sight of this **FIRST** of Exchange (Second of exchange being unpaid)
pay to the order of   MEISI FASHION (SHENZHEN) CO. LTD   或其指定人
金   额 **SAY U.S DOLLARS FIFTY–ONE THOUSAND THREE HUNDRED AND FIVE –EIGHT**
The sum of
AND CENTS FORY ONLY.

此致
To BANK OF AMERICA, NEW YORK

                                         EISI FASHION (SHENZHEN) CO.LTD.

1

Chapter 7

7. Bill of Lading

Shipper **Shanghai Grand Life Trading Co.** No 276 Dalian West Rd. Shanghai, P.R. China Tel: 86-21-62863468 Fax: 86-21-62863466		B/LNo.TD050515050		
Consignee (if "To Order so indicate) **Happy Sources Co.** 44-62 Barnett Ave Glynde SA, Australia Tel: 61-8-8337-5388 Fax: 61-8-8365-1638		中远国际货运有限公司 COSCO INTERNATIONAL FREIGHT CO. LTD. 1648 Dalian Road Shanghai 200090 China Tel：021-55963802 Fax: 021-55963804 **MULTIMODAL TRANSPORT BILL OF LADING**		
Notify party (No claim shall attach for failure to notify) **Same as Consignee**		NOT NEGOTIABLE UNLESS CONSIGNED "TO ORDER" RECEIVED by the MTO the Goods as specialized below in apparent good order and condition unless otherwise stated, to be transported to such place as agreed, authorized on the front and reverse of this Bill of Lading to which the Merchant agrees by accepting this Bill of Lading, any local privileges and customs notwithstanding.		
Place of Receipt Long,You, zhejiang	Place of Loading Shanghai, China			
Vessel Dong Feng VS 146	Port of Transhipment N/A	Port of Discharge Adelaide	Place of Delivery Adelaide	No. of Bill of Lading Three
Marks & Numbers	No. of Pkgs or shipping Units	Description of Goods & Pkgs	Gross Weight	Measurement
GLL20050314 HSS08GL1234 Made in China	25 CTNS 25 CTNS 20 CTNS 20 CTNS 20 CTNS	Park Set Toys (EN72) B/O Baby ball Set Toys Wind-up Baby Bell Wind-up Baby Bell Wind-up Baby Bell	22KGS 18.5KGS 18.5KGS 24KGS 19KGS	0.201CBM 0.215CBM 0.243CBM 0.289CBM 0.275CBM
Total Number of Containers or other Packages or Units (in words) SAY ONE HUNDRED AND TEN CARTONS ONLY				Temperature Control instruction
Freight Details, Charges etc. Prepaid FREIGHT PREPAID			Collect	Excess Value Declaration
				Ship on Board the Vessel
				Date 2006-4-16 Signature
				Place and date of issue 2006-4-16 in Shanghai
F/Agent Name for Delivery				Signed by the MTO/on behalf of the MTO

—particulars finished by shipper—

8. Packing List

Packing List	S & N Trading Co. Ltd. 99 Shennan Road East, IMC Tower A 606 Shenzhen Guangdong P. R. C. Postal Code: 518050 Tel: (0755)83018766 Fax: (0755)83018768 E-mail: export @mlexports. Com.cn		
For account and risk of Messrs.	Commercial Invoice No.		Date
	Letter of Credit No.		Date
	Issuing Bank		
Buyer's P.O. or Contract No.	Date	Import Permit/License No.	Date
Buyer's Department/Store No.		Marks & Numbers	
Carrier-Voyage/Flight No.	Shipment on or about		
From (Port of Loading)	To (Port of Discharge)		
Via (Transship at)	For Transhipment to		

Package No.	Item No.	Description of Goods	Quantity	Weight (kgs/Lbs)	Measurement

S & N Trading Co. Ltd.
(Signature and/or Stamp)
E. & O. E.

9. Insurance Policy/Certificate

中保财产保险有限公司
The People's Insurance(Property)Company of China, Ltd.

发票号码 Invoice No. TL. 050515	保险单号次 Policy No. BX050513
	ORIGINAL

海洋货物运输保险单
MARINE CARGO TRANSPORTATION INSURANCE POLICY

被保险人：上海宏生贸易公司
Insured: Shanghai Grand Life Trading Co.

中保财产保险有限公司(以下简称本公司)根据被保险人的要求，及其所缴付约定的保险费，按照本保险单承担险别和背面所载条款与下列特别条款承保下列货物运输保险，特签发本保险单。

This policy of Insurance witnesses that The People's Insurance(Property)Company of China, Ltd. (hereinafter called "The Company"), at the request of the Insured and in consideration of the agreed premium paid by the Insured, undertakes to insure the under mentioned goods in transportation subject to the conditions of this Policy as per the Clauses printed overleaf and other special.

保险货物项目 Descriptions of Goods	包装单位数量 Packing Unit Quantity	保险金额 Amount Insured
Park Set Toys(EN72) B / O Baby ball Set Toys Wind—up Baby Bell Wind—up Baby Bell Wind—up Baby Bell	110 CARTONS	USD8,234.60

承 保 险 别
Coverage
ALL RISKS+ WAR RISK

货 物 标 记
Marks of Goods
GLL20070315

总 保 险 金 额： US DOLARS EIGHT THOUDAND TWO HANDRED AND THIRTY-FOUR
　　　　　　　AND CENTS
Total Amount Insured: SIXTY ONLY………………………………………………………………

保费　　As arranged　　载运输工具　DONGFENG VSl408　　开航日期　MARCH 15,2007
Premium…………： 　Per conveyance s. s …………………… Slg. on or abt. …………………

起运港 SHANGAHI CHINA　　　　　　　目的港 ADELAIDE AUSTRALIA
From……………………………………To…………………………………………………………

所保货物，如发生本保险单项下可能引起索赔的损失或损坏，应立即通知本公司下述代理人查勘。如有索赔，应向本公司提交保险单正本(本保险单共有　　份正本)及有关文件。如一份正本已用于索赔，其余正本则自动失效。

In the event of loss or damage which may result in a claim under this Policy, immediate notice must be given to the Company's Agent as mentioned hereunder. Claims, if any, one of the Original Policy which has been issued in Original(s)together with the relevant documents shall be surrendered to the Company. If one of the Original Policy has been accomplished, the others to be void.

中保财产保险有限公司
THE PEOPLE'S INSURANCE(PROPERTY)COMPANY OFCHINAA, LTD.

赔款偿付地点　　ADELAIDE　AUSTRALIAUA
Claim payable at………………………………………………………………………………………

日期 MARCH 15,2007;　　　　　　　　　　　　　　　在 SHANGHAI　CHINA
Date………………………………………………at…………………………………………………….

地址：858 PEOPLE ROAD SHANGHAI
Address： FAX!02l—63267557 PICC CN.

10. Customs Declaration Form

WELCOME TO THE UNITED STATES	欢迎来到美国
DEPARTMENT OF THE TREASURY UNITED STATES CUSTOMS SERVICE	财政部 美国海关署
CUSTOMS DECLARATION	海关申报表

Each arriving traveler or head of family must provide the following information (only ONE written declaration per family is required):

1. Family Name _____ First (Given) _____
   Middle _____

2. Birth date

   _____ Day _____ Month _____ Year

3. Number of family members traveling with you:

4. U.S. Address:

5. Passport issued by (country)

6. Passport Number

7. Country of Residence

8. Countries visited on this trip prior to U.S. arrival

9. Airline/Flight No:

10. The primary purpose of this trip is business.
    ○ YES   ○ NO

每位入关的旅遊者或一家之主必須提供以下資料 (一個家庭只須申报一份):

1. 姓氏_____名字_____
   中間名_____

2. 出生日期：

   _____日_____月_____年

3. 与你同行的家庭成员人数：

4. 在美地址：

5. 护照发照(國家)

6. 護照號碼

7. 居住国家

8. 到美国前造访过的国家

9. 航空公司／航班号：

10. 此次旅程的主要目的是商务？
    ○ 是   ○ 否

(To be continued)

(Continued)

11. I am/we are bringing fruits, plants, meats, food, soil, birds, snails, other live animals, farm products, or I/we have been on a farm or ranch outside the U.S. YES ○ NO ○	11. 您携帶水果、植物、肉类、食品、土壤、鸟类、蝸牛、其他动物和农产品，或您一直居住在美國以外的农村或牧场嗎？ 是 ○ 否 ○
12. I am/we are carrying currency or monetary instruments over $10000 U.S. or the foreign equivalent. YES ○ NO ○	12. 您携帶現金或珍貴物品，其价值超過一万美金或相当于一万美金的外币吗？ 是 ○ 否 ○
13. I have (We have) commercial merchandise? (articles for sale, samples used for soliciting orders, or goods that are not considered personal effects.) YES ○ NO ○	13. 您有携帶任何商品嗎？(販卖之商品、订购之样本等任何非属私人之物品) 是 ○ 否 ○
14. The total value of all goods I/we purchased or acquired abroad and am/are bringing to the U.S. is (see instructions under Merchandise on reverse side; visitors should report value of gifts only):$ _____ U.S. Dollars	14. 您境外购买或獲得並帶入美國所有物品总价值(参看 背面商品栏目；访问者只須申报礼品价值)：$ _____ 美元
I have read the important information on the reverse side of this form and have made a truthful declaration. SIGNATURE _____ Date _____	我已阅读过这表格背面之重要須知，並据实以报。 签名_____ 日期_____

Useful Phrases & Technical Terms

export license	出口许可证
import license and foreign authorization	进口许可证和外国授权书
certificate of origin	原产地证明书
certificate of inspection	商品检验合格证书
consular invoice	领事发票
commercial consulate	商务领事
customs invoice	海关发票
pro forma invoice	形式发票
commercial invoice	商业发票
quality certificate	质量证明书
weight certificate	重量单
financial documents	财务凭证
drafts	汇票
promissory notes	本票,期票
letter of credit	信用证
transportation documents	运输单据
bill of lading	提单
shipping note	装船通知单
packing list	包装清单,装箱单
consignment note (for rail and road)	托运单(用于铁路和公路)
road consignment note	公路托运单,公路发货通知书
air waybill	空运提单,航空运货单
combined transport document	联合运输单据
arrival notification	到达通知
insurance documents	保险单据
insurance policy	保险契约,保险单
insurance certificate	保险凭证
open policy	开口保险单,预约保险单

Notes

1. In an attempt to reduce the error rate and ensure the timely payment, exporters are recommended to review their documents thoroughly for accuracy and to weed out any errors before the documents are presented.

为了尽可能减少出错,确保按时交货,建议出口商在提交单据之前,仔细审验各种相关单据以防出错。

2. A commercial invoice is one of the most important documents which identifies the seller and the buyer of goods or services, numbers such as invoice number, date, shipping date, mode of transport, delivery and payment terms, and a complete list and description of the goods or services including prices, discounts and quantities

   商业发票是最重要的单据之一,内容一般包括发票号码、日期、装运日期、运输方式、交货和付款条件以及含有货物的名称、价格、折扣、数量的整套单据。

3. In China, this certificate is generally issued by the Import and Export Commodity Inspection Bureau, or China Council for Promotion of International Trade.

   在中国,该证书一般由中国进出口商品检验局或中国国际贸易促进会出具。

4. Customs invoice is required by the importing country in order to clear the customs, to compile statistics, to verify country of origin for import duty and tax purpose, to compare exporting price and domestic price, and to fix anti-dumping duty. It is issued on a special form prescribed by the customs authorities of the importing country.

   为了通关,编制统计数据,确定原产地国进口关税,比较出口与国内销售的差价,核定反倾销税,进口商要求出口商开立海关发票。

5. Open policy is recommended for exporters and importers who do a large volume of business.

   预约保险单,也叫开口保险单,建议买卖双方成交大批生意时使用。

Practical Drills

❖ Questions for Discussion

1. Please list at least four names of documents used in the international trade.
2. What are the contents and function of transportation documents?
3. What's the difference between sight draft and time draft?
4. What is the function of documentation in the international trade?

❖ Case Study

The Advising Bank's Refusal

A Dalian exporter signed a contract with a UK company to sell 10 M/T of apples. The L/C amount was US $30,000. According to the contract, the seller had the option to ship 3% more or less. The seller loaded 10.2 M/T of apples and opened a commercial invoice for 30,600 USD. When the seller went to the bank for negotiation, the advising bank refused. Why?

❖ Role Play

Talking about Credit Card

A: Mr. Wang, Would you please tell me what's a letter of credit like?

B: Yes, a letter of credit is one of the most used methods of payment in international transactions. It provides advantages to both the exporter and the importer. In essence, it substitutes the credit of the bank for the credit of the buyer.

A: Mr. Wang, How would you define the letter of credit?

B: Well, I would say that the letter of credit is a letter which is addressed to the seller by bank acting on behalf of the buyer. In the letter, the bank promises to pay a specified amount of money upon presentation of stipulated documents.

A: So a letter of credit is different from a draft, isn't it?

B: Yes. The letter of credit is a promise to pay rather then a means of payment. Actual payment is accomplished by means of a draft.

A: We've often learned that credits may be revocable or irrevocable, unconfirmed or confirmed. It seemed rather complicated. Would you please explain it to me?

B: OK, in general speaking, "revocable" or "irrevocable" relates to the liability of the issuing bank, whereas "unconfirmed" or "confirmed" related to the responsibility of the correspondent bank or other bank.

A: Then what's the difference between a revocable credit and an irrevocable one?

B: A revocable credit can be amended or cancelled at any time while an irrevocable credit can only be amended or cancelled with the consent of all parties to it. Besides, in the case of a revocable credit, the issuing bank is bound to pay drawings under the credit which is negotiated by the advising bank of the transmitting bank prior to the receipt by it of the notice of revocation or of amendment, whereas an irrevocable credit carries the irrevocable undertaking of the issuing bank to pay of drawings which are made in terms of the credit.

A: I think the revocable credit gives the importer greater control over the activities of the exporter, doesn't it?

B: Right, that's why an importer may choose to open a revocable credit rather than an irrevocable one.

A: What is a confirmed credit then?

B: A confirmed credit involves a confirming bank, which may either be the issuing bank or an intermediary bank. Where the confirming bank adds confirmation to an irrevocable letter of credit, the credit is a confirmed credit, or more exactly, a confirmed irrevocable is a confirmed credit, or more exactly, a confirmed irrevocable credit.

A: I see. A confirmed credit must be also an irrevocable credit. And an exporter will enjoy the benefit of a confirmed credit. Do you agree with me?

B: Yes, I quite agree. I hope you know the reasons for heavy reliance on the letter of credit.

A: I think I do. Thank you very much, Mr. Wang.

Chapter 7

Extended Activities

I. Answer the following questions.

1. What information should be included in a commercial invoice?
2. What is pro forma invoice?
3. What is the difference between a commercial invoice and a pro forma invoice?
4. What are the three major functions of an ocean bill of lading?
5. What are the contents and functions of packing list?

II. Look at the terms in the left-hand column and find the correct definitions in the right-hand column. Copy the corresponding letters in the blanks.

1. _____	beneficiary	a. a draft payable as soon as it is presented
2. _____	open account	b. formal agreement between 2 or more parties
3. _____	contract	c. a signed agreement to pay a draft
4. _____	sight draft	d. party in whose favor a credit is established
5. _____	honor	e. a contract between a carrier and a shipper
6. _____	negotiable	f. arrangement in which payment is made after goods are sold
7. _____	bill of lading	g. that can be exchanged for money
8. _____	acceptance	h. keep an agreement by making a payment.

III. Read the following pairs of sentences carefully and discuss with partner the different meanings of the words in each pair.

1. customs
    A. Social <u>customs</u> vary greatly from country to country.
    B. How long will it take us to pass the <u>customs</u>?
2. party
    A. The freshmen are going to have a <u>party</u> at Christmas Eve.
    B. The agreement are among three <u>parties</u>.
3. negotiable
    A. The manager said that the company's claim for compensation is not <u>negotiable</u>.
    B. Don't you think an insurance policy is a <u>negotiable</u> instrument?
4. clause
    A. A compound sentence contains two or more <u>clauses</u>.
    B. Which <u>clause</u> in the agreement refers to payments?

5. mature

   A. The rice is <u>maturing</u> fast in the favorable weather.

   B. The draft drawn on our branch is to <u>mature</u> in 90 days.

6. title

   A. The <u>title</u> of the new play is "Financier."

   B. A bill of lading is a document of <u>title</u>.

7. draft

   A. The director prepared three different <u>drafts</u> of his speech before he had it in the final form.

   B. The <u>draft</u> drawn on Bank of China was dishonored because of some discrepancies in documentation.

8. accept

   A. His concept of the "invisible hand" is widely <u>accepted</u> even today.

   B. When a draft is accepted, the accepting bank has it dated and stamped "accepted".

IV. Read the following passage and fill in the brackets with appropriate words. The first letter of some of them has been given.

Documentation is the engine of exports in global trade. Documentation facilitates the m_____ of freight, transfer of title, processing of payment, and customs clearance. Without d_____, the shipment is at a standstill. Even with the continuing advances in technology playing a greater role in i_____ business, documentation is still r_____ by all parties involved in global trade. Why is this so? The answer is surprisingly simple.

On an average, customs authorities worldwide physically inspect only from 4 to 8 percent of the cargo that moves through their borders. There are some e_____, such as Saudi Arabia, but as a general rule, the local customs a_____ do not physically inspect most import shipments.

If this statistic is correct, then how does customs manage their affairs in all the gateways of the world? How do customs authorities control the m_____ crossing the border and entering into commerce? They do this through the documentation provided by the importer and the importer's customhouse broker. Importers receive their import documentation from the e_____, thereby making documentation the engine that moves the freight through the borders. In the United States, exporters create their documentation at the time the f_____ is being exported. For a typical export shipment, the only export document actually required by the Bureau of Export Administration, in conjunction with US Customs, is the Shipper's Export Declaration (SED) or a validated Export L_____. The other documentation created — such as the commercial invoice, packing list, c_____ of origin, health and sanitary certificate, bill of lading, certificate of conformance, and certificate of analysis — are all for the account of the importer to meet the c_____ clearance requirements in their country, thereby making export documentation into import documents.

V. Decide whether the following statements are true or false by writing "T" for true and "F" for false in the bracket besides each statement.

( ) 1. Export licenses are used by many countries as a means of facilitating exports.

( ) 2. If the exporter fails to make shipment within the validity period of the inspection certificate, he can usually ask that the validity of the certificate be extended automatically.

( ) 3. when a mate's receipt is issued, the shipper can use it to obtain a B/L after paying the freight.

( ) 4. Documents such as commercial invoice, export license, copy of sales contract and inspection certificate are usually needed for clearing the customs.

( ) 5. When disputes arise from international trade, the parties concerned can resolve their disputes through consultation. arbitration or legal proceedings.

( ) 6. Generally speaking, a sales contract must be made in written form.

( ) 7. A sales contract normally consists of three parts, namely. the beginning part, the body part, and the part that specifies language, number of copies and the signature.

( ) 8. Unlike other documents such as bill of lading, an inspection certificate usually does not contain a validity period.

VI. Translate the following sentences into English.

(1) 汇票只不过是一种要求支付的命令。
(2) 作为一种融资工具,信用证对进、出口商都有利。
(3) 即期汇票,顾名思义,是要求银行见票即付。
(4) 作为一种物权凭证,海运提单可以由出口商用作获得支付的手段。
(5) 检验主要针对进出口商品质量,数量及包装等方面展开。
(6) 货物的质量必须与样品严格一致。我们拒收一切质量低于样品的货物。
(7) 商品检验既可以在出口国进行也可以在进口国进行。
(8) 请尽早备妥我们的订货,并在备妥前几天通知我们,以便我们能及时地告知装船要求。

VI. Translate the following into Chinese.

To ensure timely payment, exporters should check all the documents carefully before these documents are presented. In general, it is important to maintain consistency between all the documents relating to the same transaction. For example, the description of goods, the value of the goods, and other terms in different documents should be the same. If documentary credits are used, then all the documents must be made out according to the L/C terms. More details should/must be given when documents are discussed individually.

International Cargo Transportation

*F*ocal *L*earning

After the completion of this chapter, you're required to know:
- different means of cargo transport;
- the advantages and disadvantages of each mode of transport;
- ocean freight of various categories and the terms used in ocean transport;
- the basics of road transport, rail transport, air transport, multimodal transport;
- different means of transport and the best alternatives for your needs;
- the exploitation of containerization, palletization and pipeline in China.

*L*ead-in *V*ocabulary

remunerative	adj.	有利的
ply	v.	经常从事于(船、车等)定期往返或航行
lighters	n.	驳船
dead freight	n.	空仓费
prorate	adj.	(拉丁语)按比例,成比例
lay-time	n.	装卸货时间
demurrage	n.	滞期费
dispatch money		速遣费,派遣,分派
liability	n.	责任,义务
deviation	n.	绕航,变更航路
demise	v.	让渡,转让
deteriorate	v.	使恶化
obsolescence	n.	荒废,退化
premium	n.	保险费
deviation demise		出租,转让

deteriorate	v.	变质,腐烂
premium	n.	保险费
containerization	n.	集装箱化
palletization	n.	托盘化运输
pipelines	n.	管道运输

With the lowering of international trade barrier, international bilateral or multilateral trade increases to three or four times faster than the growth of some national economies. Transport plays increasingly important roles with the development and exploitation of economic resources. In order to fulfill an export transaction and transport goods or commoditres in a safe, efficient, speedy, prompt and economical way, a businessman will find it helpful to command a good knowledge of transport.

Carriage of goods can be achieved by means of sea, rail, air, road, inland waterway, parcel post, containerization and palletization and multi-modal transport.

Section I
Ocean Freight

Ocean freight, also called Ocean Shipping, Ocean Carriage, or Marine Transportation, is the most widely used mode of transportation in international trade as well as the most efficient form in terms of energy. Two thirds of the world total volume and over 80% of China's imports and exports now are transported by sea. The first advantage is the easy passage since about 70% of the earth surface is covered by water. It still has the attraction of being a cheap mode of transport for delivering large quantities of goods over long distances. Because of the large capacity of ocean shipping, the unit distribution cost is reduced. Furthermore, ocean transport has good adaptability to cargoes of different size, weight, shape etc. However, it is slow, vulnerable to bad weather and less punctual if compared with road or air transport. Therefore before a shipment is made, the exporter has to consider many different factors influencing his transport considerations such as cost, safety, speed and convenience.

Here are the major ocean carriage modes.

1. Conference Shipping

These ships are operated by a liner, a conference carrier or members of a shipping conference. Conference means shipping conference, steamship conference or liner conference, which is an association, formed by a number of shipping companies or vessels operators of various nationalities. Such vessels represent over 50% of world shipping, for the protection of their interest as well as those of the shipper. Periodical meetings are held between representatives of the member shipping lines to discuss policies and to fix freight rates for the different classes of cargoes.

The purpose of the conference is to maintain freight rates at a remunerative level and ensure that a sufficient minimum of cargo is always forthcoming for the regular service they undertake to provide. The ships belonging to the shipping conference are always liner vessels that ply regularly between two ports or a group of ports. The liners run fixed schedules, follow fixed routes and charge standard rate called conference rates. The scheduled services enable shipping, industrial and marketing operations to be planned well in advance.

2. Non-conference Line Vessels

Non-conference line vessels, sometimes called outside shipping, are operated by an independent carrier or shipping companies that do not belong to conference, but provide scheduled services. They determine their own freight rate, sailing schedule, ports of call etc., without reference to any agreement with any other line. It is important that non-conference lines are still "liner services" operating a regular service between two or more ports. The non-conference lines are flexible but they sometimes may have the problem of insufficient cargo supply, and even sometimes they are perceived as less reliable than conference shipping

3. Tramp Ships

Tramp ships follow no firm schedule, have no regular routes or times and sail off to where the goods are available. The tramp is quite like a marine taxi-cab, ready at any time to undertake a particular voyage according to its capacity. These ships trade in all parts of the world in search of cargo, primarily bulk shipment. Such cargo includes coal, grain, timber, ores, fertilizers, etc., which are carried in complete shipload. Their rates are not fixed but are determined by bargaining or the demands of the market. Tramp vessels are engaged under chartering mainly on the basis of voyage and occasionally are chartered to supplement existing liner services to meet peak cargo shipment demands. Generally, various cargo vessels are designed to suit the needs of different cargoes and shipment.

❖ A general/packed cargo vessels is built to carry various cargoes.

❖ An oil tankers is responsible for the movement of crude oil or fuel oil. Fifty percent of the world merchant fleet, about 500,000 deadweight tons of cargoes are carried by oil tanker.

❖ A container vessel is designed to carry from 200 to over 4,000 standard containers of 20 feet in length, which is more often called a twenty-foot equivalent unit (TEU).

❖ An OBO (Oil/Bulk/Ore) carrier is a multi-purpose ship designed for large, bulk shipments of oil and grain, fertilizer and ore.

❖ A Roll-on-Roll (Ro/Ro) vessel is specially designed for loaded trailers or any vehicles for switching between to be driven onto the vessel to facilitate faster loading and unloading.

❖ A Lighter Aboard Ship (LASH) is a vessel designed to carry lighters on which cargoes are loaded, ideal for shallow waterways. A LASH can carry from 70 to 100 lighters, totaling 35,000 to 45,000 tons and it does not need a pier for loading and unloading. Lighter are towed away after they are unloaded. It offers high efficiency and is ideal on shallow inland waterways.

❖ A refrigerator ship is designed with freezing facilities inside the ship for carrying perishable cargoes.

❖ Timber ship is mainly used to carry timber or wood logs with spacious holds and heavy lifts.

4. Chartered Ships

These ships are chartered or hired for the carriage of an entire cargo of goods. Charter shipping is usually used for bulk cargoes like oil, coal, ore and grain. Charter shipping has the lowest freight rate and it is only justifiable for larger orders. The most commonly used charter ships are conference line vessels, which make regular journeys and offer special discounts to exporters/importers who use them on a regular basis. Generally, there are three kinds of chartering:

❖ **Voyage Charter**

Under a voyage charter, a ship is chartered for a single journey which may involve more than one port of call. The ship operator crews and operates the ship and the operator's own ship's master is in control of the ship. The payment by the charterer is usually based on an agreed rate per ton for a full and complete cargo. Should he fail to provide sufficient cargo to fill the ship he is liable for what is termed dead freight, a prorate payment for the space not used. A voyage charger also stipulates the number of days known as lay time for loading and unloading. Should these be exceeded, the charterer is liable for a demurrage charge for each day in excess, and conversely the charter is entitled to dispatch money for each day not taken up. The liability of the ship owner is to provide a ship that is seaworthy and to avoid unjustifiable deviation en route.

❖ **Time Charter**

Sometimes a government or shipping company wishing to strengthen its fleet temporarily will charter a ship for a specified period of time. In most cases, it is the trading company who charters the ship for a certain time span. In this condition, the contract of time charter may call for a specific or unlimited number of voyages within the agreed time. When a ship is chartered, control also remains with the owner, and the master and crew continue to be his servants. Under the time charter, if the arrangements are made for a complete lease or demise of the ship, the master and crew then become the servants of the charterer.

❖ **Bare Boat Charter**

The term bareboat means a ship without crew and ship's master. The charterer is responsible for crewing, provisioning and fuelling, maintaining and even paying different taxes or duties within a period of time. The charterer has to pay an agreed sum of freight to the owner within the agreed time of charter. This kind of charter is less popular than time charter and voyage charter. It is mainly used when there is an unexpected or sudden increase of export goods to be shipped.

Section II
Air Transport

Air transport is one of the youngest forms of distribution. It is reported that air cargo represents 13% of world airline revenue or 540 billion annually and increases at the rate of 7%-8% each year. Most air cargoes are carried on passenger airliners, about 80% of air cargoes are transported by IATA (International Air Transport Association) members.

Air freight is most desirable for consumer cargoes such as fresh flowers and fruits which will deteriorate easily, fashionable articles that have a short selling life, seasonal goods or merchandise of high value but low volume.

The most outstanding attraction of air freight is quick transit. Quick, reliable transits eliminate the needs for warehouse and reduce the risk of stockpiling, obsolescence, deterioration and capital tied up in warehouse and stock provision. Low risk of damage and pilferage with consequent competitive insurance premium is another advantage. However, the average aircraft capacity is only 2,000-25,000 kg, air transport is subject to a high operating cost when compared to its overall capacity. In addition, when airlines or air cargo companies issue an air waybill, it is often a straight waybill, the buyer is named as the consignee on the waybill, so he can claim the cargoes from the carrier by simply showing proof of identity. For this reason, air freight must be a risky way to ship goods.

Air transport services are divided into three categories: scheduled airlines, chartered carriers, and consolidated consignments by freight forwarders.

1. Scheduled Airlines

Schedule airlines operate on a scheduled service, over a fixed airline and between fixed airports. They are suitable for conveying fresh, emergent and seasonal goods.

2. Chartered Carriers

Chartered carriers are the rent of an aircraft by a shipper or several shippers to deliver cargoes, They are ideal for carrying cargoes of large quantities or carrying cargoes of different shippers to the same destination.

3. Consolidated Consignments

These means of transportation stand for that the air freight forwarder usually assembles a number of individual shipments into one consignment and dispatches them on one air waybill to one common destination. Many shippers prefer this kind of shipment as the freight rate is 7% -10% lower than that of a scheduled airline published by IATA.

Airline rates are normally based on actual weight for heavy cargo or measurement weight for large volume cargo.

Section III
Other Means of International Cargo Transportation

1. Road Transport

Road transport, is dominantly used in cross-border deliveries and playing significant parts in shipping international cargoes to and from sea ports and airports. It is a versatile means of transport with flexible operation, especially when circumstances demand a change in routing through road works or road blockage or disrupted shipping service. It has a high distributive ability of offering a door-to-door service without immediate handling. Compared with rail and air freight, road freight is very competitive if the transit distance is up to 1,000 kilometers. Furthermore, road transport is ideal for general merchandise and selective bulk cargoes in small quantities.

However, road freight has limited capacity and relatively high operating cost. There is also a high risk of pilferage and damage although the driver accompanies the vehicle throughout the transit. One of the problems facing road transport is the complication concerned with customs examination and possible duty payments when a vehicle is involved in crossing several frontiers.

2. Rail Transport

Rail transport is a major means of transport in terms of capacity, second only to ocean carriage. It is very popular in multi-modal transport and transshipment especially in land bridge. It is capable of achieving relatively high speed and is particularly economical if it provides the complete trainload for a shipper on a regular basis. Besides, it is less prone to interruption by poor weather conditions. Rail transport can be divided into international combined rail transport and domestic rail transport. The most important document for rail transport is consignment note. Once the forwarding railway station has accepted the goods for carriage together with the consignment note, the contract of carriage comes into existence.

3. Inland Waterway Transport

The inland waterway system is usually linked to the seaport and thereby acts as a distributor and feeder to the shipping services. In some countries, especially underdeveloped ones, inland waterways are a major form of distribution as the road and rail systems are unable to cope with or are nonexistent in many areas. Inland waterway transport can relieve port congestion through overside loading and discharge. This spares the cargoes from the port warehouse which can prove costly in tariffs and time-consuming through customs. It also has the advantage of low rate, and suitable for a range of commodities ranging from general cargoes to bulk shipment of coal, oil, timber and chemicals. However, the transits are slow compared with road or rail.

4. Containerization

Containerization is a mode of distributing merchandise in a unitized form, suitable for ocean, rail and multimodal transport. It is the most modern form of physical international distribution and is highly efficient in terms of reliability, cost, quality of service, advanced technology and so on. It offers a door to door service, or in case of need, services from door to container freight station or container yard, from container freight station to door or from container freight station or yard to container freight station, while there is no need to reload or check the cargo during the transit. With standardized special equipment, it can be handled quickly and easily and can thus save labors and loading and unloading charges. In addition, the low risk of cargo damage and pilferage enables more favorable cargo premiums to be obtained, compared with break-bulk cargo shipments. During transit, usually there is only one carrier in conjunction with multimodal transport, which will help to achieve high efficiency and security.

Less packing is required for containerized consignments. In some cases, particularly with specialized ISO (International Standards Organization) containers such as refrigerated ones or tanks, no packing is required, which produces substantial cost savings in the international transit and raises service quality.

5. Palletization

Palletization is a simplified version of containerization by which cargoes are carried on flat wood or metal frames. A typical size is 1,000 × 1,200 mm, which has a capacity of two tons and it is like a platform on which the cargo is placed. An aperture is provided at each side to enable the fork lift truck to mobilize or handle the pallet. Wooden pallets by which the cargo is anchored are very common in air freight, thereby facilitating cargo handling. The pallet accompanies the cargo throughout the transit.

The advantages of palletization are that it will reduce cargo packing and facilitate handling, counting and stowage, thereby, the transport cost will be reduced by 5% to 12%.

However, due attentions have to be paid when palletization is used. First, cargoes belonging to the same consignee should be squarely stowed on the pallet and the packing should be strong enough and waterproof, then each pallet should be properly marked and have the same quantity and weight of cargoes, only in this way will the consignor and the consignee benefit most.

6. Pipelines

Pipeline networks are mainly used for the distribution of gas and oil. The advantage of the pipeline is the low cost of distribution as very few labors are needed in the network. Another one is the 24-hour availability of the network. Besides, the network needs little maintenance during operation. From an environmental point of view, pipeline networks cause little disruption to the environment during installation and create no noise or fumes during distribution of cargo. On the other hand, the disadvantage of pipeline networks is its limited capacity, high cost of installing such a system. The market growth is somewhat restricted unless a new pipeline is installed.

7. International Multimodal Transport

Following the containerization of international transport, a brand new mode of transport, international multimodal transport has been introduced into the transport industry. It is the carriage of goods by at least two different modes of transport from a place in one country at which the goods are taken in charge by the multimodal transport operator to a place designated for delivery situated in a different country.

Although different modes of transport are used, a multimodal transport operator is solely responsible for the goods from his taking in charge of the goods from the consignor to his delivery of the goods to the consignee. No matter how many carriers participate in the transport, a multimodal transport operator (MTO) concludes a multimodal transport contract and assumes the responsibility of taking the cargo from the consignor and delivering then to the consignee, which adds simplicity to the transport.

Because of the simplicity and the use of containers in multimodal transport, it means higher efficiency, better quality of transport, lower cost and less time required for cargo movement between the place of origin and the place of delivery. As multimodal transport uses only one multimodal transport document, the documentation process can also be more efficient and economical.

Useful Phrases & Technical Terms

modes of transport	运输方式
ocean freight	海运运费
conference shipping	（航运）公会运输
non-conference line vessels	非公会线路船只
tramp ships	不定期轮船
charter ships	租船运输
lay time	装卸货时间
road transport	公路运输
air transport	空运
rail transport	铁路运输
inland waterway transport	内陆水道运输
international multimodal transport	国际多式联运

Notes

1. Because of the large capacity of ocean shipping, the unit distribution cost is reduced.
   因为海洋运输容量较大，单位平摊成本相应降低。

2. Tramp ships follow no firm schedule, have no regular routes or times and sail off to where the goods are available.
   租船运输没有固定的船期与路线，哪里有货物，船只开往哪里。

3. Under a voyage charter, a ship is chartered for a single journey which may involve more than one port of call.
   在定程租船方式下，所租用的船可用做有多个停靠港的单程运输。

4. The advantage of the pipeline is the low cost of distribution as very few labors are needed in the network. Another one is the 24-hour availability of the network. Besides, the network needs little maintenance during operation.
   管道运输的优点在于运营成本低，所需劳动力少，全天候工作，运行维修少。

5. Although different modes of transport are used, a multimodal transport operator is solely responsible for the goods from his taking in charge of the goods from the consignor to his delivery of the goods to the consignee.
   尽管可以使用不同的运输方式，但是，多式联运的负责人要承担从发货人交给他货物到收货人收到货物期间的责任。

Chapter 8

Practical Drills

❖ Questions for Discussion

1. Do you have an idea about transport?
2. What are the two chief advantages of air transport?
3. What does the freight forwarder do for the carrier and the shipper?
4. What are the basics of ocean shipping?
5. What are the disadvantages of air transport?

❖ Case Study

What Would the Exporter Do?

A bicycle manufacturer based in Tianjin signed a contract with an American merchant, selling 2000 bicycles. When the countersigned copy returned, the exporter noticed the merchant had added "C. K. D" to packing requirement "packed in wooden case". What does "C. K. D." mean? What would you recommend the exporter do?

❖ Role Play

Late Delivery

White: Mr. Wang, the late delivery of the dolls will make us miss the selling season and your company should be responsible for it.

Wang: I'm very sorry for the late delivery, but the carrying vessel had a serious accident.

White: What happened to the vessel?

Wang: The vessel loading the dolls hit a rock during the voyage and had to be repaired.

White: Was the accident evidenced by any authority?

Wang: Yes, here's the certificate issued by the repairer.

White: I see. But, Mr, Wang, you should have let us know about the accident in time. You know, your delay may make us lose our best customer.

Wang: We did send you a fax exactly the day the accident occurred. I'm so surprised that you didn't receive our notification.

White: Really? But I never saw the fax. To whom did you send the fax?

Wang: We sent it to your agent at the destination who is supposed to wait for the consignment at the port.

White: All right. I will ask our agent about the matter. Anyway, I hope you can get direct contact with us so that we could take effective measures to avoid any inconvenience or loss.

Wang: I'll certainly do so. Please accept my apology for negligence on our part.

White: That's all right, Mr. Wang.

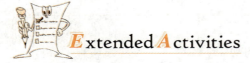

Extended Activities

I. Answer the following questions.

1. What are some of the major types of transportation?
2. What is the most important contribution of transportation to the society?
3. What are the special features of ocean transport?
4. What factors contribute to the formation of freight rate?
5. Please describe the general procedure of ocean transport by liners.

II. Please define the following terms in English. If necessary, please refer to the text.

1. general cargo vessel
2. OBO
3. oil tanker
4. refrigerated ship
5. timber ship

III. Translate the following sentences into Chinese.

1. Transport is the carriage of passengers and merchandise by road, rail, air and water. Good transport is vitally important in commerce because food, raw material and other commodities must be moved as quickly and cheaply as possible from producer to wholesaler and consumer.
2. The air transport industry supports a wide range of businesses.
3. A number of shipping companies of various nationalities have formed an association known as "Shipping Conference", which consists of many member countries, representing over fifty percent of the world shipping, for the protection of their interests as well as those of the shipper.
4. The exporter has to consider many different factors influencing his transport considerations such as cost, safety, speed and convenience.
5. Ocean freight is still one of the most popular forms of transportation in use in the business cycle as well as the most efficient form in terms of energy. It still has the attraction of being a cheap mode of transport for delivering large quantities of goods over long distances.

Chapter 8

IV. Fill in each blank of the following sentences with one of the words or phrases in the list given below and make changes if necessary.

| as well as | tie up | isolation | convenience | advantage |
| reliability | cycle | in terms of | obstacle | raw |

1. The delay in delivery was caused by a shortage of _____ materials.
2. You should believe me, for I got the news from a very _____ source.
3. He was very famous in the music _____ at that time.
4. The house I rent can offer me the _____ of living near shops, and schools.
5. _____ actual sales the book hasn't been very successful.
6. The writer lived in complete _____ in the country in his late years.
7. The little boy is clever _____ sensible.
8. Her teaching experience gives her a big _____ over the other applicants for the job.
9. She felt that her family was an _____ to her work.
10. They didn't agree on several terms of the contract, because they had the risk of _____ their money.

V. Read the following passage and fill in the blanks with appropriate words (some words are given the first letter or first several letters).

The transport of goods in containers not only reduces shipping times and loading/unloading costs, but also reduces the r_____ of the theft and damage as the goods should be appropriately packaged and stowed in secure containers. Co_____ can also reduce the amount of packaging required for the con_____, as the metal container itself becomes a part of the packaging. From the ship owner's perspective, containers permit better ut_____ of space, and therefore capacity, through their ability to be loaded and st_____ in uniform rows.

Chapter 9

International Cargo Transportation Insurance

Focal **L**earning

After the completion of this chapter, you're required to know:
- the basic concepts in international trade insurance practices;
- the fundamental insurance coverage and additional insurance coverage;
- the procedures of marine insurance;
- the insurance of land, air and postal transportation.

Lead-in **V**ocabulary

insurer	n.	保险业者,保险公司
insured	n.	保户,被保险者,投保者
technicalities	n.	技术性 专门性
broker	n.	保险经纪人
calamity	n.	灾害
inherent vice		内在缺陷
contamination	n.	污染
Total Loss		(保险用语)全部损失;[经](保险)全损
intermixture	n.	混合,混合物
special additional risks		特别附加险
premium	n.	保险费
claimant	n.	索赔人
fortuitous	adj.	偶发的
deterioration	n.	变坏,恶化
taint	n.	沾染,玷污

Chapter 9

Section I
Fundamental Concepts in the International Cargo Insurance

In the international trade, goods travel long distances to another country. Both the exporter and the importer face all kinds of possible risks or losses all the time, and therefore goods must be insured against loss or damage at each stage of their journey. In other words, no matter what means of transport is being used, insurance exists to protect the importer or exporter against the possible financial losses which he would otherwise suffer in case damage or loss was inflicted upon him. Without adequate insurance and protection of the interests of those with goods in transit, international trade cannot be guaranteed.

1. Parties Involved

Insurance is the contract by which one party undertakes to indemnity the other party against the loss or damage incurred from certain perils or risks. And risk, the chance of loss, exists in most business decisions and transactions. The parties to be involved in insurance are the insurer and the insured. In some cases, there may be an insurance broker in between.

❖ **Insurer**

Insurer is the party of the insurance contract who provides the insurance services and promise to make compensation in case of losses, which is usually represented by the insurance company or the individuals who run an insurance firm. In international cargo insurance practice, another term "underwriter" is commonly used. Etymologically, it is derived from the Corporation of Lloyd's in the seventeenth century, London, where the insurer was required to sign his name under the insurance policy as a party to the contract. Ever since then underwriter has become synonymous with insurance companies.

❖ **Insured**

Insured refers to the one who is insured against any possible perils or losses and to whom compensation is made from the insurer or the insurance company. The insured may be the buyer under FOB contract, or the seller under CIF contract, or the shipping company, which may have on insurable stake such as the carrying vessel.

❖ **Broker**

The insurance broker is the middleman in insurance business. The broker has the advantage of being familiar not only with the technicalities of marine insurance, but also has an unbiased view over the coverage and premium rates offered by all insurance companies. He is in a good position to obtain for his client the coverage that best fits his needs at the lowest possible cost.

❖ Claimant

Once damages occur, the party who suffers will lodge a claim against the insurance policy. This party is called the claimant. Whenever an actual loss occurs, the insured can get fair, efficient and rapid adjustment of his claim. While insurance may be arranged by the exporter, the importer is the rightful owner consequently; claims are usually made by the importer, after discovering a loss.

2. Insured Amount

The insured amount is the sum of money the underwriter agrees to cover the insured goods against the damages or losses, namely, it is the upper limit of compensation payable to the insured in case of loss. In international practice, the insured amount is always the CIF value of the consignment plus 10%. The added 10% compensates for the loss of profit expected from the transactions.

3. Premium

The premium is the money paid to the insurer for the services provided. It is always presented as a percentage based on the value of the goods covered and the statistical probability of loss. Insurance underwriters take a series of factors into consideration when they decide on the rate of premium, for example, the nature of packing used, the type and value of the merchandise to be insured and the nature of transit and the related warehouse accommodation.

4. Insurance Policy

The insurance policy is the most commonly used document that contains all the details concerning the goods, coverage, premium and the insured value. All this information must be sufficient enough for the insured party to assess the risk and make insurance decision. It is always filled out by the insured. When all is fixed, the insurer will normally return the duplicate to the insured with their rubber seal. The signed insurance policy will become the legal document that serves as the shipping document evidencing assurance cover.

The insurance certificate is the simplified version of the insurance policy serving the same functions in the transaction.

The open policy is recommended for exporters and importers who do a large volume of business. An open policy provides coverage for all goods shipped by the insured while the policy is in effect. The duration of this policy may last indefinitely. China's exports, by using such a policy, are automatically covered with the pre-agreement of the PICC.

Section II
Marine Transportation Insurance

Marine insurance is defined as a contract of insurance whereby the insurance company returns for premiums collected and compensates the insured the losses to the extent agreed against marine losses.

1. Risks Covered by Marine Insurance

Risk is a cause to the loss of or damage to the goods. Marine insurance generally covers two risks: Perils of Sea; Extraneous Risks.

❖ **Perils of the Sea**

Perils of the Sea include both natural calamity and fortuitous accidents. Natural calamities include heavy weather, lightening, earthquake, volcanic eruption, tsunamis and so on. Fortuitous accidents are events such as fire, explosion, stranding, grounding, sinking, capsizing missing of vessels and collision, or contact of vessel with any external object other than water, etc. However, fire caused by inherent vice or nature of the cargoes excluded. In addition, all the perils must occur at sea and must be because of sea, otherwise, the insurance will not cover them. A vessel intentionally sunk by its owner is not an accident because of sea and therefore will not be covered by marine insurance. Similarly, natural deterioration, wear and tear in transit are not perils of sea either.

❖ **Extraneous Risks**

Extraneous Risks includes General Extraneous Risks and Special Extraneous Risks. General Extraneous Risks includes theft and pilferage, contamination, leakage, breakage, sweating and/or heating, taint of odor, rusting, hook damage, fresh and /or rain water damage, short-delivery and non-delivery, shortage in weight, clashing and so on. Special Extraneous Risks includes war, strike, and failure to deliver due to some special laws or regulations.

2. Losses Covered by Marine Insurance

In the insurance business, loss is referred to in most cases as the special term "average", which actually has nothing to do with its normal meaning. Marine insurance defines its coverage in terms of the nature of the loss or damage, the extent of the loss or damage, and the conditions under which it occurred. Hence, the losses caused by the high seas fall into two categories: Total Loss and Partial Loss.

❖ **Total Loss**

Total Loss is further divided into Actual Total Loss and Constructive Total Loss. Actual Total Loss means the complete loss of the insured cargo in value. For instance, an actual total loss is supposed to occur to a missing cargo ship since it has missed for certain time span (say, two months). In case of Actual Total Loss, the insured can get indemnity against the total loss of the insured value of cargo.

Constructive Total Loss may occur if the cargo is not actually lost, but is so seriously damage as to make the goods no longer any use for the purpose for which they were originally intended. A constructive total loss may also occur when the actual loss of the insured goods is unavoidable, or the goods or the ship has to be abandoned since the cost of salvaging would be more than the value of the ship and the merchandise on arrival.

❖ **Partial Loss**

Partial Loss means a partial damage to or the total loss of part of the insured cargo (e.g. The loss of one case out of a shipment of seven). Partial Loss can be divided into General Average and Particular Average.

General average is a partial, deliberate and reasonable sacrifice of the ship, freight or goods undertaken when the whole ship was threatened by a peril of the sea, for the common interests or safety. Sometimes, in this case, the general average will be shared proportionately among all the interests affected and all those whose property does not suffer any loss, which are then refundable from the insurance company.

Particular Average means a partial loss suffered by part of the cargo and solely borne by the owner of the lost property. It occurs when a storm or fire damages part of the shipper's cargo and no one else's cargo has to be sacrificed to save the voyage. Particular Average is recoverable from the insurance underwriter if it has been covered.

3. Expenses Incurred for the Rescue of Insured Cargo

When the ship runs into risks at sea, there are mainly two types of expenses incurred for the rescue of the insured cargo: Sue and Labor Expenses; salvage Charges.

❖ **Sue and Labor Expenses**

Sue and Labor is the responsibility of the insured undertaken to keep the losses of his insured goods at a minimum. Reasonable charges incurred for this purpose are generally collectible under the insurance policy. For example, when a shipment of canned goods with some leakage arrived, the leaking cans must be taken out to minimize the possibility of rusting and label damage. The expense incurred in this operation may be recovered under the insurance policy.

❖ **Salvage Charges**

Salvage Charges is the compensation paid for the rescue of a ship, its cargo or passengers from a loss or possible loss at sea, or from a wreck or fire. The insurer is bound to such charges incurred.

4. Major Categories of General Insurance Coverage

There are mainly two types of Insurance coverage: Basic coverage and Additional coverage. Basic coverage mainly includes FPA, WPA and All Risks, while additional coverage in cludes general additional coverage and special additional coverage.

❖ Basic Coverage

FPA Coverage (Free from Particular Average) is a limited form of cargo insurance under which no partial loss or damage is recoverable. It only provides coverage for total losses of cargoes together with the ship or aircraft, and general average.

FPA is the minimum coverage and offers limited protection. However, there are two exceptions in which partial loss or damage is recoverable. First, if the lost object is a separate package in a shipment such as one case out of a ten-case shipment. And second, if the vessel is stranded, sunk or burnt, partial loss or damage is also recoverable. In this sense, FPA actually covers parts of the partial loss.

WPA/WA (With Particular Average/With Average) is a wider coverage than FPA. It provides extensive cover against all loss or damage due to marine perils throughout the duration of the policy, including partial loss or damage which may be attributed to natural calamities like heavy weather.

All Risks is the most comprehensive of the three basic coverage under which the insurer is responsible for all total or partial loss of, or damage to the goods from sea perils or general external causes. However, it does not cover loss, damage or expenses caused by delay, inherent vice or nature of the goods insured, or special external risks of war, strike, etc.

❖ Additional Coverage

Additional Coverage includes general additional coverage and Special additional coverage: General additional risks covers losses caused by extraneous risks and be classified into 11 categories: TPND (Theft, Pilferage and Non-delivery), Fresh Water Rain Damage, Risk of Shortage, Risk of Intermixture and Contamination, Risk of Leakage, Risk of Clash and Breakage, Risk of Odor, Damage caused by Heating and Sweating, Hook Damage, Risks of Rust, etc. These additional risks can not be covered independently and should go with FPA or WPA and are included in All Risks coverage.

Special additional risks include War Risk, Strikes Risk, Failure to Delivery Risk, Import Duty Risk, On Deck Risk, Rejection Risk, Afltoxin, Fire Risk Extension Clause, etc., among which war risk and strikes risk are more common. These additional coverages are usually taken out together with FPA, WPA and All Risks.

5. Procedures of Marine Insurance

In export trade, who will effect insurance depends on the particular trade terms adopted. Under CIF terms, it is the seller who arranges insurance with an insurance company, under the terms as FOB, CFR, the buyer effects insurance, but he may ask the seller to arrange insurance on behalf of the buyer: They may start by inquiring and choosing the right coverage and then negotiate insurance premium rates. Sometimes, brokers may be used whose assistance can be of enormous benefit as they are highly skilled specialists and can obtain sound and reliable coverage, together with competitive premium rates. An insurance policy is issued when goods are insured, but it is also usual for a certificate of insurance to be issued for documentary purposes. In completing the insurance contract, either party, buyer or seller will undergo different steps, they are the following.

❖ To Apply for Marine Insurance

In some countries, the first step the insured party should take is to apply for insurance from a certain insurance company. The applicant should fill in the special form or the proposal form, which gives all the details concerning ownership, value, time span insurance will be for, risks and coverage, etc.

❖ To Determine the Insurance Value or the Goods to Be Insured

The value to be insured is measured on the value of the commercial invoice; the recommended minimum amount is the total CIF value plus 10% for other fees and normal margin of profit. Probably the best way of determining needed insurance is to estimate market value of the goods at the port of destination and to obtain coverage for that amount. Other approaches to evaluate the goods may also be agreed upon by the insurer and insured to meet individual needs. The calculation and determination of the value to be insured vary from country to country.

❖ To Determine the Insurance Average and Coverage

Determination of the right coverage sometimes can be made only on the basis of the following factors: the nature of the product, packing considerations such as sacks or paper boxes; use of the products such as chemicals and tea; the carriers of the transport such as difference of air and sea transport, shipping route and ports considerations such as any transshipment on the way to the final port, etc.

❖ To Determine Insurance Premium Rates

The rates charged by the insurance company are based on such factors as the type of coverage desired, shipping routes, modes of transport, duration of the voyage, and nature of the goods and packing. Also important is each individual shipper's past loss experience. After a period of favorable experience, rates may be lowered. Conversely, a shipper with a bad loss record may find his premiums increased. Generally, the greater the risks that the consignment is exposed to, the higher the premium will be.

❖ To Sign an Insurance Policy

Before filling in and signing an insurance policy, it is essential to have a good understanding about what an insurance policy is, and the kind of insurance policies, the most extensively used policies now in the international trade are insurance policy, insurance certificate and open policy. As far as the details of these documents are concerned, please refer to Section 1 of this Chapter.

❖ To Lodge an Insurance Claim

Whenever an actual loss occurs, claims can be made by the shipper, the buyer or even a carrier that has first lien on goods. It is of vital importance that the insured must be able to prove a loss by perils against which he was insured. The one who registers a claim should get the survey report conducted by the expert, together with a copy of the bill of lading, the commercial invoice, the insurance policy, and a covering letter requesting payment, and then send them to the insurance company for processing.

Most insurance company policies require that immediate notice be given to the nearest branch or agency in the event of damage giving rise to a claim. This notice means that a claim has been filed. A delay in giving the notice might result in the underwriter's refusal to process the claim. When notified of damage, the insurance company will appoint a suitable surveyor to inspect the goods and to report on the nature and extent of the damage. As a common practice, a report or certificate of loss together with the surveyor's findings will be issued to the consignees, who pay the fee. This certificate of loss is included with the claim papers and, if the loss is recoverable under the insurance cover, the fee is refunded to the claimants.

In some circumstances, the claim papers are returned to the place where the insurance was carried out and subsequently to the underwriters. However, especially where goods are sold on CIF terms and the policy is assigned to the consignees; arrangements are made for any claims to be paid at destination. In such cases, the consignees approach the agents named in the policy for payment of their claims. Of course, the claims procedure will vary by circumstances, but undoubtedly a quicker settlement should be secured in the event of loss or damage. As a matter of fact, settling a claim is not so easy; it needs patience, evidence and knowledge.

Section III
Insurance of Land, Air and Postal Transportation

A high volume of business is now transmitted by rail and road. It is of great importance that sufficient coverage be obtained for the land carriage.

1. Insurance Coverage for Land Transportation

Insurance coverage for land transportation can be classified into two categories: Land Transportation Risk and All Risks, while the former is almost equivalent to WPA, the latter is almost equivalent to All Risks of marine cargo transport.

2. Insurance Coverage for Air Transportation

In terms of short transit time, lighter packing, quick clearance at destination and, in most places, stricter theft-pilferage control of air transportation, a considerable number of export cargoes are dispatched by air nowadays. Apparently, the speed and ease of air freight handling makes an insurance risk attractive to the insurer and premium rates attractive to the insured. In air freight transport, two types of coverage are involved: Air transportation risk and Air transportation All Risks. Air transportation risk is similar to WPA, while air transportation All Risks is similar to Marine All Risks.

3. Parcel Post Insurance

Parcel post insurance covers the losses or damage to the parcels caused by natural calamities, fortuitous accidents or external risks. It includes Parcel Post risk and Parcel post All Risks. On the basis of these two basic coverages, some additional risks may also be added if circumstances require.

Useful Phrases & Technical Terms

insured amount	投保价值
insurance policy	保险单
insurance certificate	保险凭证
marine insurance	海上保险
perils of the sea	海险, 海难
extraneous risks	外来风险
total loss	全损, 全损险
partial loss	(投保货物的) 部分损失
general average	共同海损
particular average	单独海损
FPA coverage	(平安险)
WPA/WA (With Particular average/With Average)	水渍险 (单独海损可保)
all risks	一切险
additional coverage	附加险
general additional risks	一般附加险
special additional risks	特殊附加险

Notes

1. Perils of Sea include both natural calamity and fortuitous accidents. Natural calamities include heavy weather, lightening, earthquake, volcanic eruption, tsunamis and so on. Fortuitous accidents are events such as fire, explosion, stranding, grounding, sinking, capsizing and collision, missing of vessels, contact of vessel with any external object other than water, etc.

海事险包括自然灾害与偶发事件。自然灾害包括恶劣天气、闪电、地震、火伤喷发、海啸等。偶发事件包括火灾、爆炸、搁浅、沉船、倾倒、船只丢失、船只与水以外的物体接触产生的危险等。

2. However, it does not cover loss, damage or expenses caused by delay, inherent vice or nature of the goods insured, or special external risks of war, strike, etc.

但是,一切险的责任范围并不包括由于延迟、内在缺陷或投保货物的性质而导致的货物的灭失、损坏及其费用,或战争、罢工等引起的损坏。

3. Determination of the right coverage sometimes can be made only on the basis of the following factors: the nature of the product, packing considerations such as sacks or paper boxes; use of the products such as chemicals and tea; the carriers of the transport such as difference of air and sea transport, shipping route and ports considerations such as any transshipment on the way to the final port, etc.

选择合适的险种应该考虑以下因素:商品的性质、包装、用途、运输形式、运输路线以及到岸港口等。

4. Special additional risks include War Risk, Strikes Risk, Failure to Delivery Risk, Import Duty Risk, On Deck Risk, Rejection Risk, Aflatoxin, Fire Risk Extension Clause, etc。

特殊附加险包括战争险、罢工险、交货不到险、进口关税险、仓面险、拒收险、黄曲霉素险、火险条款等。

Practical Drills

❖ Questions for Discussion

1. What sort of property insurance do you prefer if you run a business?
2. What do insurance premiums mean?
3. What should the insurant do if an undesirable event happened to him?

❖ Case Study

Refusal of Compensation

A Chinese company exported some fruits to Japan. The price term employed was CIF Tokyo. During transshipment in Hong Kong, part of the cargo was soaked by heavy rain. When the ship arrived at the port of destination, the importer claimed compensation from the insurance company. However, the insurance company refused to compensate, claiming that damage caused by rain was not included in W.P.A coverage.

Role Play

An Exporter Discusses Insurance of an Order with a Buyer

Exporter: Yes, we'll need to insure your shipment of bikes.

Importer: What is the major purpose of insurance?

Exporter: It protects against damage or loss of goods during shipping.

Importer: You're an experienced exporter. Why don't you explain how goods are valued for insurance purposes? I suppose there's more than one factors that goes to make up insured valuation.

Exporter: Right, the primary factor is the cost of the goods at the point of delivery. Then, too, it depends on whether goods are shipped FOB or Ex-factory.

Importer: I'd like to hear something about those unfamiliar terms.

Exporter: F.O.B. means free on board. This means the seller is responsible for delivery of the goods to the carrier, and from there the buyer is responsible. Ex-factory means from the point of origin. This means the buyer pays all shipping costs from the factory.

Importer: How should we go about shipping the bikes?

Exporter: Our firm uses a freight forwarder. As soon as the order is ready, my company issues as order to our freight handler. They prepare all the documents needed for shipping, including the certificate of insurance.

Importer: I understand freight forwarders handle packing and insurance as well as the other documents needed for export.

Exporter: Right.

Importer: What sort of documents do you need to provide to the freight forwarder?

Exporter: We must submit a commercial invoice which provides accurate information about the goods, their value, their quantity, and the names of the consignor and consignees.

Importer: But it's the freight forwarder who chooses the insurance company?

Exporter: Yes, they only deal with reputable firms, so you can be sure of dependable coverage.

Importer: The insurance is protection against loss arising from damage?

Exporter: Yes, we're usually covered for loss or damage. As soon as the insurance company gets the export declaration — if they agree to insure — they write a policy fixing the terms and the premium.

Importer: And then the consignee pays the premium?

Exporter: And the insurance company issues a receipt for the premium called a covering note. That secures the goods until the actual policy is written.

Importer: So from that point on we're protected against loss or damage?

Exporter: Some policies cover TLO, so in that case we're covered for total loss of goods only, not for partial loss or damage. But all this is always spelled out in advance.

Importer: Well. Thanks for the information.

Chapter 9

Extended **A**ctivities

I. Answer the following questions.

1. Why is insurance indispensable to international trade?
2. What are the fundamental principles of insurance that firms must follow when they seek cover for goods?
3. What documents are needed in processing a claim for compensation?
4. Explain the two major types of ocean marine risks.
5. Can you give some examples to illustrate "Insurable interest"?

II. Look at the terms in the left-hand column and find the correct definitions in the right-hand column. Copy the corresponding letters in the blanks.

1. _____ risk
2. _____ insurance policy
3. _____ insurance
4. _____ liability insurance
5. _____ claim
6. _____ the insured
7. _____ insurer
8. _____ insurance premium
9. _____ property insurance
10. _____ coverage

a. agreement in which you pay a premium in exchange of protection from the specified undesirable event
b. a person or company that purchases insurance
c. kinds of risks to be insured
d. a condition in which loss or losses are possible
e. a written agreement between an insurance company and a policyholder
f. insurance for direct or indirect financial losses caused by fire, windstorm and theft.
g. sum of money paid regularly to an insurance company in exchange of protection against the specified undesirable event
h. a demand for compensation due to damage, etc.
i. a company that sells insurance
j. protection against loss arising out of legal liability.

III. Complete the following sentences by translating the parts given in Chinese.

1. Among all kinds of insurance, _____ (汽车保险是最近出现的保险).
2. _____ (如果发生索赔), the insured must present relevant documents, such as insurance contract, the policy, etc.
3. One of the chief problems _____ (风险管理不得不克服的) has been to differ itself from insurance.

149

4. Nowadays, people purchase _____ (健康保险多于其他保险)。

5. _____ (为了投保), an applicant must demonstrate that he or she has an insurable interest in the property or life insured.

6. In France, _____ (只有30%多一点的保险公司) were nationalized in 1945.

IV. Fill in the blanks (1)—(8) with the most suitable information about Marine Cargo Transport Insurance given in the text.

Risks	Perils of the sea	(5)
		Fortuitous accidents
	(2)	General extraneous risks
		Special extraneous risks
Loss	Total loss	(6)
		Constructive total loss
	(3)	Particular average
		General average
(1)	Sue and labor expense	
	Salvage charges	
Scope of insurance coverage	Basic coverage	(7) (EPA)
		With Particular Average (WPA)
		(8)
	(4)	General additional coverage
		Special additional coverage

V. Fill in each blank of the following sentences with one of the words or phrases.

Misfortune can arise in many forms, all of them leading to some form of lo_____. For example, the sole breadwinner of a family may meet with an ac_____ and die. The dependents face two immediately obvious forms of loss: emotional and financial.

The natural question to ask then is: "what arrangement can be made to overcome or at least re_____ the effects of misfortune that may befall any one person?"

In answering the above question, we have to ad_____ that not all forms of loss can be made good. For instance, the emotional trauma arising from the death of a loved one cannot be made good by any conceivable compensation system.

Perhaps, what can be done is to devise a compensatory system which will at least seek to reduce the impact of financial loss that is consequent to an unfortunate event. One such possible arrangement whereby the financial loss arising as a consequence of an unfortunate incident, such as death or a fire, can be through the institution of ins_____.

VI. Decide whether the following statements are true or false by writing "T" for true and "F" for false in the bracket besides each statement.

1. (   ) Ocean marine insurance covers two types of losses, partial loss and total loss.
2. (   ) Three types of risks are covered by oceans marine insurance, namely the perils of the sea, the extraneous risks and the force majeure.
3. (   ) Without insurance, international trade is simply impossible to take place.
4. (   ) According to "lost or not lost concept", the insurance contract is valid if the assured did not know of the loss at the time of contract of insurance.
5. (   ) In ocean marine insurance, general average is to be borne by the carrier, who may, upon presentation of evidence of the loss, recover the loss from the insurance underwriter.
6. (   ) Ocean marine insurance covers ships and their cargo only on the high seas and not on inland waterways.
7. (   ) In essence, floating policy is the same as the time policy.
8. (   ) Partial loss or damage is never recoverable with FPA.
9. (   ) In ocean marine insurance, the insured can recover more than actual loss provided that he can provide evidence of further losses contingent on the actual loss.
10. (   ) Special additional coverage such as War risks, strikes and so on must be taken out together with FPA, WA or AR.

VII. Complete the following charts according to what you have learned from the text.

Procedures for Marine Cargo Insurance

To Determine the _____ or the Goods to Be Insured

↓

Determine the Insurance Average and _____

↓

To Determine Insurance Premium _____

↓

To Sign _____

↓

To Lodge an Insurance _____

Chapter 10

International Trade Payment

Focal Learning

After the completion of this chapter, you're required to know:
- the definition and the role of international trade payment;
- the payment instruments of international trade ;
- the methods of payment;
- the terms of payment in sales contract.

Lead-in Vocabulary

settlement	n.	结算
proceeds	n.	货款,收入,所得
counterpart	n.	相对应的人
foreign exchange	n.	外汇
inventory	n.	库存
party	n.	当事人
remittance	n.	汇款业务
clearing system	n.	清算业务
cover	n.	头寸
dishonor	v.	退票
recourse	v.	追索
maker	n.	出票人
endorsement	n.	背书
holder	n.	持票人
issue	v.	出票
tenor	n.	期限
collection	n.	托收
marine	a.	海运的,航海的
credit standing		信用状况
working capital		流动资金
discount	v.	贴现

Chapter 10

Section I
Payment Instruments of International Trade

As we know, financial documents, called instruments, too, are widely used in international trade and payment. They clearly record currency to certain extent, circulating among participants, facilitating the transfer of credits, acting as payment and credit tools in merchandise exchange. In international trade, the main instruments of payment are the currency and bills (i.e. bill of exchange, promissory note, and cheque).

1. Bill of Exchange

The bill of exchange or draft has played a vital part in the world's commercial and financial life for some countries. Also, it is widely used for settlement in international trade.

A bill of exchange or draft is an unconditional order in writing prepared by one party (drawer) and addressed to another (drawee) directing the drawee to pay a specialized sum of money to the order of a third person (the payee), or to the bearer, on demand or at a fixed and determinable future time.

In conjunction with the definition, Figure 1 specimen: bill of exchange may be dissected as follows:

(1) An unconditional order in writing;
(2) Addressed by one person/party (the drawer);
(3) To another (the drawee);
(4) Signed by the person (the drawer) giving it;
(5) Requiring the person to whom it is addressed (the drawee or payer) to pay;
(6) On demand, or at a fixed or determinable future time;
(7) A sum certain in money;
(8) To, or to the order of, a specified person, or to bearer (the payee).

Figure 1 Specimen: Bill of Exchange

```
No. 920                    Bill of Exchange
USD 350                                      New York, 20 May, 2003

    On demand pay to Peter Smith to bearer the sum of U.S. Dollars three
hundred and fifty only.

                                              (signed) John Jones

To: Mr. Michael Hanks
San Francisco
```

2. Promissory Notes

A promissory note is an unconditional promise in writing made by one person (the maker) to another (the payee or the holder) signed by the maker engaging to pay on demand or at a fixed or determinable future time a sum certain in money to or to the order of a specified person or bearer. From definition of promissory note, it is easy to find that there is no accepter, only the maker and the other parties are the payee, endorser, bearer and holder. The maker has prime liability while the other parties have second liability. Should the promissory note be made by two persons, then they are jointly and severally liable to the note according to its tenor.

Bill of treasuries, bank notes and so on are daily used examples of promissory note. Main contents are stated as follows:

(1) The words "Promissory Note" clearly indicated;
(2) An unconditional promise to pay;
(3) Name of the payee or his order;
(4) Maker's signature;
(5) Place and date of issuing;
(6) Tenor of payment;
(7) A certain amount of money;

The details are shown in Figure.

Figure 2 Specimen: Promissory Note

```
Promissory Note
                                              Manchester
                                              September 23, 2001
USD 600
       Thirty days after sight, we promise to pay Thomas Martin or order the sum
of U.S. Dollars six hundred only.

                                              James Brown
                                              William Jones
```

3. Cheques

A cheque is defined as an unconditional order in writing drawn on a bank signed by the drawer, requiring a bank to pay on demand a sum certain in money to the order of a named person or to the bearer.

The meanings of the different parts of the definition are:

(1) Unconditional

Payment can not hinge on certain conditions being met, for example "Pay Mr. White USD

200 provided my salary cheque has been paid into my account".

(2) Writing

It must be in writing, pen, ballpoint pen, print, even pencil can be used although the latter is not recommended because details can easily be altered.

(3) Signed

A cheque must be signed by the drawer who is person paying the money.

(4) On Demand

It is expected that the cheque will be paid as soon as it is presented to the other bank.

(5) certain amount

The amount of the cheque must be definitive, both in words and figures.

(6) Named Person or Bearer

The cheque must be payable to someone by name or payable to "the bearer".

Basically, there are five essential elements in a cheque. They are mentioned as follows:

(1) Indicating the word "cheque" or "check";

(2) Detailed name of the drawee, i.e. the paying bank;

(3) Name and signature of the drawer;

(4) Date and place of issuance;

(5) Currency and a certain amount.

Section II
Methods of Payment

Nowadays, how to choose a certain payment method among them is the result through analysis and comparison and a contest for both buyer and seller. In this chapter, we mainly introduce these methods as follows: remittance and collection, letter of credit and banker's letter of guarantee.

1. Remittance

Remittance is one of banking customer services, in which funds will be transferred from one person to another. When two persons live in the same country, this type remittance is called domestic remittance, while the remittance will be a foreign banking business if two persons live in different countries.

Originally, there are four parties involved in this business: (1) Remitter—who applies to transfer money to another person; (2) Payee or Beneficiary—to whom the money will be transmitted; (3) Remitting Bank—it is entrusted to remit the funds outward; (4) Paying bank—it is entrusted by the remitting bank to make payment to the payee.

There are three basic ways for a bank to transfer funds for its clients from home country to abroad. They are telegraphic transfer, mail transfer and demand draft.

❖ Telegraphic Transfer (T/T)

By telegraphic transfer, payment instruction given by the remitting bank to the paying bank will be transmitted by telecommunication, such as cable, telex or computer system. The key point is that the paying bank must authenticate whether the instruction is given really by the remitting bank indicated in the telecommunication, for the funds should eventually be reimbursed by this remitting bank to the paying bank.

The whole procedure of T/T is illustrated by following Figure 3.

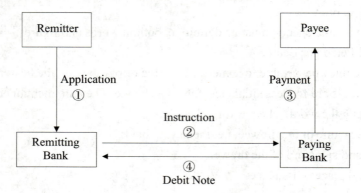

Figure 3 Procedure of telegraphic transfer

❖ Mail Transfer (M/T)

A Mail transfer means that payments instruction given by the remitting bank is transmitted by mail or by courier.　Payment instruction is in a form of payment is in a form of Payment Order. Procedure of M/T is almost the same as the T/T. (See Figure 8.3). Owing to the mail time being much longer than that of telecommunication, the M/T is not broadly used in international trade.

❖ Demand Draft (D/D)

Demand Draft is also called remittance by banker's demand draft. The payment instruction is written down directly on the surface of the bank draft. A bank draft is a negotiable instrument

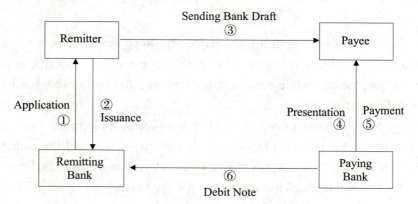

Figure 4 Procedure of demand draft

drawn by the remitting bank in its overseas correspondence bank, ordering the latter to pay on demand the stated amount to the holder of the draft. It is often used when the client wants to control the funds-transfer. After being issued, the bank draft should be handed over to the remitter, who may dispatch or even bring it to the beneficiary abroad.

Little different from T/T, the procedure of D/D is shown in Figure 4.

2. Collection

Collection means instructing others to collect money. Generally speaking, collection serve as a compromise between open account and payment in advance in settlement of international trade. So collection is a kind of payment system, in which creditors submit financial documents or commercial documents or both for obtaining proceeds to the remitting bank and ask it to entrust his relation bank (collecting bank) to make the documents available to the payer.

Normally, there are four main parties which are involved in collection. They are the principal (seller/exporter/drawer), the remitting bank (principal's/seller's bank), the collecting / presenting bank and the drawee (buyer/importer).

The documentary collection procedure involves the step-by-step exchange of documents giving title to goods for either cash or a contracted promise to pay a later time. Collections can be sorted into two categories, i.e. clean collection and documentary collection.

❖ Clean Collection

Clean collection refers to collection of financial documents not accompanied by commercial documents. It is often used to collect remaining funds, advance in cash, sample expenses, etc. in international trade payment. The seller draws merely bills of exchange on buyer, not accompanied by any shipping documents, and entrusts bank to collect funds from the buyer.

❖ Documentary Collection

Documentary collection means a collection of financial documents accompanied by commercial documents or commercial documents not accompanied by the financial documents. Documentary collection is broadly used in international trade payment, which will be introduced as:

(1) Documents Against Payment (D/P) at Sight

After shipment of the goods, the exporter shall draw a sight bill of exchange and send it as well as shipping documents to his bank (remitting bank), through which and whose correspondence bank the documentary draft is presented to the importer. The importer shall pay against documentary draft drawn by the seller at sight. Actually, D/P at sight requires immediate payment by the importer to get hold of the documents.

The whole procedure of D/P at sight is shown by Figure 5.

(2) D/P after Sight

After shipment of the goods, the exporter shall draw a draft and send it as well as shipping

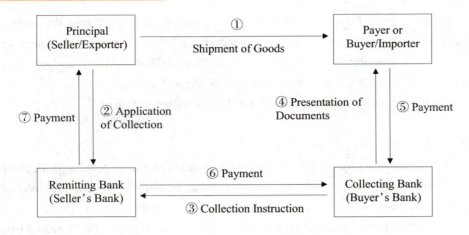

Figure 5   Procedure of D/P at sight

documents to his bank (remitting bank), through which and whose correspondent bank (collecting bank) the documentary draft is presented to the importer. The importer shall accept the draft, and make payment on the due date of the draft.

Under D/P after sight, the importer is given a certain period to make payment, such as 30, 45, 60 or 90 days after the first presentation of the documents, but he is not allowed to get hold of the documents until he pays.

In this case, in order to push sales of the goods in time, the importer may consult with the collecting bank to borrow the bills of lading before the maturity of the drafts against the trust receipt (T/R), and make payment on the due dates of drafts. This method is called accommodation.

The whole procedure of D/P after sight is shown by Figure 6.

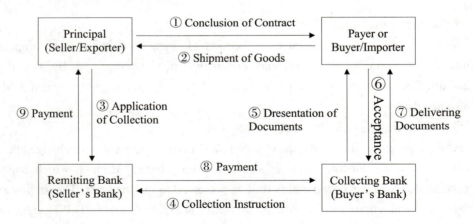

Figure 6   Procedure of D/P after sight

❖ **Documents against Acceptance (D/A)**

D/A called for delivery of documents against acceptance of the draft drawn by the exporter. D/A is always after sight.

D/A makes the importer get hold of shipping documents and take delivery of the goods before payment. So the exporter would have to take great risks.

The whole procedure of D/A after sight is shown by Figure 7.

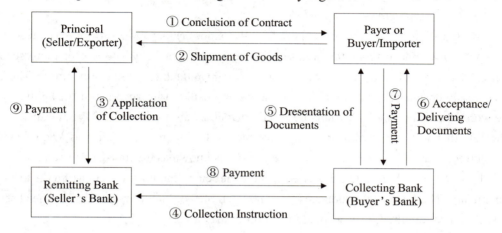

Figure 7   Procedure of D/A

3. Letter of Credit

A letter of credit, abbreviated as L/C, stands at the center of international commercial transactions. Issued by a bank at the request of an importer, the letter of credit states that the bank will pay a specified sum of money to a beneficiary, normally the exporter, on presentation of particular, specified documents.

The terms and conditions of a documentary credit revolve around two issues: (1) the presentation of documents that evidence title to goods shipped by the seller and (2) payment. Generally speaking, L/C can fall into different categories in international trade, they are:

❖ **Sight and Time L/C**

If the L/C terms demand that the bill of exchange drawn by the exporter is the type which requires the importer to pay at sight, i.e. when the bill is presented to him by the reimbursing bank, L/C with such terms is called Sight L/C. On the other hand, the L/C which has terms allowing the importer a deferred payment is called Time L/C.

❖ **Revocable and Irrevocable L/C**

A revocable L/C is issued in favor of the beneficiary in accordance with the instructions of the applicant and gives the buyer maximum flexibility, since it can be amended, revoked or cancelled without the beneficiary's consent and even without prior notice to the beneficiary up to the moment of payment by the bank at which the issuing bank has made the documentary credit available.

Under Irrevocable L/C terms, L/C cannot be cancelled or withdrawn after is has been opened and notified to the exporter (who is the beneficiary of L/C) as long as there is no agreement on cancellation or withdrawal among the applicant of L/C, opening bank and the beneficiary. However, in the case of Revocable L/C, it can be cancelled anytime upon the applicant's request. Therefore, L/C should be irrevocable from the exporter's point of view. The exporter has to be aware that any L/C received which does not specify either as being revocable or irrevocable, will be regarded as being revocable.

❖ **Transferable and Non-transferable L/C**

In a transferable L/C, the first beneficiary (the exporter) may request the paying, accepting or negotiating bank to make the credit available in whole or in part to one or more second beneficiary. The second beneficiary can be an export-manufacturer or an export-trader. The L/C is expressly designated "transferable" by the issuing bank on instructions of the applicant. If the words "transmissible", "assignable", and "divisible" are used, the L/C is not transferable. The L/C that was transferred or made available to the second beneficiary is known as the transferred credit. The bank that makes the transfer is known as the transferring bank.

In a non-transferable letter of credit, the beneficiary cannot transfer the credit to other beneficiary. The L/C usually indicates "non-transferable" or "not transferable." In the absence of such indication, the L/C is deemed to be non-transferable.

❖ **Confirmed and Non-confirmed Credit**

The confirmed L/C is the one which is confirmed and guaranteed by a third party bank for the payment in the event that the opening bank becomes bankrupt. The exporter can be assured of a safe transaction if the L/C is confirmed by a leading bank. Non-confirmed credit means that the local bank must send the paperwork to the originating country for approval and only after that approval is given will the local bank pay on the L/C.

❖ **Documentary and Clean Credit**

Documentary credit is an arrangement whereby the applicant (the importer) requests and instructs the issuing bank (the importer's bank) or the issuing bank acting on its own behalf, pays the beneficiary (the exporter) or accepts and pays the draft (bill of exchange) drawn by the beneficiary, or authorizes the advising bank or the nominated bank to pay the beneficiary or to accept and pay the draft drawn by the beneficiary, or authorizes the advising bank or the nominated bank to negotiate against stipulated document(s), provided that the terms and conditions of the documentary credit are fully complied with. For purpose of maintaining uniformity in the text, the words "letter of credit", "credit" and "L/C" are used to refer to the documentary credit.

Clean credit is a letter of credit with no documentary requirements other than a demand for payment, usually a draft.

❖ **Reciprocal and Back-to-back Credit**

A reciprocal credit is usually concerned with a barter transaction. It is in all respects similar to an ordinary commercial credit except that the opener of the original credit may assume the position of the beneficiary of the reciprocal credit, while the beneficiary of the original credit may become the opener of the reciprocal credit. In other word, they are both importers and exporters at the same time.

Back-to back credit is a new letter of credit issued to another beneficiary on the strength of a primary credit. The second L/C uses the first L/C as collateral for the bank. Used in a three-party transaction.

Procedure of L/C is shown in Figure 4.1. Keep in mind, there are important variations on this basic procedure, which is related to confirmation of the payment or the availabilities of the payment. In addition, such procedure would be changed when discrepancies are checked out by banks and correspondences take place several rounds between parties involved.

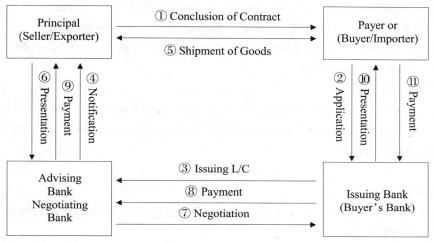

Figure 8　Procedure of L/Coperation

4. Banker's Letter of Guarantee

Originally, there are three parties involved in this business, i.e. principal, beneficiary, and guarantor.

There are two types of banker's letter of guarantee, i.e. guarantee under import and export contracts and bank guarantee for loan. Furthermore, guarantee under import and export contracts includes tender guarantee, performance guarantee, advance payment guarantee, guarantee under import contract and guarantee under compensation trade.

Section III
Terms of Payment in the Sales Contract

1. Payment by Remittance

There should be methods, time, money and approaches of remittance in the contract. For example, the Buyers shall pay 50% of the sales proceeds in advance by M/T to reach the Sellers not later than Feb. 15th 2000.

2. Payment by Collection

There should be classification, acceptance by importer and terms of payment in the contract.

❖ **Payment by D/P at Sight**

Upon the first presentation buyers shall pay against documentary draft drawn by sellers at sight. The shipping documents are to be delivered against payment only.

❖ **Payment by D/P after Sight**

Buyers shall duly accept the documentary draft drawn by the maturity. The shipping documents are to be delivered against payment only. Or buyers shall pay against documentary draft drawn by sellers at... days after date B/L. The shipping documents are to be delivered against payment only.

❖ **Payment by D/A**

Buyers shall duly accept the documentary draft drawn by seller at... days sight upon first presentation and make payment on its maturity. The shipping documents are to be delivered against acceptance only.

3. Payment by the Letter of Credit

There should be classification of L/C, date of opening L/C, period of validity of L/C and so on in the contract.

❖ **Payment by Sight L/C**

Buyers shall open through a bank acceptable to sellers an irrevocable sight L/C to reach sellers... days before the month of shipment, valid for negotiation in China until 15th day after shipment.

Useful Phrases & Technical Terms

bill of exchange	汇票
promissory notes	本票
telegraphic transfer (T/T)	电汇
mail transfer (M/T)	信汇
demand draft (D/D)	票汇
clean collection	光票托收
documentary collection	跟单托收
documents against payment (D/P) at sight	即期付款交单
D/P after sight	远期付款交单

Chapter 10

documents against acceptance (D/A) 承兑交单
sight and time L/C 即期和远期信用证
revocable and irrevocable L/C 撤销和不可撤销信用证
transferable and non-transferable L/C 转让和不可转让信用证
confirmed and non-confirmed credit 保兑和未保兑信用证
reciprocal and back-to-back credit 对开和背对背信用证

Notes

1. A promissory note is an unconditional promise in writing made by one person (the maker) to another (the payee or the holder) signed by the maker engaging to pay on demand or at a fixed or determinable future time a sum certain in money to or to the order of a specified person or bearer.
   本票是一个人(开票人)向另一个人(收款人)签发的,保证于见票时或定期或在可以确定的将来的时间,对某人或其指定人或持票人支付一定金额的无条件的书面承诺。

2. Under D/P after sight, the importer is given a certain period to make payment, such as 30, 45, 60 or 90 days after the first presentation of the documents, but he is not allowed to get hold of the documents until he pays.
   在远期付款方式下,(卖方开具远期汇票)要求进口方到一定时间支付货款,比如第一次见票后30、45、60、90天付款,但是在进口方付款之后,方可拿到单据。

Practical Drills

❖ Questions for Discussion

1. What is remittance and how many remittances are there?
2. Why is L/C and how many letters of credit are there?
3. What risks has L/C for the buyers and the sellers?
4. What are the differences between L/C and banker's letter of guarantee?

❖ *Case Study*

1
A FOB Contract

Seller: Huaxin Trading Co. Ltd.
  14th Floor, Kingstar Mansion
  789 Jinling Road, Shanghai, China
  Tel: 021-5679420 Fax: 5679358

Buyer: James Brow & Sons
  340 Lalan Street, Toronto, Canada
  Tel: (01) 7709923 Fax: (01) 7702240

The sellers agree to sell and the buyers agree to buy the mentioned goods on the terms and conditions stated below.

(1) Name of Commodity, Specifications Packing terms and Shipping Marks	(2) Quality	(3) Unit Price	(4) Total Amount
35-piecice Dinnerware Setand teaset Art No. Hx116 Packing: 1 set/carton Shipping Marks: James Brown 　　　　　　　SHHX027 　　　　　　　TORONTO 　　　　　　　C/NOS. 1-588	600 sets	USD 18.00 per set FOB Toronto	USD 12,000

(5) Time of shipment: Before March 30, 2002, not allowing partial shipment

(6) Port of Loading: Shanghai

(7) Port of Destination: Toronto

(8) Insurance: To be effected by the sellers for 110% of invoice value covering WPA and War Risk with PICC (1/1/1981)

(9) Terms of payment: By sight L/C

By irrevocable L/C in favor of the sellers payable at sight against presentation of shipping documents in China, without partial shipments and with transshipment allowed. The covering L/C must reach the sellers before the contracted month of shipment and remain valid in the above loading port until the 15th day after shipment, failing which the sellers reserve the right to cancel the contract without future notice and to claim against the buyers for any loss resulting therefrom.

Chapter 10

2
Letter of Credit

Bank of America

TRADE OPERATIONS CENTER #5655
333 SOUTH BEAUDRY AVE., 19TH FLOOR   Place:
LOS ANGELES, CA 90017

Cable Address: BankAmerica

☐ This refers to our preliminary teletransmission advice of this credit.

IRREVOCABLE DOCUMENTARY LETTER OF CREDIT NO. 000000	APPLICANT
	ABC TOYS IMPORT, INC.
	300 MAIN STREET
DATE OF ISSUE: JANUARY 6, XXXX	SAN FRANCISCO, CALIFORNIA 94000
ADVISING BANK REFERENCE NO.	BENEFICIARY
BANK OF AMERICA	XYZ TOYS EXPORT LTD.
G. P. O. BOX 472	8TH FLOOR, STONE BLDG.
HONG KONG, HONG KONG	45 KOHAN ROAD
	KOWLOON, HONG KONG
DATE AND PLACE OF EXPIRY	AMOUNT
AUGUST 15, XXXX	US$85,350.00 (U.S. DOLLARS EIGHTY FIVE
HONG KONG	THOUSAND THREE HUNDRED FIFTY AND 00/100)

Covering   100   % invoice value

Credit available with   ANY BANK
by ☐ sight payment   ☐ deferred payment   ☐ acceptance   ☒ negotiation
against presentation of the documents detailed below and your draft(s) at SIGHT
drawn on   BANK OF AMERICA, LOS ANGELES

Partial shipments: ☒ allowed   ☐ not allowed   Transhipments: ☐ allowed   ☒ not allowed

Shipments/dispatch/taking in charge from/at   HONG KONG PORT   SHIPMENT LATEST: 08/10/XX
for transportation to   SAN FRANCISCO/BAY AREA, CALIFORNIA, USA

MERCHANDISE DESCRIPTION:

INFLATABLE TOYS
P.O. NO. 1234 25000 PCS @ US$3.00 EACH.
P.O. NO. 6789 10000 PCS @ US$1.035 EACH
CIF SAN FRANCISCO/BAY AREA, CALIFORNIA, USA.

DOCUMENTS REQUIRED:
1. SIGNED COMMERICAL INVOICE IN TRIPLICATE.
2. MARINE AND WAR INSURANCE POLICY OR CERTIFICATE FOR 110 PERCENT OF INVOICE VALUE IN DUPLICATE.
3. CERTIFICATE OF ORIGIN FORM 'A' WHERE APPLICAPBLE, OR BENEFICIARY'S SIGNED CERTIFICATE THAT NONE IS REQUIRED.
4. PACKING LIST.
5. FULL SET ORIGINAL CLEAN ON BOARD VESSEL MARINE BILLS OF LADING, TO ORDER OF SHIPPER, BLANK ENDORSED, MARKED FREIGHT PREPAID AND NOTIFY CLEARING AGENT, 100 MAIN STREET, SAN FRANCISCO, CALIFORNIA 94000.

SPECIAL INSTRUCTIONS:
1. WE WILL DEDUCT US$XX FROM PROCEEDS ON EACH SET OF DOCUMENTS CONTAINING DISCREPANCIES.
2. ALL BANKING CHARGES OTHER THAN OURS ARE FOR BENEFICIARY'S ACCOUNT.
3. ALL DOCUMENTS MUST BEAR OUR LETTER OF CREDIT NUMBER.

Documents to be presented within   5   days after the date of issuance of the shipping document(s) but within the validity of the credit.

We hereby issue this Documentary Credit in your favour. It is subject to the Uniform Customs and Practice for Documentary Credits, 1993 revision, ICC Publication No. 500, and engages us in accordance with the terms thereof. The number and the date of the credit and the name of our bank must be quoted on all drafts required. If the credit is available by negotiation, each presentation must be noted on the reverse of this advice by the bank where the credit is available.

All documents to be forwarded in one cover, by airmail, unless otherwise stated above. Negotiating bank charges, if any, are for account of beneficiary. The advising bank is requested to notify the credit to the beneficiary without adding their confirmation.

This document consists of   1   signed page(s)

Mary Smith AUTHORIZED COUNTERSIGNATURE   John Doe AUTHORIZED SIGNATURE

Please examine this instrument carefully. If you are unable to comply with the terms or conditions, please communicate with your buyer to arrange for an amendment. This procedure will facilitate prompt handling when documents are presented.

❖ *Role Play*

Decision on Mode of Payment

A: What is the mode of payment you wish to employ?

B: Confirmed, irrevocable letter of credit, of course.

A: We are old friends, and you should have faith in us. Is the wording of "confirmed" necessary for the letter of credit?

B: Yes, it is. This is the normal terms of payment in international business, by which payment is assured.

A: Is it at sight or after sight?

B: It's at sight, of course. So long as the documents are in full conformity with the contract, you are kindly requested to pay for the shipment immediately after your receipt of all the necessary shipping documents.

A: Can you send the papers to the bank soon after shipment?

B: Yes, we can. Please don't worry. Generally speaking, we can forward all the papers to the bank three days after shipment. By the way, when will you open the letter of credit?

A: One month before shipment. We are worried that you cannot effect shipment on time.

B: I'm sure that shipment will be effected according to the contract stipulation. Please open letter of credit in good time.

A: I believe what you said. We'll open the letter of credit on time. The only thing is that we pay too much for such letter of credit arrangement, as it will tie up our capital.

B: Sorry. There is very little we can do about it. Besides, the total amount is so big and the world monetary market is not stable at the moment. We cannot accept any other terms of payment. Furthermore, the same kind of letter of credit is adopted for our imports from your country.

A: Yes, that's the fact. I agree to use letter of credit at sight, but hope that you will be more flexible next time.

B: All right, we'll discuss it then.

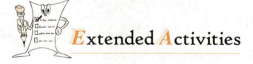

Extended Activities

I. Answer the following questions.

1. What is the role of bank in international trade?
2. What are the differences between collection and L/C?
3. Which method of payment is the safest?
4. What is the difference between a commercial draft and a banker's draft?

5. What is the advantage and disadvantage of transferring money through D D compared with T T?

II. Choose the correct answers.

1. When financing is without recourse, this means that the bank has no resource to the _____ of such drafts are dishonored.
   A. drawee   B. payee   C. payer   D. drawer

2. A _____ is drawn by the exporter and sent to the buyer.
   A. draft   B. promissory   C. I.O.U   D. cheque

3. A cheque must be signed by _____
   A. the drawer   B. the drawee   C. the payer   D. the payee

4. If it is not stated as D/A or D/P, the documents can be released _____.
   A. against payment   B. against acceptance
   C. in either way   D. against acceptance pour aval

5. The operation of collection begins with _____.
   A. the customer and the remitting bank
   B. the remitting bank and the collecting bank
   C. the presenting bank and the drawee
   D. the collecting bank and the presenting bank

6. A credit can be transferred by _____.
   A. the first beneficiary   B. the second beneficiary
   C. the third beneficiary   D. any person

7. Under _____, the obligation of the issuing bank is extended only to the beneficiary in honoring drafts or documents and usually expires at the counters of the issuing bank.
   A. the revocable credit   B. the irrevocable credit
   C. the irrevocable straight credit   D. the confirmed credit

8. The credit may only be confirmed if it is so authorized or requested by _____.
   A. the issuing bank   B. the advising bank
   C. the applicant   D. the beneficiary

9. Back-to-back credits are advantageous to _____.
   A. all consumers   B. all manufactures
   C. all customers   D. all traders

10. M/T is sent to the correspondent bank _____, unless otherwise instructed by client.
    A. by courier service   B. by ordinary mail
    C. by airmail   D. by sea mail

III. Decide whether the following statements are true or false by writing "T" for true and "F" for false in the bracket besides each statement.

1. (   ) D/D stands for Demand Draft.

2. (　) Among T/T, M/T and D/D, T/T is the cheapest method of payment.
3. (　) A bill of exchange is a conditional order to pay in writing.
4. (　) A cheque is a demand bank draft.
5. (　) A promissory note is an unconditional order to pay in writing.
6. (　) The principal is usually the importer.
7. (　) Normally D/P will apply with sight drafts and D/A will apply with usance drafts.
8. (　) Unless otherwise stated in the credit, a transferable credit can be transferred once only.
9. (　) Most of the promissory notes in use today are issued by individuals rather than by firms.
10. (　) When an L/C expressly indicate that it is a transferable one, it means that such an L/C must be transferred.

IV. The following is a list of special terms. After reading it, you should find the items equivalent to those given in Chinese in the table below.

A—Telegraphic Transfer(T/T)
B—Mail Transfer (M/T)
C—Demand Draft (D/D)
D—Bill of exchange
E—Bill of lading
F—Promissory note
G—Cheque
H—D/P at sight
I—D/A
J—D/P after sight
K—Remitting bank
L—principal
M—Revolving documentary credit
N—Confirming bank
O—Standby credit
P—Red clause documentary credit

Example: (H) 即期付款交单　　　(P)红条款信用证
1. 提单　　　　　　　　　　6. 委托人
2. 备用信用证　　　　　　　7. 本票
3. 信汇　　　　　　　　　　8. 保兑行
4. 汇票　　　　　　　　　　9. 支票
5. 远期付款交单　　　　　　10. 票汇

Chapter 10

V. Translating the following sentences into Chinese.

1. If a usance draft is presented, the drawee takes up the obligation of payment when the draft becomes due by putting the word "accepted", his signature and the date of acceptance on the face of the draft.
2. A check can be made to order, to bearer, crossed with two parallel lines for account deposit only, or certified by a bank that is going to pay.
3. By nominating a bank will process the documents and forward them to the issuing bank for payment at maturity.
4. Since this is a rather substantial order, we hope that 90% of the credit amount be paid against the presentation of documents and the rest is to be paid after the machines are proved satisfactory on trial.
5. If we again fail to receive your L/C in time, we shall cancel our sales confirmation and ask you to refund to us the storage charges we have paid on your behalf.

VI. Translating the following sentences into English.

(1) 我们要求在45天之后付清,如果预付现金则享有15%的折扣。
(2) 我们将开立以你方为收益人的信用证,以美元结算。
(3) 如果你们能提供售后服务,我们同意支付100%货款。
(4) 我们希望的付款方式是保兑的,不可撤消的信用证。
(5) 如果单据跟合同不符,你们可以拒付。

Chapter 11

Inspection, Force Majeure, Claim and Arbitration

Focal Learning

After the completion of this chapter, you are required to know:
- the inspection practice in international trade;
- the demarcation of force majeure and its classification;
- the claim clause in sales contract and the prerequisites for claim;
- the procedures of arbitration.

Lead-in Vocabulary

indispensable	adj.	不可缺少的, 必要的
differences	n.	误差
verify	v.	证实
theoretically	a.	理论上
penalty	n.	处罚
veterinary	adj.	兽医的
sanitary	adj.	卫生的
disinfection	n.	消毒
bacteria	n.	细菌
fulfill	v.	完成
defendant / respondent	n.	被诉方, 应诉方
plaintiff / claimant	n.	起诉人, 原告
tribunal	n.	审判庭
borne	v.	承受, 承担

Chapter 11

Section I
Commodity Inspection

Commodity inspection is an activity, which relates closely to the two parties concerned. It refers to the fact that both imports and exports are inspected to see that the ordered goods are the same as what the importer intends to buy.

1. Necessity of Commodity Inspection

Commodity inspection is an indispensable link of the smooth handling of international transaction. Since the buyer and the seller are thousands of miles apart, it is quite possible that export and import goods are subject to damages or shortage in transit.

It is likely that the quality of the goods received by the buyer may not be in agreement with the sales contract. Therefore, it is not difficult to understand why a buyer wants to inspect the goods he is purchasing. A buyer wants to make certain that the goods delivered to him are exactly the goods described by the contract he has signed with the seller in terms or quality, quantity, packing etc.. On the other hand, a seller also wants to inspect the goods he is selling for two reasons. First, a seller wants to control the quality of the goods so that his image will not be damaged and the market will be developed. Second, a seller wants to prove with an inspection document that the goods delivered have met the relevant contract terms so that he will not be responsible for any problems in the goods after delivery.

In these conditions, it is advisable that the goods be inspected by a third party and an inspection certificate issued, the certificate will be served as a proof to ascertain the trouble and which party is to blame.

2. Time and Place of Inspection

The time and place of inspection is the first item in an inspection clause. It stipulates when and where the inspection should be conducted and is associated with the terms of delivery used, the nature of the commodity and packaging, and the laws or regulations of different countries.

If arrival terms such as DDU or DDP are used, the inspection should be conducted at the named place in the country of importation where the goods are made available to the buyer. When the departure term (EXW) is used, it is clear that the commodity should be inspected at the factory or warehouse where the delivery is made. However, for some terms such as FOB, CFR or CIF, it could be difficult or impossible to carry out the inspection right at the place of delivery of the commodity, especially for some commodities and types of packaging when the facilities or personnel of inspection are not available. Besides delivery terms, commodity and packaging, laws and regulations must be observed. Some countries, for example, require all imports to be inspected before loading at the exporting country by a nominated inspection agency or a surveyor.

In international trade practice, there are three modes to stipulate the time and place of inspection.

❖ **Shipping Quality and Whipping Weight**

In this way, inspectors from both sides conduct a joint inspection, usually at the seller's factory or at the port of shipping, the inspection certificate issued will serve as the final proof of the quality and quantity of the commodity shipped. Such an arrangement will ensure that the seller ships qualified goods. The buyer will bear all the risks once the goods leave the factory. Theoretically, buyers can reinspect at the port of destination but cannot claim for compensation unless there is a big discrepancy in quality. In other words, such arrangement deprives the buyer the right to reexamine the goods upon arrival and it is disadvantage to the buyer.

❖ **Landed Quality and Landed Weight**

In this mode of inspection, both the seller and buyer agreed that the inspections of the quality, quantity (weight) of the commodities are carried out at the port of destination, and the inspection certificate issued by the inspection organization is final. Under this condition, any loss or damage in quality or quantity in transit will be borne by the seller; in this sense, such inspection is favorable to the buyer.

❖ **Inspection at the Port of Shipment and Re-Inspection at the Port of Destination**

With this method of inspection, the seller and the buyer both agree to inspect the quality and quantity (weight) of the commodities in the place of shipment, the certificate issued at the port of shipment will be used as one of the documents for payment, but the buyer retains the right to re-inspect the goods in the place of destination and to claim for compensation if the merchandise is not in conformity with the contract.

While this mode of inspection looks relatively fairer to both the buyer and the seller than the previous two, and it is most widely used in international trade. However, it also has a problem: if the quality or weight of the goods changes in transit, then inspection results at ports of shipment and destination would be different, sellers and buyers might have different arguments about the discrepancy.

In practice, for small differences (e.g. 0.5% more or less), the result of inspection at the port of shipment is considered final or the difference is divided between the buyer and the seller. When the difference is big, it needs to be settled by negotiation or by arbitration. Before making a claim against the seller, the buyer should make sure that the insurance company or the shipping company is not liable for the difference. For example, if the inconformity has been the result of natural disasters or accidents that have been covered by insurance, the buyer should ask for compensation from the insurance company. If the inconformity is the result of the carrier's negligence, then the carrier should be responsible for the loss or damage.

3. Inspection Agency and Certificate

❖ **Inspection Agency**

The inspection agency is the third party which takes an impartial or neutral position in the inspection of the goods. There are both governmental and non-government inspection institutions. The agency chosen to carry out inspection should be permitted by relevant laws or should be acceptable to both the buyer and the seller if there is no specific requirement of law. In China, the inspection of export and import goods is undertaken by China Entry and Exit Inspection and Quarantine Bureau and China Export and Import Commodities Inspection Company Ltd. and its branch. The inspection agencies in China carry out the duties of legal inspection, supervision and superintending and surveying services.

❖ **Certificate**

After the inspection of the imported or exported goods, the inspection institution will issue inspection certificate. Most frequently used inspection certificates can be classified into following categories: Inspection Certificate of Quality, Weight, Quantity, Origin, Value, Damaged Cargo, and Health. For commodities such as frozen meat or leather, Veterinary Inspection Certificate might be required to prove that the commodity is free from diseases of animals. When feather or human hair is traded, Sanitary or Disinfection Inspection Certificate is required to prove that the commodity is free from harmful bacteria. For some special transaction, one or more of the above inspection certificates are required. It should be clearly stated in the contract what certificates are needed according to the nature of the goods and the laws of the importing country.

Inspection Certificates are used to verify whether the goods are in conformity with the terms of contract. If the verification is positive, the certificates are the documents for payment negotiation. If not, they are the documents for refusal of the goods and claim for compensation.

Section II
Force Majeure

In business contracts or confirmations, parties of international trade usually stipulate Force Majeure clause to safeguard their interests, for occasionally some natural or social accidents or events beyond their control happened, any party involved shall not be liable for the loss or damage incurred.

1. Concept of Force Majeure

A force majeure event, also called Act of God, is one that can generally be neither anticipated nor brought under control. As a matter of fact, force majeure clause usually excuses a party who breaches the contract because the party's performance is prevented by the occurrence of an event that is beyond the party's reasonable control. A force majeure clause may excuse performance on the occurrence of such events as natural disasters, labor strikes, bankruptcy, or failure of subcontractors to perform.

2. Consequences of Force Majeure

There are two consequences of force majeure: natural disasters like flood, storm, heavy snow earthquake etc. and social disturbances like war, strike, sanctions, etc. In case of a force majeure event, the party who quotes the clause should give prompt notice to the other party within a specified time limit. A force majeure event should also be verified by a certificate that attests such an event. The issuer of the certificate should be mentioned in the clause.

If possible, specific events such as the scope of force majeure events, consequences, time limit of notice to the other contractor, certificates and the agencies who issue them should be clearly agreed upon and listed in contract to avoid any dispute.

However, if a force majeure clause is not expressively included in a contract; a legal action may be undertaken on the basis that such a clause should be implied under the doctrine of commercial frustration or commercial in practicability.

In cases of natural disasters or other events that have made it impossible to fulfill the contract, the contract can be terminated. While in cases of events (such as transportation stoppage caused by an earthquake) that will only delay the fulfillment of a contract, the contract can be postponed but not terminated since it is still possible for the seller to carry out his contract obligations.

Section III
Claim

In international trade, complaints and claims from the customers, and disputes between the buyers and the sellers may arise although the parties work very carefully in the performances of a contract.

1. The Definition of Claim

When one party to a contract fails to fulfill his obligations and causes the other party financial losses, the latter would demand the former to compensate him for the losses. This demand is called a claim. In international trade practice, there are roughly three categories of claim: a claim between the seller and the buyer; a claim against the carrier; and a claim against the insurer.

2. Settlement of Claim

For a moderate contract of general merchandise, a discrepancy and claim clause is often included. In case the goods delivered are inconsistent with the contract stipulations for quantity, quality, packaging, etc, the buyer should make a claim against the seller within the time limit of re-inspection and claim under the support of an inspection certificate or a survey report issued by a nominated surveyor accepted. If the claim is justified, prompt and well-supported, it can be settled in the following methods: main refund and compensation for the direct losses or expenses, selling the goods at lower rates according to the degree of inferiority, extent of damage and amount of losses, or replacing the faulty goods with perfect or new ones conforming to the specifications, quality and performance as stipulated in the contract.

For a contract covering a huge shipment of goods or high value equipment such as a complete plant, a penalty clause might also be included and quoted when one party fails to implement the contract such as non-delivery, delayed delivery, delayed opening of L/C etc. Under this clause, the party who failed to carry out the contract must pay a fine, a certain percentage of the total contract value; however, paying the penalty does not mean that the contract can be avoided. In other words, the party that has failed to implement the contract must carry out his contract obligations in spite of his payment of the penalty.

To file or to settle a claim, the following points should be paid due attention to: whether the claim is justified by the contract; whether the claim is made in time; or whether the claim is well supported by good documentation. Failing to have positive answers would mean difficulties in settling the claim.

Section IV
Arbitration

Arbitration is the resolution of a dispute between two parties through a voluntary or contractually required hearing and determination by a impartial third party chosen by the parties in controversy or a higher or disinterested body. In international trade, the main arbitration body is the International Chamber of Commerce (ICC).

1. Procedures of Arbitration

In international trade practice, when disputes arise, friendly negotiation or mediation is the best choice of all and will benefit to both parties. However, not all disputes can be settled by amicable negotiation of mediation, arbitration will be the second alternative.

The arbitration clause in an international contract should specify an arbitration agency, which is of prime importance and a matter of great concern to either contracting party. There are normally two types of arbitration agency: permanent arbitration agency which provides facilities and personnel; and temporary arbitration tribunal, set up only for a special dispute.

In addition, the place for arbitration should be included in the contract. The location can be anywhere from the seller's country, the buyer's country to a third party. If no location is specified in the contract, the parties may, upon the occurrence of dispute, consult with each other for a decision as to where to hold the arbitration.

The general arbitration procedures are to submit dispute to arbitration, appoint arbitrators, hear a case, and issue an award.

❖ **Submitting Disputes to Arbitration**

If a dispute is to be submitted to a permanent organization, the application is sent directly to the tribunal and to the defendant (also called respondent). If the dispute is to be submitted to a temporary organization, the application is sent directly to the defendant, then arbitrators should be appointed.

❖ **Appointing Arbitrators**

Two points must be considered in appointing arbitrators: number of arbitrators and qualifications of arbitrators. If two arbitrators are conducting the hearing, it may be that both parties are appointed by a neutral party. If there is to be a presiding arbitrator, then he can also be appointed by a neutral party, or jointly selected by the two arbitrators nominated by the disputants. Sometimes, the disputing parties may also jointly choose a sole arbitrator to arbitrate singly. Both disputing parties should be contractually bound by the decision of the arbitrators, who may hear evidence on oath and have powers to seek all necessary documentation. The appointed arbitrators and the presiding arbitrator shall work impartially, not representing any party's interests.

❖ **Case Hearing**

Case hearing can be carried out by face-to-face reply or correspondence. In some countries, the tribunal can give the order of interim measures of protection while the arbitration is going on. For example, the object can be placed under a third party's control or perishable goods can be sold and the proceeds are placed under the tribunal's control.

❖ **Issuing an Award**

An award is the decision made by the arbitration tribunal. It must be in written form with or without explanations or reasons. An award is final and binding in China and most of the other countries, provided that there are no illegal actions by any party involved in the arbitration process. If one party refuses to obey the award, the other can ask a court to enforce the implementation of the award.

2. Cost of Arbitration

In addition, how the cost of the arbitration is to be divided and the scopes of arbitration are normally stipulated in the clause. Fees can be borne by the losing party of the dispute, can be divided between the two parties or can be paid according to the award. It is also necessary to stipulate a reasonable time limit for arbitration to take place to reduce the risk of one obstructive party using delaying tactics to his benefit.

Useful Phrases & Technical Terms

be subject to	以……为条件，以……为效
make certain	保证
shipping quality and shipping weight	离岸品质和离岸重量
landed quality and landed weight	到岸品质和到岸重量
port of shipmen	装运港
port of destination	目的港
inspection agency	检验机构
quarantine bureau	检疫局
China Entry and Exit Inspection and Quarantine Bureau	中国出入境检验检疫局
China Export and Import Commodities Inspection Company Ltd.	中国进出口商品检验有限公司
force majeure	人不可抗力
International Chamber of Commerce (ICC)	国际商会

Notes

1. When one party to a contract fails to fulfill his obligations and causes the other party financial losses, the latter would demand the former to compensate him for the losses. This demand is called a claim.
   当合同一方没有履行它的义务而使另外一方遭受经济上的损失，后者将要求前者赔偿他的损失，这一要求就是索赔。

2. Since the buyer and the seller are thousands of miles apart, it is quite possible that export and import goods are subject to damages or shortage in transit.
   因进出口双方相距甚远，所以进出口货物有必要以货物在运输过程中的损失或短缺为确认条件。

3. With this method of inspection, the seller and the buyer both agree to inspect the quality and quantity of the commodities at the place of shipment, the certificate issued at the port of shipment will be used as one of the documents for payment, but the buyer retains the right to re-inspect the goods at the place of destination and to claim for compensation if the merchandise is not in conformity with the contract.

采用这种检验方法,买卖双方应都同意在装货地检验商品的品质和数量,装运港的检验证明将被用作支付的单据之一,但是当商品与合同的规定不一致时,买方保留在目的地重新验货和索赔的权利。

4. When one party to a contract fails to fulfill his obligations and causes the other party financial losses, the latter would demand the former to compensate him for the losses.'

当合同一方没有履行他的义务而使另外一方遭受经济损失,则后者将要求前者赔偿他的损失。

5. To file or to settle a claim, the following points should be paid due attention to: 1) whether the claim is justified by the contract; 2) whether the claim is made in time; 3) or whether the claim is well supported by good documentation.

提交索赔或理赔时,应随时注意以下几点:1)合同内容证明索赔是否正当;2)索赔要求是否及时;3)索赔单据是否齐全。

6. If a dispute is to be submitted to a permanent organization, the application is sent directly to the tribunal and to the defendant (also called respondent).

如需向某一永久性组织提交争议,申诉书应直接递交给法庭和辩护方(也称应诉方)。

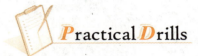

Practical Drills

❖ Questions for Discussion

1. Why is inspection an indispensable part of international trade?
2. What factors need to be considered when drafting the force majeure clause?
3. For a Chinese exporter, if the inspection clause reads: "Quality and weight certified by the China Commodity Inspection Bureau as per their respective certificates which are to be taken as final", what is the mode of inspection?
4. What are some of the major characteristics of a force majeure event?

❖ Case Study

Arbitration of Dispute

A trading company in Guangzhou signs a sales contract with an Italian company to supply some electronic products in the year 2004. The two parties agreed on China as the place of arbitration. A dispute arises on the quality of the goods supplied and the importer sues the exporter in its local court. In this case, how should the Chinese exporter proceed?

Chapter 11

❖ *Role Play*

Damage

Jim: I regret to tell you that a number of cotton price goods were water stained or soiled because of improper packing. We have to file a claim with you.

Tom: That sounds strange. Inside the strong cardboard cartons the goods were wrapped with plastic bags and fastened with nylon twine. It was possibly caused by rough handling. You know, even the strongest packing can give way under improper handling.

Jim: I can assure you there was no rough handling when the goods were unloaded. The damage might have happened during loading.

Tom: How much of the contents of the damaged goods is still usable?

Jim: 80%. And the shipping charges cost us a lot. The goods are in urgent need, however, we have to keep our customers waiting. Shall we return the goods to you or you allow a 20% reduction in price?

Tom: Let's compromise on a 15% reduction in price on the shipment.

Jim: Well. We might as well accept your proposal.

Extended Activities

I. Answer the following questions.

1. What are the three types of inspection agency?
2. Please explain the three major ways of stipulating the place and time of inspection.
3. Please list at least 5 types inspection certificates.
4. Please list the possible places where re-inspection can be conducted.

II. Term Translation.

索赔	不可抗力	仲裁条款	首席仲裁员
听证	提出仲裁申请	国际商会	特别审判庭
裁决书	兽医卫生许可证	卫生防疫许可证	装运港
处罚条例	到岸质量和重量	检验机构	

III. Decide whether the following statements are true of false according to the text. If it is true, please write "T" in the blanks beside each statement, otherwise "F".

1. (   ) If cargo should be damaged or lost during transit, the carrier bears no responsibility whether or not the damage or loss is due to the carrier's negligence.

2. (   ) If shipping quality is used in inspection, the inspection must be conducted at the

seller's factory only.

3. (   ) In practice, the small differences (e.g. 0.5 of weight), inspection result at the port of the shipment is considered final or the difference is divided between the buyer and the seller.

4. (   ) For one contrast, only one method and one standard should be used to ensure consistency in inspection.

5. (   ) Arbitration can be used to settle criminal cases as well as civil cases.

6. (   ) An arbitration award must be in written form with or without explanations or reasons.

7. (   ) Usually an arbitration tribunal can be composed of one, two or three arbitrators.

8. (   ) In international trade, the party that has failed to implement the contract may choose not to carry out his contract obligations if he has paid the required penalty.

IV. Read the following passage and fill the blank with one word, some of which the first letter has been given.

Among the available d_____ resolution alternatives to the courts, arbitration is by far the most commonly used internationally. Arbitral award is considered f_____ and binding. While several mechanisms can help p_____ reach an amicable settlement—for example, through conciliation under the ICC Rules of Conciliation—all of them depend, ultimately, on the goodwill and c_____ of the parties. A final and enforceable decision can generally be o_____ only by recourse to the courts or by arbitration. As arbitral a_____ are not subject to appeal, they are much more likely to be final than the judgments of courts of first instance.

Although arbitral awards may be s_____ to challenges (usually in either the country where the arbitral award is rendered or where enforcement is sought), the grounds of challenge available against arbitral awards are limited.

Arbitral awards enjoy much greater international r_____ than judgments of national courts. About 120 countries have s_____. The 1958 United Nations Convention on the Recognition and Enforcement of Foreign Arbitral Awards, known as The New York Convention. The C_____ facilitates enforcement of awards in all c_____ states. There are several other multilateral and bilateral arbitration conventions that may also help enforcement.

Arbitration is also noted for its neutrality. In arbitral p_____, parties can place themselves on an equal footing in five key respects: 1) place of arbitration; 2) language used; 3) procedures or rules of law applied; 4) nationality; 5) legal representation

Arbitration may take place in any country, in any language and with a_____ of any nationality. With this flexibility, it is generally possible to structure a neutral procedure offering no undue advantage to any party.

V. Translate the following sentences into Chinese.

1. In general, discrepancies between the two parties can be resolved through amicable consultations.
2. We hereby lodged a claim against you on the basis of BCIB's survey report.
3. This is to certify that we, the undersigned, have inspected the quality of the above mentioned goods and found the results as follow...
4. The buyer has lodged a claim against the seller on the shipment for $2,500 for short weight.
5. Such deviation between the products and the sample is normal and permissible. Therefore, the claim for compensation cannot be allowed.

VI. Translate the following sentences into English.

(1) 如果进口商经检验发现商品数量与合同不符,就将拒收货物。
(2) 他们检查了这些货物,看是否短重。
(3) 装运品质以广州商检局出具之检验证书为证明并作为最后依据。
(4) 你们的产品质量低劣,与我方市场的销售标准相距甚远。
(5) 收到你方发来的30箱速溶咖啡,但很遗憾,检查结果表明5箱显然由于包装不良而严重损坏。

VII. Complete the following chart according to the text.

Procedure of Arbitration

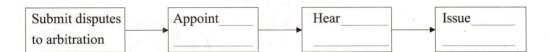

Chapter 12

Marketing Organizations Abroad

Focal Learning

After the completion of this chapter, you are required to know:
- the agency arrangements;
- branch offices and subsidiaries abroad—foreign acquisitions;
- sole distribution agreements, licensing and franchising.

Lead-in Vocabulary

principal	n.	委托人（授权另一人代表其行事的人）
remuneration	n.	报酬，酬劳；赔偿，补偿
purport	v.	声称
ratify	v.	批准，认可
contingency	n.	或有费用，临时费，应急费，意外费用
cartage	n.	火车运输；货车运费
lighter age	n.	驳运，驳运费
intermediary ship	n.	媒介关系
bailment	n.	委托，寄托（把物品或个人财产移交给另一个人管理的行为）
jurisdiction	n.	权限（管辖或控制范围）
equity	n.	普通股，优先股；资产净值
franchising	n.	特许经营权转让协议
licensee	n.	许可证持有人，获许可的人
deductible	a.	可减免的，可扣除的（尤指收入所得税可减免的）

Chapter 12

Section I
Agency Arrangements

Exporting firms range in size from the very small exporter to the large multinational company and the methods of marketing will naturally vary according to their size, the type of goods and the nature of the market. There are obvious advantages to the exporter of selling direct to the overseas buyer without using an intermediary such as an agent or export house. Direct selling means having direct communication between a representative of the exporting company and the buyer. But there are considerable disadvantages in selling direct to the foreign buyer. Generally speaking indirect selling is more popular with a new exporter because it involves less investment and is less risky, while direct selling becomes more worthwhile as export sales increase and the exporter's knowledge of both the techniques of exporting and the problems of particular markets develops. Indirect selling involves the employment of an agent or distributor overseas. All of these offer the exporter their knowledge of the market and their network of customers, and save him the expense of setting up his own sales force and seeking his own customers.

1. Self-employed Agents Abroad

The characteristic feature of this form of marketing is that the exporter enters into direct relations with the customer abroad by means of a contract procured on his behalf, by a representative who resides abroad and who is not his employee.

An agent in the legal sense is a person who has authority from another person, the principal, to represent him or act on his behalf and legally bind him in relation to third parties.

The remuneration of a self-employed agent is usually based upon a commission on the price of the goods sold by or through him, while the remuneration of an employee is normally a fixed salary, sometimes augmented by bonuses commissions.

A contract of agency creates a confidential relationship, and the agent has, in certain terms or to receive the purchase price from him. The exporter should make searching inquires about the personal reputation and financial standing of the agent before reposing his trust in him. These inquiries are often made through the exporter's bank or through his forwarder. When they result in a satisfactory reply, two further points should be observed.

First, a precautionary measure is usually included in the contract. Second, personal contact should be established and maintained between the principal and agent.

2. The Nature of the Contract of Agency

In the export trade, the authority which the exporter gives the self-employed agent abroad normally takes one of the following two forms: First, the agent may be authorized to introduce third parties in his territory to the principal, leaving the decision as to whether he wants to contract to the latter; second, the agent has authority to conclude contracts with third parties on behalf of the principal.

Every agent agreement creates three relationships.

(1) Relationship between the Principal and the Agent

It is the internal arrangement between the principal and the agent, the contract of agency proper; it settles the rights and duties of these two parties, the scope of authority granted to the agent and the remuneration due to him.

(2) Relationship between the Principal and the Third Party

Relationship existing between the principal and the third party is a normal contract of sale, with certain features which arise from the fact that seller concluded the contract through an agent.

(3) Relationship between the Agent and the third Party

It only occurs in exceptional circumstances.

3. The Agent's Authority

An agent's authority to act may be actual, implied, ostensible (or apparent), usual, customary or by operation of law. Actual authority arises although there is no such agreement between principal and agent. For the remainder, the agency relationship arises although there is no such agreement between principal and agent, or where there is such agreement but the agent has exceeded his actual authority. An implied authority may arise from the relationship between principal and agent or from conduct. An agency relationship may also occur where there is no agreement between principal and agent but where the principal has consented to the agent acting on his behalf and the agent has consented so to act.

❖ **Actual authority**

Actual authority is the express authority given to the agent by agreement with the principal. An "actual" authority is a legal relationship between principal and agent, created by a consensual agreement to which they alone are parties. Its scope is to be ascertained by applying ordinary principles of construction of contracts, including any proper inference from the express words used, the usages of the trade, or the course of business between the parties. Such an agreement may be by deed, in writing or oral.

❖ **Implied, usual and customary authority**

The agent's implied authority may be inferred from the relationship between the principal and the agent or from conducts. The agent may perform acts which are subordinate and incidental to those expressly authorized and when it is inferred from the conduct of the parties and the circumstances of the case.

It is well established that the agent's implied authority also permits him to act in conformity with custom or what is usual, as long as these acts are reasonable and do not conflict with the scope of this express authority. Naturally what is customary or usual in the trade will vary according to the particular circumstances of each trade or profession.

❖ Ostensible Authority

Implied authority is to be distinguished from ostensible or apparent authority, although it may sometimes be difficult to draw the distinction. In an ostensible authority the agent either has no actual authority to act on the principal's behalf or has exceeded his actual authority. Ostensible or apparent authority is the authority of an agent as it appears to others. It is clear from the authorities that ostensible authority operates as estoppels, preventing the principal from asserting that he is not bound by the contract. Actual authority and apparent authority are quite independent of one another. Generally they coexist and coincide, but either may exist without the other and their respective scope may be different.

The elements necessary to establish ostensible authority are: a representation; a reliance on the representation; an alteration of your position resulting from such reliance.

The representation must be made by the principal or by a person duly authorized by the principal; it cannot be made by the agent.

❖ Ratification

Where an agent exceeds his authority or has no actual or implied authority to act on behalf of another, but purports to conclude an agreement with a third party on behalf of his principal, then that purported principal may ratify the purported agreement. Once the purported principal has ratified the unauthorized agreement the ratification relates back and is deemed equivalent to an antecedent authority and ratification, as we all know, has a retroactive effect. The effect of ratification by the principal puts all three parties in the same position as where the agent has an express authority, i.e. both principal and third party may enforce the agreement against each other; the agent is no longer liable for exceeding his authority, nor personally liable to the third party, and has earned his commission.

A void agreement may not be ratified but a voidable one can be. Ratification may be express or implied from conduct or acquiescence.

4. Rights and Obligations of the Agent and the Principal

❖ Duties of the Agent to His Principal

The general requirement of the self-employed agent is that the agent must look after the interests of his principal and act dutifully and in good faith. In particular, the commercial agent must: (1) make proper efforts to negotiate and conclude the transactions he is instructed to take care of; (2) communicate to his principal all the necessary information available to him; (3) comply with reasonable instructions given by his principal.

The main common law duties of the agent are: (1) to use reasonable diligence; (2) to disclose all material facts; (3) not to accept bribes or to make secret profits; (4) not to divulge confidential information; (5) to account to the principal.

❖ Duties of the Principal

Like the agent, the principal must act dutifully and in good faith. In particular, the principal must: (1) provide the agent with the necessary documentation concerning the goods and information to enable the agent to carry out the contract; (2) advise the agent in reasonable time if the anticipates that the volume of business will be lower than expected and inform the agent of his acceptance, rejection or non-performance or any contract involving the agent.

The following are the main duties of the principal: (1) to pay commission; (2) to pay agent's expenses and indemnity; (3) to deal with orders emanating from agent's territory but not procured by him; (4) to repeat orders.

❖ **Exclusive Trading Rights**

The agency agreement may provide that the self-employed agent shall have sole, or exclusive, or sole and exclusive trading rights in a particular territory. The character of the agency is here territorial and not personal. The agent is normally paid commission on all sales emanating from his territory, whether procured by his own efforts or those of other persons, and he usually undertakes to promote systematically in the territory reserved to him the distribution of the principal's goods by an organization of sub-agents, advertisements or other means. As far as the exclusivity of trading rights is concerned, agency agreements are, similar to distribution agreements, but the essential difference between an agent, who contracts on behalf of a principal, and a distributor, who contract on his own account and for his own benefit, remains. In particular, the contract of agency should state expressively that the agent has to sell in the principal's name.

5. Special Types of the Agents

Commercial practice has evolved certain types of agency agreements that play an important role in the export trade.

❖ **The Commission Agent**

A commissionaire is a person who internally, i.e. in his relationship to his principal, is an agent but externally, i.e. in his relationship to the third party, is a seller or buyer in his own name. Where a commissionaire has acted for the principal, no privity of contract can be constituted between the principal and the third party. As an agent, the commission is accountable to his principal for the profit from the transaction, must use reasonable diligence in the performance of his duties, and must not make an undisclosed profit or take a bribe. The principal, on the other hand, cannot claim the price from the third party directly, nor is he liable in contract for any defects of the goods.

❖ **The Del Credere Agent**

A del credere agent is an agent who undertakes to indemnify the principal for any loss which the latter may sustain, owing to the failure of a customer introduced by the agent to pay the purchase price.

The advantages of the del credere arrangement are evident: (1) The principal is not sufficiently in touch with the foreign market in which the agent operates to judge the financial soundness of the customer who orders goods; (2) Credit terms cannot always be avoided if it is desired to market the goods on a competitive basis, and even where no credit terms are granted, the exporter might find himself entangled in complicated and costly insolvency proceedings if the customer fails.

These pitfalls are avoided by the agent agreeing to accept the del credere for the customers introduced by him and, incidentally, the principal can be assured that the agent will not place considerations of turnover higher than the solvency of the customers whose orders he solicits. It is usual to pay an additional commission, called the del credere commission, to the agent who accepts a del credere responsibility. The del credere agreement need not be evidenced in writing; it is a contract of indemnity against loss and not a contract of guarantee. The del credere agent undertakes merely to indemnify the principal if the latter, owing to the insolvency of the buyer or some analogous cause, is unable to recover the purchase price, but the agent is not responsible if a perfectly solvent buyer refuses to pay the price on the ground that the principal has not duly performed the contract.

❖ **The Agent Carrying Stock**

Agents resident abroad have either authority to solicit or accept orders and pass them on to the principal, who then dispatches the goods to the customer directly, or they are entrusted with a store or consignment of stock lines, spare parts, etc. and have authority to supply customers directly from their store. Agents of the latter type are mercantile agents, agents who in the customary course of the business have authority to sell goods, or to consign goods for sale, or to buy goods or to raise money on the security of goods.

❖ **The Confirming House**

In the export trade an overseas importer may buy through a confirming house, although in recent years the number of independent confirming houses has decreased, many having been absorbed by banks. In modern practice confirming houses are called export house.

(1) Nature of the Confirming House

A confirming house usually enters into two legal relationships, namely, with its overseas customer, who asks it to procure certain goods for him, and with the seller in the home market, with whom it places the order or indent. The relationship with the overseas customer is normally that between principal and agent, whereas the relationship with the seller in the home market depends on the nature of the contract which the confirming house concludes with him.

Three possibilities exist in that respect: first, when placing the order with the seller, the confirming house may buy from the seller. The second possibility is that the confirming house places the order with the seller "as agents on behalf of our principals", either naming them or not. A third arrangement is that the confirming house may place the client's order as agent of the overseas importer, but may indicate at the same time that it intends to hold itself personally responsible for the price.

In practice, confirming houses, when carrying out orders received from their customers abroad, use two types of forms: one in which they order the goods from the supplier in the home market under their own liability, and the other in which they merely pass on the order of the overseas importer as his agent.

(2) Obligations of the Confirming House

The confirming house, which has made itself liable to the supplier, is under a personal obligation to the supplier to pay the price for the goods.

As regards the client, the confirming house undertakes to give the supplier proper shipping instructions but—and this has to be emphasized—it does not undertake liability for the conformity of the goods with the contract, and in particular for their quality and quantity.

(3) Insolvency of the Confirming House

If the confirming house becomes insolvent, the question arises whether the seller can still claim the price from the overseas buyer. If the confirming house has re-ordered the goods from the seller, the answer is clear: the seller can claim the price from the buyer on the contract of purchase originally placed by the buyer. If the confirming house has confirmed the buyer's order, the position is more difficult. If the intention of the parties was that the obligation of the confirming house shall be the sole obligation to the seller, there would be no claim against the overseas buyer. That conclusion would, however, be exceptional. Normally, the confirmation by the confirming house, like the confirmation of the advising bank under a letter of credit, provides only conditional discharge and the seller has still his claim against the overseas buyer.

Section II
Branch Offices and Subsidiaries Abroad

Often the most effective method of overseas marketing is the establishment of a local branch or subsidiary in the country to which the exports are directed.

1. General Understanding of Branch Offices and Subsidiaries Abroad

❖ **The choice between Branches and Subsidiaries**

The exporter who wishes to establish a permanent presence in an overseas country will ask himself whether it is more advantageous to establish a branch office in that country or to work through a subsidiary incorporated there. There is no general answer to this question and it depends on the circumstances of the individual case.

Two matters have to be considered: first, whether the local legislation, particularly relating to employment, companies, taxation and foreign investment, is more favorable to one of these alternatives; secondly, whether the exporter wishes to co-operate with local interests.

❖ **The Legal Distinction between Branches and Subsidiaries**

The decisive difference between these two types of business organization is that the subsidiary has a separate and independent legal personality in the overseas country in which it is incorporated, but a branch office is merely an emanation of the exporter in the overseas country and, through it, he is himself present in that country.

A subsidiary which requires bank credit might be unable to offer sufficient security and the bank may ask for a guarantee by the parent company to secure the debts of the subsidiary. No such guarantee is required in the case of a branch office, because its debts are automatically those of the head office.

2. Dealings between Branch Offices Abroad

Exceptionally, e.g. in string contracts in the commodity trade, dealings between two branches of the same legal entity are treated like dealings between two separate legal entities, provided that these dealings are regarded in the trade as genuine trading transactions. Foreign branches of banks are treated as separate from the head office.

3. Subsidiary Companies Abroad

❖ The Overseas Subsidiary

The overseas subsidiary is incorporated under the law of that country. It possesses an independent and separate legal personality and enjoys in the country of its incorporation the same status as an indigenous trading corporation. The control of the overseas subsidiary is vested in the parent firm. It is exercised by various means, such as:

(1) holding a majority of shares in the subsidiary company;
(2) holding a majority of the voting power of the subsidiary company;
(3) reserving the right to appoint its directors or managers.

But these examples are illustrative only and not exhaustive.

The overseas subsidiary is capable of entering into same contractual relations with the parent firm as can be entered into by every other enterprise trading in the overseas country. The relations between these two enterprises may be:

(1) ordinary contracts of sale concluded on FOB,CIF or other trade terms;
(2) the parent firm may arrange a sole distribution agreement with the subsidiary;
(3) the parent firm may employ the subsidiary as its commission agent;
(4) the parent firm may employ the subsidiary as its resident representative abroad.

A question is whether the parent company can be regarded as being within the jurisdiction of the court, by virtue of the subsidiary having its place of business there. As the parent and the subsidiary are two different legal persons, the question has, in principle, to be answered in the negative.

❖ The Multinational Enterprise

By establishing one or several subsidiaries overseas, the parent company becomes a multinational or, as it is sometimes called, transnational enterprise. Such an enterprise has been defined as "companies of different nationalities, connected by means of shareholdings, managerial control, or contract and constituting an economic unit."

On the international level no effective regulation of multinationals has yet been established. On the national level, two legal problems arise with respect to multinational enterprises:

First, the interests of the host country in which the subsidiary is formed may conflict with those of the home country in which the controlling company has its seat. Secondly, in some circumstances the veil of separate legal status of the various constituent companies of the multinational enterprise is pierced and the multinational is treated as an economic unit.

❖ **Foreign Acquisitions**

As enterprise which is cash rich or has a leverage facility may consider expanding its export potential by acquiring a company to establish in an overseas country. It can then utilize the marketing outlets of that company for the distribution of its own products and need not build up a permanent representation from the beginning in that market.

The usual, and best, method of a foreign acquisition is that of an agreed takeover bid. The bidding company will purchase the equity, or at least the majority of the voting shares, in the target company from its shareholders. The effect of this transaction is that the target company has become a subsidiary of the bidding company and the observations made earlier on subsidiary companies abroad apply to the acquired company.

If it is intended to establish a permanent representation abroad, in addition to the general considerations which have to be taken into account, two special areas of law have to be examined; the local law relating to takeovers and competition law of the country in question.

Section III
Sole Distribution Agreements, Licensing Agreements and Franchising

The various legal forms of overseas marketing can be grouped as follows: The exporter may conclude a sole distribution or licensing or franchising agreement with an importer abroad; or he may entrust his representation to an exclusive agent abroad or ask his overseas customers to use the services of a confirming house in this country; or he may provide his own unincorporated or corporate marketing organization in the overseas country by establishing a branch office or subsidiary there, or by a foreign acquisition, i.e. by acquiring an enterprise already carrying on business in the target country and possibly having established market outlets there; or he may combine with an enterprise in the overseas country in a joint venture or adopt another form of joint export organization, e.g. the European Economic Interest Grouping (EEIG).

In this section, we will focus on sole distribution, licensing and franchising.

Chapter 12

1. Sole Distribution Agreements

❖ Nature of Sole Distribution Agreements

(1) Sole and Exclusive Agreements

In distribution agreements, and in agency agreements, the distributor or agent is often granted "sole" or "exclusive" rights of representation. It has to be ascertained in every case what the parties meant by them. The best course for the parties is to spell out in their agreement the precise rights which they intend the representative to have. If these rights are not defined in the contract, it should be borne in mind that in modern commercial usage the following meanings are often attributed to the terms "sole" and "exclusive". Both terms imply that the principal shall not be entitled to appoint another distributor or agent for the territory of the representative. If the representation is "sole", the principal himself may undertake sales in the territory of the representative on his own account without any liability to the representative. If the representation is "exclusive", the principal is not allowed himself to compete with the representative in the allotted territory.

Sometimes a distribution or agency agreement provides that the representative shall have "sole and exclusive" rights of representation.

(2) Sole Distribution Agreements Distinguished from Contracts of Sale and from Agency Agreements.

Sole distribution agreements, as customary in the export trade, are different from contracts of sale and agency agreements. They provide, in essence, that the seller, a manufacturer or merchant in a country, grants the buyer, an overseas merchant, sole trading rights within a particular territory with respect to goods of a specified kind while the buyer may undertake to rely on the seller as the sole source of supply she never desirous of buying goods of the specified kind in the country.

The sole distribution agreement is not a contract of sale of specific goods. It merely lays down the general terms on which later individual contracts of sale will be concluded. Although its mandatory clauses are dependent on the conclusion of individual contracts of sale in the future, its restrictive clauses are immediately effective and remain in force for the duration of the agreement even when individual sales are never concluded.

Further, the sole distributor is not an agent of the manufacturer or trader in the legal sense. Unlike an agent, the sole distributor does not act on behalf of the principal and is not accountable to him for the profits derived from the resale of the goods in his own country or territory. The profit of the sole distributor normally is the difference between the buying and selling price whereas the profit of the agent is usually the commission which they earn when concluding a sales contract on behalf of his principal or when the principal concludes a sales contract with a customer introduced by the agent.

(3) Sole Distribution Agreements and Licensing and Franchising Agreements

The sole distribution agreement is sometimes described by commercial men as the grant of a sale license. From the legal point of view, this is an inaccurate description because the distribution agreement provides for the conclusion of straightforward contracts of sale and not for the grant of licenses.

Licensing and franchising agreements are very different from sold distribution agreements. By a licensing agreement the owner of an intellectual property right authorizes another person, the licensee, to use that right, subject to certain conditions. The intellectual property right may be a patent, trademark, business name or a particular business method. A franchise agreement is a contract whereby the franchiser grants the franchisee a license to carry on a particular business under a name belonging to the franchiser and making use of his business methods, which the franchiser communicates to the franchisee. Normally the franchiser is entitled under this agreement to exercise a strict degree of control over the franchised business during the period of the license. Licensing and franchising agreements will be considered later on.

❖ Clauses in Sole Distribution Agreements

Sole distribution agreements require careful drafting. An infinite variety of arrangements is possible there. The parties have complete liberty of contracting and should use that discretion for the purpose of creating by their contract a charter of trading which is fair and equitable to both of them, and closely adapted to the particular requirements of their trade and can be relied upon, whether the market is a seller's or a buyer's market. In view of the variety of forms admitted by law, it is impossible to give an exhaustive catalogue of the clauses embodied in these agreements. It is believed that the main points to be considered are indicated under the following heads.

(1) Definition of the Territory

The following points have to be considered by the parties:

A. The geographical definition of the territory which may consist of several political units, or of one political unit, or of part of a political date;

B. The extension of the territory at a future date;

C. The seller's obligation not to sell directly to customers in the territory;

D. The seller's obligation to refer direct enquires from consumers in the territory to the buyer;

E. The buyer's obligation to pass on enquires from outside the territory to the seller;

F. The buyer's obligation to keep customers or retailers' lists and to supply them to the seller on request;

G. The territory in which the buyer is bound to buy exclusively from the seller.

(2) Definition of the Price

Sometimes the distributor agreement contains provisions relating to the ascertainment of the price which the distribution shall pay when ordering goods under that agreement. The difficulty is here that the distribution agreement is intended to be of considerable duration but that the prices of the goods, which shall be bought from time to time by way of individual sales contracts under the terms of the distribution agreement may be affected by inflation or other events or may fluctuate if quoted on world markets.

The parties refer sometimes in the distribution agreement to a definite price ruling on a particular date, such as the date of conclusion of the sales contract or the delivery of the goods. In other cases the parties agree that the distributor shall pay the most favored customer price, i.e. the best price which the supplier would obtain from another customer at the critical date, possibly subject to a rebate.

2. Licensing Agreements

The exporter who owns a patent, trademark or other form of intellectual or industrial property in relation to goods may exploit such ownership abroad through licensing another to exploit that property overseas. The licensor therefore avoids the necessity of providing the capital needed in the designated territory to exploit the property and further avoids the commercial risk of the transactions carried out in relation to the goods. The licensor needs to be mindful of certain important matters when drawing up the license:

(1) quality control;
(2) the question of relevant laws;
(3) the impact of relevant laws.

Quality control may generally be ensured by a provision that samples of the goods sold abroad will be tested on a regular basis. The question of taxation relates to the issue of whether tax is deductible at source or not and the consequences of such deduction for the licensor.

3. Franchising

Where it is desired that the licensee operates under the corporate image already established by the licensor franchising, a particular form of licensing may be adopted. Under this arrangement the licensee will carry on the licensed business under the franchiser's name, style, get up, etc., and indeed in accordance with a system already developed by the franchiser. The purpose is to ensure that the retail outlets, wherever they may be, are easily recognized by the customer, who is therefore not able to distinguish between the outlets owned and run by the franchiser and those run by the franchisee. The difference is behind the scenes. The franchisee will own the outlets maintained by him and risk his own capital.

Such arrangements are mainly associated in the mind of the public with catering outlets such as "fast-food" and coffee chains but of course franchising arrangements are not confined to this trade. The franchise industry is not only involved with provision to customers but also in provision of goods and services to other businesses. Such is the nature and size of the franchising industry that in certain areas there may be a franchise association whose members will subscribe to the Code of Ethics which was established by the International Franchise Association. The ICC have produced a Model Franchising Contract with a detailed commentary to which potential franchisers may make reference.

Useful Phrases & Technical Terms

credit terms	赊销付款条件；信用证条款，贷款条件
precautionary measure	防范措施
express authority	明示权限
retroactive effect	追溯效力
privity of contract	合同关系不涉及第三人原则
del credere	保证收取货款
del credere commission	保证收取货款佣金
confirming house	保付行，保付公司
constituent company	子公司
intellectual property	知识产权

Notes

1. An agent in the legal sense is a person who has authority from another person, the principal, to represent him or act on his behalf and legally bind him in relation to third parties.
   代理商是指在法律方面受他人或者负责人的委托，全权代表他人或者代表他们从事活动，并且法律上有权与第三方达成协议的企业或个人。

2. First, a precautionary measure is usually included in the contract. Second, personal contact should be established and maintained between the principal and agent.
   首先，合同中应包括注意事项；然后，经销商与代理商才能建立合同关系。

3. Sole distribution agreements, as customary in the export trade, are different from contracts of sale and agency agreements. They provide, in essence, that the seller, a manufacturer or merchant in a country, grants the buyer, an overseas merchant, sole trading rights within a particular territory.
   出口贸易中的独家分销协议与销售效益、代理协议不同。事实上，独家分销协议规定卖方、生产商或者某一国的商家授予买方，或海外商家在某一区域独家销售指定商品。

4. First, whether the local legislation, particularly relating to employment, companies, taxation and foreign investment, is more favorable to one of these alternatives; secondly, whether the exporter wishes to co-operate with local interests.
   首先，当地的有关就业、公司经营、税收以及海外投资的法律是否有利于这些做法。其次，出口商是否希望与当地相关各方合作。

5. self-employed: 自雇的，非受雇于人的（直接经营自己的行业或业务而非受雇于他人来谋生的）

6. consensual: 两厢情愿的(未经文件或手续上的格式化而由双方同意所产生或达成的)

Questions for Discussion

1. What items should be embodied in sole distribution agreements?
2. Can you give a brief introduction of agent's authority?

Case Study

Sole Agency Agreement

November 1, 2006

Camellia Machinery and Equipment Co. Ltd. ,45 Beijing Rd., Kunming, Yunnan, 650011, China (hereinafter called **Party A**) and **Road Construction Supply Co. Ltd. , 22 Tran Xuan Soan Street, Hanoi, Vietnam** (hereinafter called **Party B**), desiring to develop business based on the principles of equality and mutual benefit, have agreed as follows through friendly negotiations:

(1) **Appointment of agency:** Party A agrees to appoint party B to act as its sole agent in Hanoi, Vietnam for the sale of the under-mentioned commodity, and therefore no sales of competing bulldozers shall be made in Vietnam, either on Party B's account or on account of any other firms or companies. At the same time Party A is not allowed to appoint other sole agents in Vietnam for the same product during the life of the agreement.

(2) **Name of commodity:** Type DJ-4 bulldozers with the brand name of Dongfeng.

(3) **Price and quantity:** Party B is under an obligation to push sales energetically at the competitive price quoted by Party A. Each transaction is subject to Party A's final confirmation. It is mutually agreed that during the validity of this agreement, Party B shall place orders with Party A for not less than 5,000 bulldozers. Party B shall order at least 2,000 bulldozers in the first six months from the date of signing this agreement. Should Party B fail to fulfill the above-mentioned quantity (namely 2,000 bulldozers) in this duration, Party A shall have the right to sell the goods under this agreement to other customers in Vietnam. In case Party B places orders for less than 1,000 bulldozers in the three months from the date on which the agreement is signed, Party A shall have the right to terminate this agreement by giving notice in writing to Party B.

(4) **Reimbursement:** Party A owes Party B a duty of reimbursement, i.e. Party A repays

Party B for the expenses that Party B incurs in carrying out Party A's instructions. But Party A pays no subsidy for Party B's sales promotion or publicity to canvass business if any.

(5) **Liability:** Party B is not liable for the contracts it negotiates for Party A unless it acts outside the scope of its authority, for example, Party B intentionally participates in fraud or misrepresentation.

(6) **Payment:** Payment is to be made by confirmed, irrevocable letter of credit, without recourse, available by sight draft upon the presentation of shipping documents. The letter of credit for each order shall reach Party A 30 days prior to the date of shipment. Should Party B fail to establish the letter of credit in time, Party B shall be liable for any loss or losses including bank interest, storage, etc. which may incur upon Party A. all goods supplied are to be invoiced by Party A direct to customers, with copies sent to Party B.

(7) **Commission:** Party A agrees to offer Party B a commission of 3% (three percent) on the basis of FOB value of orders. For the bulldozers sold in excess of the quota, Party A will give Party B 1% additional commission. The commission is to be paid to Party B only after the full payment for each order is received by Party A. As an international practice, it should be noted that the commission shall also be paid to Party B on orders secured and executed by Party A itself in Vietnam—that is , when business is done on principal-to-customer basis. All customers' orders are to be transmitted to Party A immediately for prompt supply. Customers settle their accounts directly with Party A, who sends Party B an up-to-date statement at the end of each month of all payments it received. The commission is transferred to Party B's bank account.

(8) **Transactions with governmental bodies:** Transactions concluded between governmental bodies of Party A and Party B are not restricted by the terms and conditions of this agreement, nor shall they be considered as the target fulfilled by Party B under this agreement.

(9) **Market report:** ...

(10) **Validity of the agreement:** This agreement is to remain in force for a period of one year, i.e. commencing on November 1,20... and terminating on November 1,20.... Both parties have the power to terminate the agency relationship. If either party considers it necessary to renew the agreement, the proposing party may take the initiative to conduct a negotiation with the other party one month before its expiration.

(11) **Notarization and witness:** ...

(12) **Loyalty, and reasonable care and skill:** ...

(13) **Questions and termination of the agreement:** ...

(14) **Texts of the agreement:** ...

For Camellia Machinery and Equipment Co. Ltd.	For Road Construction Supply Co. Ltd,
(signature)	(signature)

Chapter 12

❖ *Role Play*

Joint Venture

A: Let's get started, OK?

B: Yes, the total amount of investment would be US$18 million. For a project producing carpets, this figure is large enough to provide the construction funds and circulation capital.

A: How much would China be prepared to invest in this venture.

B: We lay out about 51% of the total investment. This includes, of course, cash, factory buildings, the right to use the site, things like that.

A: Is there any regulation on the proportion of investment by foreign investors?

B: The regulation is rather flexible. But the investment by a foreign enterprise should not be less than 25%.

A: l see. How long will a joint venture last?

B: How long do you want?

A: 1 would suggest 10 years to start with. So long as we can rim the plant well, the period can be prolonged later.

B: An important matter I should mention is that the technology you provide should be the newest, and during the duration of the joint venture, you should continue offering us your proved technology.

A: You ask too much, Miss Huang. You certainly realize that technology has a price tag. We spend hundreds of thousands of dollars on scientific research every year. If you ask us to continually offer our improved technology, then you need to pay more for that.

B: You must be very clear that technology should be always improved, otherwise, our products cannot compete with others. And your share is 49% of the capital of the joint venture. That means near half of the profits will go to you. So I believe you certainly want this joint venture to be a successful one.

A: It is really a complex issue. I agree that if new technology is essential to competitiveness, I will share the technology with you.

B: Thank you for your cooperation , Mr. Simon. Oh, it's time for lunch. Shall we adjourn the meeting?

A: OK. Let's leave the remaining details for the next meeting.

I. Answer the following questions.

1. How many relationships are created in an agency agreement?

2. What is self-employed agent abroad? And how is it rewarded?

3. What are the duties of an agent to his principal?

4. What are the advantages of the del credere agent?

5. what is the legal distinction between branches and subsidiaries? And what should be considered when you choose to establish a branch or a subsidiary?

II. Look at the terms in the left-hand column and find the correct definitions in the right-hand column. Write the corresponding letters in the blanks.

1. _____ principal   a. overseas
2. _____ abroad   b. approve
3. _____ contend   c. privilege
4. _____ ratify   d. representative
5. _____ franchise   e. compete
6. _____ agent   f. expertise
7. _____ augment   h. intermediary
8. _____ know-how   i. increase

III. Decide whether the following statements are true or false by writing "T" for true and "F" for false in the bracket besides each statement.

1. (　) The sole distribution agreement is a contract of sale of specific goods and the sole distributor acts as an agent of the manufacturer or trader in the legal sense.

2. (　) Actual authority and apparent authority are quite dependent of one another. Generally they coexist and coincide, and they can't exist without the other.

3. (　) If the confirming house becomes insolvent, the seller can still claim the price from the overseas buyer.

4. (　) If the representation is "exclusive", the principal himself may undertake sales in the territory of the representative on his own account without any liability to the representative.

5. (　) A forwarder may act as a principal or as an agent and they may qualify more often as principals than as agents.

IV. Translate the following sentences into English.

(1) 甲方同意任命乙方为他在越南河内推销下述商品的独家代理商。

(2) 我遗憾地说,值此认识阶段,进行此事的时机尚不成熟。

(3) 甲方同意支付乙方按订单离岸价值3%的佣金。

(4) 本协议的有效期为1年,即从2006年11月1日开始到2007年11月1日结束。

(5) 经郑重考虑,我们不能给你总代理权。

(6) 为销售贵公司的产品,我们已在国内建立起了许多商业网点。

V. Translate the following passage into Chinese.

Co-operation between exporters and commercial agents should be regulated by a formal agreement stating clearly the rights and responsibilities of both parties, if possible including the responsibility for the drawing up and approval of a marketing plan. The agent knows the local market and can provide valuable information. In addition, the tough competitive conditions on the overseas market require an agent who is able to provide customers with immediate service, for example, the technical assistance at an awkward moment. Furthermore, the personal contacts built up over the years by a foreign commercial agent are extremely valuable in introducing new products. The majority of agents work on a commission basis, although in some cases such a commission may well be combined with a fixed fee. Such a system would apply to those cases where an agent commits himself to perform particular assignments, such as drawing up marketing plans, producing advertising material, or warehousing.

VI. Speaking activities.

Discussion: Which points in this passage do you agree or disagree with? And why?

Anyone who has contact with customers is a sales person that includes the telephonist who answers the telephone and the service engineer who calls to repair a machine. So that probably includes you!

The relationship between a sales person and a client is important: both parties want to feel satisfied with their deal and neither wants to feel cheated. A friendly, respectful relationship is more effective than an aggressive, competitive one.

A sales person should believe that his product has certain advantage over the competition. A customer wants to be sure that he is buying a product that is of good value and of high quality. No one in business is going to spend his company's money on something they don't really need.

Some sales people prefer a direct "hard sell" approach, while others prefer a more indirect "soft sell" approach. Whichever approach is used, a good sales person is someone who knows how to deal with different kinds of people and who can point out his product will benefit each individual customer in special ways. A successful sales meeting depends on both the sales person and the customer asking each other the right sort of questions.

Chapter 13

E-commerce

Focal Learning

After the completion of this chapter, you're required to know:
- the definition of e-commerce;
- the brief history of e-commerce;
- the process of e-commerce;
- the classification of e-commerce;
- the distinctive features of each category of e-commerce;
- the advantages and the disadvantages of e-commerce.

Lead-in Vocabulary

network	n.	网络
transaction	n.	交易
tremendously	adv.	极大的
commercialization	n.	商业化
vendor	n.	卖主
renewal	n.	更新
notification	n.	通知,报告
submission	n.	服从
forge	v.	结成
notify	v.	通知
glorified	v.	使……光荣
configure	v.	定购

Chapter 13

Section I
E-commerce and Its Historical Development

1. E-commerce

E-commerce is the direct buying and selling of goods and services, the transfer of funds, the conducting of business communication and transactions over networks. It means using simple, fast, prompt and low-cost electronic communications to transact, without face-to-face meeting between the two parties of the transaction. Now, it is mainly done through Internet and Electronic Data Interchange (EDI). Recently, with the extensively exploitation of computer, the maturity and adoption of Internet, the establishment of secure transaction agreement and the support and promotion by governments, the development of e-commerce is becoming prosperous, with people starting to use electronic means as the media of doing business.

2. Historical Development of E-commerce

E-commerce application had its beginning in the early 1970s, with such innovations as electronic fund transfer (EFT). However, its application was only limited to large corporations, financial institutions and a few daring small business. Then came Electronic Data Interchange (EDI), which expanded from financial transactions to other transaction processing and enlarged the participating companies from financial institutions to manufacturers, retailers, services and so on. Many other applications followed, ranging from stock trading to travel reservation system. Meanwhile, EDI allowed suppliers to exchange information such as prices, inventory, and delivery dates with retailers making it possible to easily track trends, new products, and much more. With the commercialization of the internet in the early 1990s and with its rapid growth, millions of potential customers popped up and the term electronic commerce come into appearance. The following table will illustrate the evolution of e-commerce.

Year	Event
1984	EDI was standardized through ASCX12. This guaranteed that companies would be able to complete transaction with one another reliably.
1992	Computer Server offers online retail products to its customers. This gives people the first chance to buy things using their computers.
1994	Netscape arrived providing users with a simple browser to surf the internet and a safe online transaction technology called Secure Sockets layer (SSL).
1995	Two of the biggest names in E-commerce are launched: Amazon.com and eBay.com.
1998	ADSL or digital subscriber line, provides fast, always on line service to subscriber across California. This prompts people to spend more time and money on line.

1999	Retail spending over the Internet reach $20 million, according to business.com.
2000	The U.S government extended the moratorium on Internet taxes until at least 2005.

(source: http://newmedia. medill.northwest.edu)

Section II
Major Categories of E-commerce

The major types of e-commerce transactions are classified based on the nature of the transaction, which includes business-to-business, business-to-consumer, consumer-to-consumer-to-business, government-to-citizen, government-to-business e-commerce.

1. Business-to-business (B2B) E-commerce

Business-to-business (B2B) market, called wholesaling on line, consists of selling goods and services from one business to another, which includes buying, selling, solicitation and research. The relationship between the businesses can be that of vendor, supplier, and customer.

Among all types of e-commerce, the business-to-business way of doing business electronically through Internet or Electronic Data Interchange has been increasing dramatically in recent years, and the business-to-business e-commerce has become the fastest growing segment within the e-commerce environment. B2B aims at improving and simplifying various business procedures within a company and increasing efficiency of transactions among companies that have business relationship.

2. Business-to-consumer E-commerce

Business-to-Consumer (B2C) e-commerce applies to any business or organization selling retail items or service to its consumer over the internet for their own use, a process sometimes called e-retailing. It has grown to include providing consumers with online services such as online auction, health information and real estate sites and online shopping, allowing consumers to shop and pay their bills online. This type of offering saves time for both retailers and consumers. Amazon.com, the online bookseller, is one of the pioneers in B2C e-commerce. It launched its site in 1995 and quickly took on the major retailers of the U.S.. Its annual sales topped US$150 million in its third year of running a website and a warehouse.

3. Consumer-to-consumer E-commerce

Online consumer-to-consumer e-commerce is another a fast-growing business area. C2C e-commerce refers to the business model that aims at providing a platform to allow an individual to trade or barter goods and services with another individual. Consumers can post their own products online through some agent websites for other consumers to bid. The most famous C2C website is eBay, which allows the consumer to buy a wide range of items.

4. Consumer-to-business E-commerce

Consumer-to-business e-commerce is a special business model on the internet, which involves individuals selling goods or services to businesses. In this case, the consumer may posts his project with a set budget online and within hours, companies review the consumer's requirement and bid on the project. The consumer will review the bids and selects the company that is qualified enough to complete the project.

5. Government-to-citizen E-commerce

Among various kinds of services provided by governments, many of them can be done through electronic media. Providing public services electronically not only provides citizens time-saving and high-quality services, but also improves efficiency and cost effectiveness. Besides, the move can also promote the development of e-commerce. The Government of the Hong Kong Special Administrative Region has launched the Electronic Service Delivery (ESD) Scheme on Internet in December 2000, providing more than 60 kinds of services round the clock. These services include payment of government bills, filing of tax return, voter registration, renewal of driving and vehicle license, change of personal address etc.

6. Government-to-business E-commerce

This mode of trading often describes the way in which government purchases goods and services through electronic media such as Internet. The Electronic Tendering System (ETS) launched in April 2000 by the Government of the Hong Kong Special Administrative Region is an infrastructure to provide online services such as registration of suppliers, tender notification, download facility for tender documents, enquiries handling, submission of tender proposals and announcement of tender results.

Section III
Business Process and Models of E-commerce

1. Business Process of E-commerce

In terms of e-commerce, a customer can order goods or services from a vendor's website, paying with credit cards (the customer enters account information by way of the computer) or with a previously established "cyber-cash account". The transaction information is transmitted to a financial institution for payment clearance and to the vendor for order fulfillment. Personal and account information will be kept confidential through the use of "secured transaction" that use encryption technology.

2. Business Models of E-commerce

The e-commerce business models include e-shops, e-procurement, e-malls, e-auctions, virtual communities, collaboration platforms, third party marketplace, value-chain integrators, value-chain service providers and information brokerage, trust etc. Generally, five distinct e-commerce business models form the basic structure for the wide variety of web sites today. The five categories are respectively vanity, information, advertising, subscription and storefront sites. Some sites focus on one type of business model, while many others sites combine several of the five identified business models.

❖ Vanity Sites

Many websites started as vanity sites, which are often created by individuals as an outlet of self expression, to share a hobby, to find others with the same interests or to promote a cause. When such a site is launched at the beginning, there is no intention of earning money, it is simply a personal site, a blog or a forum on a specific theme. The costs of this business model are covered by the individual himself or by some entities such as universities, communities, associations, libraries and even some business providing service free of charge.

❖ Information Sites

Information sites, also known as brochure or billboard sites, are designed to create awareness of its products or services by way of the web with the actual purchase or transaction taking place offline. Numerous e-commerce web sites in China are implementing such a model. Most corporate web sites benefit by providing information about their products, opportunities, employment, investment, customer services etc. through indirect purchase of the goods or services from existing physical outlets.

❖ Advertising Sites

Advertising models is always applied to network television, radio and many periodical. Advertising on the websites are usually in the form of banners, sponsorships, e-zine ads and other promotional methods.

Although this form of e-commerce model is very common, it is largely unproven on the net. One of the reasons is the shortage of useful, accurate, use-friendly statistics which hinders mass adoption by advertisers.

❖ Subscription Sites

This form is nurtured by publishers and accepted by subscribers. It caters to sites targeted at particular groups of individuals with specific needs. These sites are often specialized with timely information and expert content and the subscription fees fund the development and maintenance of the site.

Subscriptions can be paid on a weekly, monthly or annually basis. Payment carried through a credit card is very common.

❖ Storefront Sites

In terms of storefront sites, it is an electronic version of product catalog offered by websites. The virtual storefronts are built to describe the offer with some pictures and words, some even provide a "shopping cart" to help you to complete the purchase online.

Once the transaction is finished on line, the cyber enterprise arranges for product fulfillment such as delivering, shipping and handling. Now many manufacturers are passing up the intermediary wholesaler and retailers by offering their products directly to the consumers in this way.

Although the vast majority of such sites offer tangible products, they can work for service products, too. The primary characteristic of this model is its capacity to make a one-time purchase with no future obligations.

With consumer increasingly surfing the internet for physical commerce alternatives, all these five models of e-commerce will remain viable in the near future, and each model will continue to mature both in its popularity and sophistication.

Section IV
Advantages of E-commerce

As computer network facilitates information exchange in a speedy and inexpensive way, Internet now penetrates into almost every corner of the world. Small and medium sized enterprises (SMEs) can forge global relationships with their trading partners everywhere in the world. High-speed network makes geographical distance insignificant. Businesses can sell goods to customers outside traditional markets, explore new markets and realize business opportunities more easily. SMEs who cannot afford to establish overseas offices can now increase their exposure to every corner of the world. In general, businesses are lured to e-commerce by the following various factors:

1. Low Operating Cost

E-commerce expands the marketplace to national and international markets. With minimal capital outlay, a company can easily and quickly locate more customers, better suppliers and the most suitable business partners worldwide. The automation of customer service lowers costs, which may make it possible for a company to offer products at a lower price. Specifically, it reduces the staff involvement in routine tasks. With e-commerce, customer and supplier are performing the simpler tasks related to ordering, status checking and tracking, since it is more automated, there should be less errors, thus the quality will be improved. And the direct cost of sale for an order taken from a website is lower than that through traditional means, since there is no human interaction during the online electronic purchase order process. E-commerce decreases the cost for documents preparation, error detection and correction, mail preparation, telephone bill, data entry, overtime and supervision expenses. Also, e-commerce lowers the overhead costs associated with maintaining a brick and mortar (traditional business as opposed to the electronic business of cyberspace) retail outlet. Moreover, there are almost no or marginal sales taxation on the Internet, so everything is a little less expensive than in stores..

2. Large Purchase Per Transaction

For example, online bookseller Amazon. com makes personalized recommendations to customers and, along with every title offered, lists related titles. Another click or two will add one or more titles to all order. These features lead people to buy more books than they might in a traditional bookstore.

3. Integration of Business Procedures

Internet offers companies the ability to make more information available to customers than ever before. For example, a computer company that tracks each unit through the manufacturing and shipping process can allow customers to see exactly where the order is at any time.

4. Flexibility and Availability of Information

Successful websites are not just glorified mail-order catalogs. Internet offers companies the ability to configure products and build custom orders, to compare prices between multiple vendors easily, and to search large catalogs quickly. Moreover, businesses can gather information on products, buyers and competitors through Internet so as to increase their own competitiveness. Detailed client information such as mode of consumption, personal preferences and purchasing power, etc. can help businesses to set their marketing strategies more effectively.

Businesses can maintain their competitive advantage by establishing close contact with their customers and consumers at anytime through Internet by providing the latest information on products and services round the clock. On the other hand, data can be update at anytime, eliminating the problem of out-dated information.

5. Improved Interactions

E-commerce allows customers to interact with other customers in electronic communities and exchange information, ideas as well as compare experience. Internet provides companies with many markets in the cyber world and numerous chances for product promotion. Besides, relationships with buyers can also be enhanced. Online tools allow businesses to interact with customers in ways unheard of before, and at almost instant speeds. For example, customers can receive automatic e-mails to confirm orders and to notify them when orders are shipped. In addition, by the use of multi-media capabilities, corporate image, product and service brand names can be established effectively through the Internet.

Section V
Limitations of E-commerce

E-commerce is a new type of business with many advantages, some organizations are still not involved in it and some consumers are hesitant to purchases online. In order to obtain a comprehensive understanding of e-commerce, the limitations should be observed. They can be classified into technical and non-technical features.

1. Technical Limitations

E-commerce needs extra costs for technological solution compared to traditional modes. Some unstandardized protocols employed in Internet techniques, certain unreliable processes, the insufficient telecommunications bandwidth, unfixed, constantly evolving software tools greatly restrict the development of e-commerce. Moreover, the enterprises need to update their applications constantly and the vendors require certain software to show features on their pages, which is not common in the standard browser used by the majority.

2. Non-technical Limitations

Buying products through the Internet means that you cannot examine products personally and physically. Merely viewing images of the products online involves the risk of uncertainty of the quality of the product. The purchasing privacy and security cannot be guaranteed online, since anything sent over the Internet is sent through several different computers before it reaches its destination, during which unscrupulous hackers will possibly capture credit card or checking account data as it is transferred or break into computers that hold the same information.

Many businesses face cultural, legal and linguistic obstacles, besides some government regulations and standards are not refined enough for many circumstances.

Above all the limitations, the benefits of e-commerce have convinced more and more people to accept it. E-commerce is obviously a promising new trend for many businesses. In such a digital era, it poses challenges to traditional business modes and its current limitations still need to be tackled by practitioners.

Useful Phrases & Technical Terms

electronic data interchange   (EDI) 电子数据交换
electronic fund transfer   (EFT) 电子资金转账
popped up   流行
secure sockets layer   (SSL)
real estate   房地产
electronic service delivery   (ESD) 电子服务输送
electronic tendering system   (ETS) 电子投标系统
unscrupulous hackers   无耻的黑客

Notes

1. E-commerce is the direct buying and selling of goods and services, the transfer of funds, the conducting of business communication and transactions over networks. It means using simple, fast, prompt and low-cost electronic communications to transact, without face-to-face meeting between the two parties of the transaction. Now, it is mainly done through Internet and Electronic Data Interchange (EDI).
电子商务是指通过电子媒体进行的商务活动。这意味着使用简单、快捷、低成本的电子通信手段来进行交易，交易的双方不必进行面对面的会晤。如今电子商务主要是通过因特网和电子数据交换实现。

2. Then came Electronic Data Interchange (EDI), which expanded from financial transactions to other transaction processing and enlarged the participating companies from financial institutions to manufacturers, retailers, services and so on.
电子数据交换技术的发展和使用由处理金融交易扩展到其它贸易领域，从而使参与电子商务的企业从金融行业扩展到生产厂家、零售商与服务行业。

3. Moreover, businesses can gather information on products, buyers and competitors through Internet so as to increase their own competitiveness. Detailed client information such as mode of consumption, personal preferences and purchasing power, etc. can help businesses to set their marketing strategies more effectively.
另外，企业为了提高自身的竞争力，可以通过因特网收集有关产品、买主以及竞争者的信息。详细客户信息诸如消费方式、个人爱好、购买力等能帮助企业更加有效地确定营销策略。

4. As computer network facilitates information exchange in a speedy and inexpensive way, Internet now penetrates into almost every corner of the world. Small and medium sized enterprises (SMEs) can forge global relationships with their trading partners everywhere

in the world. High-speed network makes geographical distance insignificant. Businesses can sell goods to customers outside traditional markets, explore new markets and realize business opportunities more easily.

由于计算机网络能以一种迅速而廉价的方式促进信息的交换,因特网如今已延伸到世界的各个角落。中小型企业能够与世界的贸易伙伴建立联系。高速的网络使地理上的距离变得无关紧要。企业在传统的市场之外就可以更容易地销售货物、探索新的市场并识别商业机会。

5. The major types of e-commerce transactions are classified based on the nature of the transaction, which includes business-to-business, business-to-consumer, consumer-to-consumer, consumer-to-business, government-to-citizen, government-to-business e-commerce etc.

按交易的性质,电子商务可以划分为以下几类:企业对企业的电子商务、企业对消费者的电子商务、消费者对消费者的电子商务、消费者对商业机构的电子商务、政府与公民之间的电子商务、政府与企业之间的电子商务。

6. B2B application aims at improving and simplifying various business procedures within a company and increasing efficiency of transactions among companies that have business relationship.

企业与企业之间使用电子商务改善、简化公司内部或者业务关系公司之间的办事程序,提高交易效率。

7. Consumers can post their own products online through some agent websites for other consumers to bid.

消费者可以通过代理网站将自己的产品发布在网上,以便其他消费者竞价购买。

8. Providing public services electronically not only provides citizens time-saving and high-quality services, but also improves efficiency and cost effectiveness.

为公众提供电子服务不仅能为公民节省时间,提供高质量的服务,还能提高效率,节约成本。

9. The Electronic Tendering System (ETS) launched in April 2000 by the Government of the Hong Kong Special Administrative Region is an infrastructure to provide online services such as registration of suppliers, tender notification, download facility for tender documents, enquiries handling, submission of tender proposals and announcement of tender results.

2000年4月,香港特别行政区政府开始使用电子投标系统,这个系统是一项提供在线服务的基础设施。例如,用它可以做到:供应商登记、招标通告、招标文件的下载工具、询价处理、投标方案的提交以及投标结果的公布。

10. Some unstandardized protocols employed in Internet techniques, certain unreliable processes, the insufficient telecommunications bandwidth, unfixed, constantly evolving software tools greatly restrict the development of E-Commerce.

非标准化的网络协议、不可靠的程序、电信带宽不够、不断变化的软件在很大程度上限制了电子商务的发展。

Practical Drills

❖ Questions for Discussion

1. What are the importance and use of e-commerce?
2. Introduce the Development of the World Wide Web.
3. The following sites include a list of some of the best business sites: http://www.winmag.com/101/standard/cov0048a.htm/ Log on the site and examine five of these sites. How might a small business benefit from this information? What are the differences between these online sites and their offline counterparts?

❖ Case Study

Dell Computer: E-commerce in Action

Dell computer sells computers, hardware and software products directly to its customers. Dell is one of the most successful personal computer manufacturers in the world. Its business model is based on direct just-in-time inventory control system, mass customization and heavy use of the Web. Compared to its competitors, Dell enjoys lower manufacturing cost, high delivering speed, and customized products and services. Dell customers are individuals as well as business customers. Using e-commerce and JIT inventory models, Dell Computer has become the leader in built-to-order systems. In 1996, Dell started selling computers through its website. In 2000, it sold more than 50 million dollars in products each day over the net.

The Dell e-commerce model offers value, quality, mass customization and selection to its customers. Dell targets keeping inventory no more than 8-11 days at its manufacturing facilities. This is in contrast to the industry standard of 80 days. Dell uses the Web to create a community around its supply chain. Dell has created a secure and personalized site and view demand forecasts and other sensitive information. This information enables them to better manage their production schedules. For many of its customers, Dell has also created Premier Pages containing approved configurations, pre-negotiated prices, and new work flow capabilities.

Gigabuy.com, a part of Dell's e-commerce operations, sells a comprehensive list of hardware and software manufactured by Dell and other computer manufacturers. Dell's storefront enables customers to configure their desired computer and then order this system over the Web.

Chapter 13

❖ *Role Play*

Talking about Order On-line

American importer talks with a Chinese Salesman at a trade show, the importer will make the order on-line.

Salesman: Good morning. May I help you?

Importer: I wonder if you can give me more information about your toys ordered on-line?

Salesman: I'd be glad to help. Would you like a packet of our promotional literature?

Importer: Thank you. I see your products are fully made in China.

Salesman: Yes, these models are all turned out in our country.

Importer: These models seem to be quite small.

Salesman: Yes, one of the problems our company was trying to solve when we worked on this model was to do away with its size and weight.

Importer: Remarkable! There is nothing quite like seeing a problem and solving it to create a good product. Are all the components made here in China?

Salesman: Yes. May I ask what company you work for?

Importer: I represent M.E. Company. We're a high-volume, discount line-order house.

Salesman: How about talking with the designers about our upcoming models?

Importer: No, I'm afraid I don't have enough time. I'm due to fly back to the States on Friday.

Salesman: But go to the www. website, you can search for information in detail such as the catalog, sample, prices, shipping...etc. We have a large assortment of items in this line, and it's very convenient to order on line.

Importer: Yes, I think that would be useful. Thank you for your help.

*E*xtended *A*ctivities

I. Answer the following questions.

1. How many types of e-commerce are mentioned in the text? And what are they?
2. Which type of e-commerce is worthy of paying the most attention to?
3. What kind of benefits do e-commerce have?
4. What limitation do e-commerce have?
5. Why does e-commerce become prosperous in recent years?

II. Look at the terms in the left-hand column and find the correct definitions in the right-hand column. Write the corresponding letters in the blanks.

1. ____ shift   a. a person who sells something he has bought

2. _____ return   b. a person, team business organization, firm etc., trying to do better than another or others
3. _____ feedback   c. money received
4. _____ patron   d. strong belief; trust
5. _____ faith   e. a change in position or direction
6. _____ revenue   f. a series of numbers or letters that represent a scientific rule
7. _____ competitor   g. a person who uses a particular shop, hotel, etc., esp. regularly
8. _____ reseller   h. profits or income from investment
9. _____ vendor   i. advice, criticism, etc., about how successful or useful something is
10. _____ formula   j. a person who sells

III. Translate the following technique terms into Chinese.

1. digital mechanisms   2. American Online
3. EDI (Electronic data interchange)   4. online catalogue
5. electronic wallet   6. internet marketing
7. broadband network   8. office application
9. information retrieval   10. commercial network

IV. Fill in the blanks with the words or expressions given below, and change their forms where necessary.

| alliance | apply | get into | explosive | faith |
| feedback | plunge | respond | bet on | revenue |

1. Personal computers are common even to children thanks to the industry's _____ growth.
2. The economy is not what it was. Many of the restrictions no longer _____.
3. Since there are a lot of fake goods, we should buy something in good _____.
4. To managers, _____ from employees is always import, for example, ideas for new products, changes for existing products, public feeling about prices, quality, etc.
5. I've sent a reminder to ask for the repayment. Do you think they _____ in time?
6. John always _____ into risky ventures without thinking about the possible results.
7. Oil _____ has risen with the rise in the dollar.
8. Relief workers in _____ with local charities are trying to help people in great poverty.
9. The individual may be buying the option because of a desire to speculate in pound's, _____ an increase in the pound's value.
10. We should keep on developing new products and try to make them _____ the international market as soon as possible.

V. Translate the following sentences into Chinese.

1. Write a program that will let academics from across the world share information on a single site.
2. There have always been things that people are good at and things that computers have been good at. But there is little overlap between the two.
3. One of the things computers were not able to do was to store contacts from different sources. The dream behind the Web is of a common place in which we communicate by sharing information.
4. The Web is valuable because it uses a common computer language to reach people and share information.
5. New features like Web browsers and search engines were developed.

VI. Translate the following passage into Chinese.

B2B e-commerce is companies buying from and selling to each other. online. But there's more to it than purchasing. It's evolved to encompass supply chain management as more companies outsource parts of their supply chain to their trading partners.

Which business units should be involved in a B2B project? Definitely the units that do purchasing. B2B e-commerce can drastically change how buyers do their jobs, especially if your company is one that still places orders the old fashioned way. Sales and customer service departments will need to be involved with projects that affect how you receive and process orders from customers. And don't forget the folks who manage your inventory. You may need to get other departments involved, too, depending on the functionality you're building.

Fundamentals of GATT and WTO

Focal Learning

After the completion of this chapter, you're required to know:
- the basics of GATT;
- the objectives, functions and basic principles of WTO;
- the structure of WTO;
- the outline of WTO agreements.

Lead-in Vocabulary

dispute	n.	争议,争端
arbitration	n.	仲裁
litigation	n.	诉讼
conciliation	n.	调解
negotiation	n.	商议,谈判
protocol	n.	草案,协议
forum	n.	论坛,讨论会
transparency	n.	透明,透明度
signatory	n.	签字者,签名者
ratification	n.	批准

Section I
A Brief Introduction to GATT

Towards the end of the Second World War, a number of international negotiations were set in motion in order to create institutional structures for the conduct of international relations in the post-war world. One of the most important negotiating processes at the time was the United Nations Conference on Trade and Employment held in Havana, Cuba, in 1947, after lengthy preparatory stages in New York, London and Geneva. At end of the Conference, the Havana Charter for the International Trade Organization was adopted. Due to the United States' failure to ratify the Havana Charter, the Charter never entered into force. As part of the negotiations on the Havana Charter, a group of countries engaged in tariff negotiations and in 1947 agreed on substantial tariff reductions.

Prior to the entry into force of the Havana Charter, a mechanism was needed to implement and protect the tariff concessions negotiated in 1947. To do so, it was decided to take the Chapter on Commercial Policy of the Havana Charter and convert it, with certain additions, into the General Agreement on Tariffs and Trade. To bring the GATT into force, a Protocol of Provisional Application was developed. Thus, the GATT was born, as a provisional agreement until such time as the Havana Charter would be ratified.

The protocol of Provisional Application of the General Agreement on Tariffs and Trade was signed by 23 countries. It entered into force on January 1st, 1948. Throughout its 48-year history, the GATT provided the structure for a global process of steady trade liberalization through eight "round" of multilateral trade negotiations sponsored by its Contracting parties, covering progressively larger volumes of international trade.

Table 5

GATT Trade Rounds

	Year	Place/name	Subjects covered	Number of countries
1	1947	Geneva	Tariffs	23
2	1949	Annecy	Tariffs	13
3	1951	Torquay	Tariffs	38
4	1956	Geneva	Tariffs	16
5	1960—1961	Geneva (Dillon Round)	Tariffs	16
6	1964—1967	Geneva (Kennedy Round)	Tariffs and antidumping measures	62
7	1973—1979	Geneva (Tokyo Round)	Tariffs, non-tariff measures, "framework" agreements	102
8	1986—1994	Geneva (Uruguay Round)	Tariffs, non-tariff measures, rules, services, intellectual property, dispute settlement, textiles, agriculture, creation of WTO, etc.	123

Section II
A Brief Introduction to WTO

The WTO is the only global international organization dealing with the rules of trade between nations.

WTO is one of the results of Uruguay Round, and was established in the light of the Marrakesh Agreement Establishing the World Trade Organization, which is included in the Final Act Embodying the Results of the Uruguay Round of Multilateral Trade Organizations. The Marrakesh Agreement entered into force on 1 January 1995. By December, 2001, the WTO had 144 members. At the same time, the WTO had more than 30 governments observers which were in the process of acceding to the World Trade Organization.

1. Objectives, Functions and Basic Principles of WTO

❖ **Objectives**

WTO basic objectives are similar to those of GATT, which has become part of WTO. These objectives have been expanded to deal with trade in services. Furthermore, they clarify that, in promoting economic development through the expansion of trade, adequate attention has been paid to protecting and preserving the environment.

In its preamble, the Agreement Establishing the World Trade Organization reiterates the objectives of GATT. These are:

(1) to raise standards of living;

(2) to ensure full employment of members' economies;

(3) to promote the steady growth of real incomes and effective demand in their markets;

(4) to expand the production of and trade in goods and services.

❖ **Functions**

The Agreement establishing WTO provides that it should perform the following five functions:

(1) Facilitating Implementation, Administration and Operation of the Covered Agreements

The WTO facilitates the implementation, administration and operation of the WTO Agreement and the Multilateral Trade Agreements, and furthers their objectives. It also provides the framework, for those of its Members that have accepted them, for the implementation, administration and operation of the Plurilateral Trade Agreements.

(2) Providing the Forum for Negotiations on Multilateral Trade

The WTO provides the forum for negotiations on multilateral trade relations in matters covered by its various agreements. It may also, on decision by the Ministerial Conference, provide a forum for further negotiations, and a framework for the implementation of their results, on other issues arising in the multilateral trade relations among its Members.

(3) Dispute Settlement

The WTO administers the integrated dispute settlement system, which is a central element in providing security and predictability to the multilateral trading system, serving to preserve the rights and obligations of the Members of the WTO.

(4) Review of National Trade Policies

The WT0 administers the Trade Policy Review Mechanism, which is designed to contribute to greater transparency and understanding of the trade policies and practices of WTO Members, to their improved adherence to the rules, disciplines and commitments of the multilateral trading system, and hence to the smoother functioning of the system.

❖ Basic Principles

The WTO agreements are lengthy and complex because they are legal texts covering a wide range of activities. They deal with: agriculture, textiles and clothing, banking, telecommunications, government purchases, industrial standards and product safety, food sanitation regulations, intellectual property, and much more. But a number of simple, fundamental principles run throughout all of these documents. These principles are the foundation of the multilateral trading system.

(1) Non-discrimination

The basic principles of the multilateral trading system, as embodied in the WTO Agreement, derive mostly from the principles that constituted the foundations of the GATT. Trade without discrimination is one of these basic principles, guaranteed through the operation of various clauses included in the multilateral agreements on trade in goods, in the GATS, and in the TRIPs Agreement.

(2) Transparency

Provisions on notification requirements and the Trade Policy Review mechanism are set out in the WTO Agreement and its Annexes, with the objective of guaranteeing. The fullest transparency possible in the trade policies of its Members in goods, services and the protection of intellectual property rights. Article X Of GATT 1994 deals with the publication and administration of trade regulations; Article III of GATS sets out provisions on transparency as one of the general obligations and disciplines under that agreement; and Article III establishes transparency rules for the TRIPs Agreement.

(3) Predictable and growing access to markets

Predictable and growing access to markets for goods and services is an essential principle of the WTO. This principle is fulfilled through various provisions so as to guarantee security, predictability and continued liberalization of trade.

(4) Most-Favored-Nation Treatment (MFN)

The most-favored-nation clause has been the pillar of the system since the inception of the GATT in 1947. The Contracting Parties to the GATT 1947 were bound to grant to the products of other contracting parties treatment no less favorable than that accorded to products of any other country. Members of the WTO have entered into similar commitments, under the GATT 1994 for trade in goods, under the GATS in relation to treatment of service suppliers and trade in services, and under the TRIPs.

(5) National Treatment

The national treatment principle condemns discrimination between foreign and national goods or services and service suppliers or between foreign and national holders of intellectual property rights. GATT 1994 and the TRIPs Agreement provide for national treatment as one of the main commitments of WTO Members. Imported goods, once duties have been paid, must be given the same treatment as like domestic products in relation to any charges, taxes, or administrative or other regulations. With regard to the protection of intellectual property rights, and subject to exceptions in existing international conventions. Members of WTO are committed to grant to nationals or other Members treatment no less favorable than that accorded to their own nationals. GATT, however, due to the special nature of trade in services, deals with national treatment under its Part III. Specific Commitments, where national treatment becomes a negotiated concession and may be subject to conditions or qualifications that Members have inscribed in their schedules on specific commitments in trade in services.

2. WTO Structure

The structure of the WTO is dominated by its highest authority, the Ministerial Conference, composed of representatives of all WTO members, which is required to meet at least every two years and which can take decisions on all matters under any of the multilateral trade agreements.

The day-to-day work of the WTO, however, falls to a number of subsidiary bodies; principally the General Council, also composed of all WTO members, which is required to report to the Ministerial Conference. As well as conducting its regular work on behalf of the Ministerial Conference, the General Council convenes in two particular forms—as the Dispute Settlement Body, to oversee the dispute settlement procedures and as the Trade Policy Review Body to conduct regular reviews of the trade policies of individual WTO members.

The General Council delegates responsibility to three other major bodies—namely the Councils for Trade in Goods, Trade in Services and Trade-Related Aspects of Intellectual Property. The Council for Goods oversees the implementation and functioning of all the agreements (Annex 1A of the WTO Agreement) covering trade in goods, though many such agreements have their own specific overseeing bodies. The latter two Councils have responsibility for their respective WTO agreements (Annexes 1B and 1C) and may establish their own subsidiary bodies as necessary.

Three other bodies are established by the Ministerial Conference and report to the General Council. The Committee on Trade and Development is concerned with issues relating to the developing countries and, especially, to the "least-developed" among them. The Committee on Balance of Payments is responsible for consultations between WTO members and countries which take trade-restrictive measures, under Articles XII and XVIII of GATT, in order to cope

Chapter 14

with balance-of-payments difficulties. Finally, issues relating to WTO's financing and budget are dealt with by a Committee on Budget.

Each of the four plurilateral agreements of the WTO—those on civil aircraft, government procurement, dairy products and bovine meat—establish their own management bodies which are required to report to the General Council.

Table 6

WTO Structure

- Ministerial
- Geneva
  - General Council meeting as Trade Policy Review Body
  - General Council meeting as .
    - Council for Trade in Goods
    - Council for Trade-related Aspects of Intellectual Property
    - Council for Trade in Services

Committees on
Trade and Environment
Trade and Development
Subcommittee on least-Developed Countries
Regional Trade Agreements
Balance of Payments
Restrictions Budgets,
Finance and Administration

Working parties on
Accession

Working groups on
The relationship between Trade and Investment
The interaction between Trade and Competition Policy
Transparency in Government Procurement

Committee on
Market Access
Agriculture
Sanitary and Phytosanitary Measures
Technical Barriers to Trade
Subsidies and Countervailing Measures
Anti-Dumping Practice
Customs Valuation
Rules of Origin
Import Licensing
Trade-Related Investment Measures
Safeguard

Textiles Monitoring Body
Working parties on
State-Trading Enterprises

Committee on
Trade in Financial Services
Specific Commitments

Working parties on
Domestic Regulation
GATS Rules

Plurilaterals
Committee on Trade in Civil Airaft Committee on Government

Key
—Reporting to General Council (or a subsidiary)
—Reporting to Dispute Settlement Body
—Plurilaterals Committees inform The General Council of their Activities although these agreements are not sighed by all WTO members

219

❖ Representation in the WTO and Economic Groupings

The work of the WTO is undertaken by representatives of member governments but its roots lie in the everyday activity of industry and commerce. Trade policies and negotiating positions are formulated in capitals, usually with a substantial advisory input from private firms, business organizations, farmers as well as consumer and other interest groups. Most countries have a diplomatic mission in Geneva, sometimes headed by a special Ambassador to the WTO, whose officials attend meetings of the many negotiating and administrative bodies at WTO headquarters. Sometimes expert representatives are sent directly from capitals to put forward their governments' views on specific questions.

As a result of regional economic integration—in the form of customs unions and free trade areas—and looser political and geographic arrangements, some groups of countries act together in the WTO with a single spokesperson in meetings and negotiations.

The largest and most comprehensive grouping is the European Union and its 15 member states. The EU is a customs union with a single external trade policy and tariff. While the member states coordinate their position in Brussels and Geneva, the European Commission alone speaks for the EU at almost all WTO meetings. The EU is a WTO member in its own right as are each of its member states.

A lesser degree of economic integration has so far been achieved by the countries which are GATT members of the Association of South East Asian Nations (ASEAN)—Malaysia, Indonesia, Singapore, Philippines, Thailand and Brunei Darussalam. Nevertheless, they have many common trade interests and are frequently able to coordinate positions and to speak with a single voice.

Among other groupings which occasionally present unified statements is the Latin American Economic System (SELA) and the African, Caribbean and Pacific Group (ACP). More recent efforts at regional economic integration, for instance, NAFTA (Canada, US and Mexico) and MERCOSUR (Brazil, Argentina, Paraguay and Uruguay)—have not yet reached the point where their constituents frequently have a single spokesperson on WTO issues.

A well-known alliance in the Uruguay Round—bringing together a similarity of trade interests rather than a regional identity—was the Cairns Group which comprised, and still comprises, agricultural exporting nations from developed, developing and East European countries.

❖ How the WTO Takes Decisions

The WTO continues a long tradition in GATT of seeking to make decisions not by voting but by consensus. This procedure allows members to ensure their interests are properly considered even though, on occasion, they may decide to join a consensus in the overall interests of the multilateral trading system. Where consensus is not possible, the WTO agreement allows for voting. In such circumstances, decisions are taken by a majority of the votes cast and on the basis of "one country, one vote".

There are four specific voting situations envisaged in the WTO Agreement. First, a majority of three-quarters of WTO members can vote to adopt an interpretation of any of the multilateral trade agreements. Second, and by the same majority, the Ministrial Conference, may decide to waive an obligation imposed on a particular member by a multilateral agreement. Third, decisions to amend provisions of the multilateral agreements can be adopted through approval either by all members or by a two-thirds majority depending on the nature of the provision concerned. However, such amendments only take effect for those WTO members which accept them. Finally, a decision to admit a new member is taken by a two-thirds majority in the Ministerial Conference.

❖ The WTO Secretariat and Budget

The WTO Secretariat is located in Geneva. It has around 450 staff and is headed by its Director-General, Mr. Renato Ruggiero, and four deputy directors-general. Its responsibilities include the servicing of WTO delegate bodies with respect to negotiations and the implementation of agreements. It has a particular responsibility to provide technical support to developing countries, and especially the least-developed countries. WTO economists and statisticians provide trade performance and trade policy analyses while its legal staff assists in the resolution of trade disputes involving the interpretation of WTO rules and precedents. Much of the Secretariat's work is concerned with accession negotiations for new members and providing advice to governments considering membership.

The WTO budget is around US$83 million (105 million Swiss Francs) with individual contributions calculated on the basis of shares in the total trade conducted by WTO members. Part of the WTO budget also goes to the International Trade Centre

3. An Outline of the WTO Agreements

The WTO agreements are the founding charter of the organization and the basis for everything the WTO does. Most of the WTO's agreements were outcome of the 1986-1994 Uruguay Round. Some, including GATT 1994, were revisions of texts that previously existed under GATT as multilateral or plurilateral agreement. Some, such as GATS, were new. The full package of multilateral Uruguay Round agreements is called the round's Final Act are available in the legal Texts of the WTO.

Marrakesh Agreement Established the World Trade Organization. It called for a single institutional frame work encompassing the GATT, as modified by the Uruguay Round, all agreements and arrangements concluded under its auspices, and the complete results of the Uruguay Round. Institutionally, it is headed by a Ministerial Conference meeting at least once every two years. A General Council oversees the operations of the agreement and Ministerial decisions on a regular basis. This General Council acts as a Dispute Settlement Body and a Trade Policy Review Mechanism, which concern themselves with full range of trade issues covered by the WTO, and has also established subsidiary bodies such as a Goods Council, and a TRIPs Council. The WTO framework ensures a "single undertaking approach" to the results of the Uruguay Round.

Useful Phrases & Technical Terms

GATT—General Agreement on Tariffs and Trade	关税与贸易总协定
WTO—World Trade Organization	国际贸易组织
multilateral trade organizations	多边贸易组织
plurilateral agreement	复边贸易协议
MFN treatment	最惠国待遇
ministerial conference	部长级会议
committee	委员会

Notes

1. The Uruguay Round 乌拉圭回合

   It is the 8th round of multilateral trade negotiations concerning the GATT. The Uruguay Found concluded in December 1993 after seven years of talks with 117 member nations. The major goals of the Uruguay Round were to reduce barriers to trade in goods; to strengthen the role of GATT and improve the multilateral trading system; to increase the responsiveness of GATT to the evolving international economic environment; to encourage cooperation in strengthening the inter-relationship between trade and often economic policies affecting growth and development and the establishment of a multilateral framework of principles and rules for trade in services, including the elaboration of possible disciplines for individual service sectors.

2. Ministerial Conference 部长级会议

   A conference composed of the representatives of all WTO members at ministerial level which is to meet at least once every two years. It has authority to take decisions on all matter under any of the multilateral trade agreement under its jurisdiction. The five ministerial conferences so far have been held in Singapore, Geneva, Seattle, Doha, and Cancun.

3. Dispute Settlement Body 解决争端机构

   The WTO General council, when it convenes to settle disputes arising between members. The DSB has sole authority to establish panels, adopt panel and appellate reports, maintain surveillance of implementation of rulings and recommendations, and authorize retaliation in cases where its recommendations are ignored.

4. Appellate Body 受理上诉机构

   A standing body of seven persons established under the WTO understanding on rules and procedures governing the Settlement of Disputes to hear appeals arising from panel cases. The grounds for such appeals are confined to pointes of WTO law. The Appelate Body members are persons of recognized authority with the demonstrated expertise in law, international trade and relevant WTO agreements who are not affiliated with any government.

5. TRIPs Agreement TRIPS 协议是世贸组织中一部重要的知识产权保护文件，它对我国的商标立法和执法都产生了重大影响

The Program on technical cooperation in the area of Agreement on Trade-related Aspects of Intellectual Property Rights (TRIPS) aims at improving understanding of the development implications of the TRIPS Agreement, and strengthening the analytical and negotiating capacity of developing countries so that they are better able to participate in TIPRs-related negotiations in an informed fashion in furtherance of their sustainable development objects.

Practical Drills

❖ Questions for Discussion

1. What are the main principles of GATT?
2. What are core issues facing WTO?
3. How do you understand free trade?

❖ Case Study

China and WTO

China was one of the 23 orginal signatories of the GATT in 1948. After China's revolution in 1949, the government in Taiwan announced that China would leave the GATT system. Although the government in Beijing never recognized this withdrawal decision, nearly 40 years later in 1986, China notified the GATT of its wish to resume its status as a GATT Contracting Party.

On 10 November, 2001, the Doha Ministerial Conference approved by consensus the text of the agreement for China's entry into the WTO. After notifying the WTO of its ratification of its membership, China has become the WTO's 143rd full member as of 11 December, 2001.

The WTO accession has a great impact on the development of China:

1. Opportunity

(1) Be offered multilateral, unconditional and stable MFN treatment by all WTO Members. As a developing country, China will obtain some preferential treatment or transition arrangement accorded by the WTO. All these privileges will provide support for China's industries which have competitive advantages to exploit the foreign markets.

(2) As a full member, China will take part in all negotiations regarding various areas, stipulating and amending the relative regulations as well as the construction of the system of the multilateral trade system. Thus China will have more says in world affairs, especially trade areas to safeguard China's position and legal privileges in world trade.

(3) By making use of the mechanism and procedures of trade dispute settlement of the WTO, China can solve trade disputes with other countries more fairly and reasonably.

(4) By making use of the WTO forum, China may publicize its policy of reform and opening to the outside world, actively develop cooperation and communication with other countries in the field of economics, trade and technology.

2. Challenge

China shall undertake its obligations of reducing customs tariffs, publishing trade restrictions measures, opening services market, enlarging protection scopes of intellectual property rights and eliminating the restrictions in introducing foreign capitals. Thus many protection environments will no longer exist. All in all, China's domestic market will be opened more widely to foreign enterprises. Some industries with higher cost and disadvantages in non-price factors will be thrashed.

With WTO entry and increased competition from the world market, the immediate future for Chinese farmers doesn't look any better. According to WTO negotiations, foreign exporters are given the right to sell and distribute their products directly to consumers.

China has also agreed to cap its future spending on farm subsidies at 8.5% of the value of domestic farm production. By 2004, duties on agriculture products will fall from 22% to 17%, and on US priority products from an average 31% to 14%.

China will cut import tariffs on products such as rape oil, butter, mandarins and wine from 25% to 80% to a range of 9% to 18%.

The major losers because of tariff cuts and relaxed imports will be domestic grains like corn and soybeans which must compete with higher quality imports. The livestock industry will also face challenges from cheaper meat imports.

 Role Play

At the Trade Show

An American importer talks with a Chinese salesman at a trade show.

Salesman: Good morning. May I help you?
Importer: I wonder if you can give me more information about this computer model you're showing?
Salesman: I'd be glad to help. Would you like a packet of our promotional literature?
Importer: Thank you. I see your computer is fully IBM compatible.
Salesman: Yes, this model can run any software or DOS program an IBM personal computer can run.

Importer: These models seem to be quite small.
Salesman: Yes, one of the problems our company was trying to solve when we worked on this model was to do away with he bulk of IBM desk-tops and their clones. Our computer is only 11 pounds.
Importer: Remarkable! There's nothing quite like seeing a problem and solving it to create a good product. Are all the components made here in China?
Salesman: Yes, we do some subcontracting, but only in China. These computers are made here. May I ask what company you work for?
Importer: l represent Reese Computer and Supply Company. We're a high-volume, discount mail order house.
Salesman: Would you like to tour our factory and perhaps even one or two of our subcontractors?
Importer: Yes, if it wouldn't take too long to arrange. I'm due to fly back to the States on Friday.
Salesman: I'm sure we can arrange it before then. How about meeting the founder of our company? Would you be interested in talking with him about our ideas for upcoming models?
Importer: Yes, l think that would be useful. Thank you for your help.

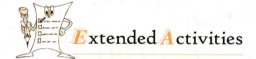

Extended Activities

I. Answer the following questions.

1. When was WTO established?
2. What are the new areas of activity of WTO?
3. What are WTO's objectives?
4. What are WTO's main functions?
5. What are the basic principles that WTO members must follow?
6. What is anti-dumping?
7. What do you think about WTO's structure?

II. Look at the terms in the left-hand column and find the correct definitions in the right-hand column. Write the corresponding letters in the blanks.

1. _____	trade dispute	a. opposing or intended to regulate business monopolies, such as trusts or cartels
2. _____	tariff	b. trade controversy
3. _____	dumping	c. the union of two or more commercial interests or corporations

4. _____ regionalism   d. duties or a duty imposed by a government on imported or exported goods
5. _____ merger   e. the sale of goods abroad at below the price charged for comparable goods in the producing country
6. _____ disintegration   f. loyalty to the interests of a particular region
7. _____ antitrust   g. the act or process of disintegrating

III. Decide whether the following statements are true or false by writing "T" for true and "F" for false in the bracket besides each statement.

1. (   ) The Uruguay Round allows countries to take limited steps to safeguard national industries.
2. (   ) The WTO stressed the importance of rules.
3. (   ) The new legal procedure for resolving disputes of WTO is different from the GATT procedure.
4. (   ) The WTO's dispute settlement procedure aims to resolve trade disputes through impartial panels after they start trade wars.
5. (   ) The US law known as Section 301 authorizes the US to retaliate unilaterally against other countries which it judges are violating a GATT provision or unfairly restricting the import of US goods or services.
6. (   ) Competition policy is not a hard issue at WTO panels.
7. (   ) Regional trading blocks have impact on global politics.
8. (   ) There is no division between the US, EU and Japan—and the many developing countries who are the majority of the WTO's members on labor standards and environmental policy.

IV. Fill in the blanks below with the most appropriate terms from the box.

| agreement | negative | issue | bilateral | negotiations |
| population | disputes | accession | domestic | |

Agriculture is the most sensitive __(1)__ in the WTO negotiations and caused the most difficult in reaching an __(2)__, as it has with other WTO member countries. Conflicts and __(3)__ on agricultural problems always result in lengthy __(4)__ among not only the developed countries themselves but also between developing countries and developed nations. China is a developing country with the largest __(5)__ in the world. Most Chinese people still live in the countryside. Many people are worried that Chinese farmers endowed with small plots of land and backward technology cannot compete with large farmers equipped with modem technology in advanced countries. such as the United States, Canada, and Australia. and that WTO __(6)__ will have substantial __(7)__ impacts on Chinese agriculture. They give US evidence that current prices of grain in Chinese markets ale already dose to or even exceed world market prices. For example, on March

1999, the price of corn in the __(8)__ market Was RMB 1. 44/kg on average; however, the average price in the Chicago Future Market Was equivalent to RMB 0. 72/kg. Therefore, some anxiety about the agricultural impact of WTO entry is understandable.

In the __(9)__ agreement between China and the U.S., agricultural trade occupies a premier position. Since the agricultural agreement with the U.S. is most comprehensive and has received most public attention, I will base my discussion mainly on the agreement between China and the U.S., supplemented the agreement between China and the EU only when it is necessary.

V. Translate the following sentences into English.
(1) 环保主义者认为如果全球变暖和雨林保护等问题不同等考虑的话,商业目的将胜出,环境就会遭殃。
(2) 无条件最惠国待遇始于2000年,它为加入WTO铺平了道路。
(3) 令美国沮丧的是,评审团裁决日本没有违反WTO规则,因为在政府行为和日本的市场结构之间没有联系。
(4) 所有国家都享有公认的保护国家利益的权利,但是这个原则以及他们对WTO规则的理解都可能存在很大的差别。
(5) 一个被审讯团裁定违反贸易规则的国家可以向审理上诉的机构进行上诉。

VI. Translate the following passage into Chinese.
While the WTO, like GATT, represents a multilateral approach to trade liberalization, regional trade agreements have grown in importance in the post-war period. These are formed between countries in a broad geographic area, such as the continents of Europe and North America. They are designed to bring down trade barriers among their member states, thus opening up regional markets for national producers. However, their impact can be much broader, as strong regional markets can have a significant impact on world trade patterns. Political considerations also play a key role, as economic integration is inseparable from the political power balance within any region, and regional trading blocks are influential in global politics.

VII. Speaking activities.
Oral presentation
Form groups of three or four and prepare jointly for the oral presentation topic below. Then vote for a representative in a group to make a 8-15 minute presentation before the whole class.

China now has entered the WTO. Many people say the WTO membership of China is like a double-edged sword which brings opportunities and challenges to China's economy. And now many people are concerned about the economic safety of China. What is your view on this argument? How can China make good use of WTO membership and meanwhile protect its economy?

Chapter 1

I. Answer the following questions.
   Omitted.

II. Look at the terms in the left-hand column and find the correct definitions in the right-hand column. Write the corresponding letters in the blanks.
   1. c   2. a   3. h   4. b
   5. g   6. d   7. e   8. f

III. Decide whether the following statements are true or false by writing "T" for true and "F" for false in the bracket besides each statement.
   1. F   2. F   3. T   4. F   5. T   6. T   7. T

IV. Complete the following diagram according to what you have read in the text.

Types of Trade Restrictions

Trade restriction
- Tariffs
  - Revenue tariff vs. Protection tariff
  - Import duty vs. Export duty
  - Import surtax
    - Countervailing
    - Anti-dumping
    - Variable levy
- Non-tariff
  - Quota
  - License
  - Advance deposit
  - Foreign exchange control
  - Technical standards
  - Health & sanitary regulations

Keys

V. **Translate the following sentences into English.**

(1) Trading globally gives consumers and countries the opportunity to be exposed to goods and services not available in their own countries.

(2) International trade allows wealthy countries to use their resources—whether labor, technology, or capital—more efficiently.

(3) Multinational firms, as opposed to local ones, undertake their business operations on a global basis.

(4) For recent years, China has registered fast and sustained growth in foreign trade volumes.

(5) International trade continues to be dominated by advanced industrialized countries, the trade volume of which accounts for over half of the world's total.

VI. **Translate the following passage into Chinese.**

经济"全球化"是一个历史过程,是人类创新和技术进步的结果。它是指全世界各国经济之间,特别是通过贸易和金融活动,实现的不断加强的一体化。有时候这个词汇也指人员和知识的跨国境流动。更广泛的讲,也存在着文化、政治和环境的方面全球化,这里就不予讨论了。

从根本上说,全球化并没有什么神秘的。自从20世纪80年代以来,这个词汇就已经被经常使用了,反映了技术的进步,使国际交易——贸易和金融活动——更快更容易地完成。它是指几个世纪以来一直活跃于各层次人类经济活动中的市场力量在国外的延伸(或拓展)。

VII. **Speaking activities.**

Omitted.

Chapter 2

I. **Answer the following questions.**

Omitted.

II. **Look at the terms in the left-hand column and find the correct definitions in the right-hand column. Write the corresponding letters in the blanks.**

1. b   2. a   3. g   4. h
5. e   6. e   7. f   8. d

III. **Decide whether the following statements are true or false by writing "T" for true and "F" for false in the bracket besides each statement.**

1. F   2. F   3. T   4. T   5. F   6. F

IV. **Fill in the blanks below with the most appropriate terms in appropriate forms from the box.**

1. relating to   2. work on   3. involves
4. otherwise   5. are conscious of   6. put into practice

V. Explain the following terms in English.

1. International subcontracting—is a cross between licensing and investment, and is also known as outsourcing or contract manufacturing. In subcontracting, a company gets the technology of a product from an independent manufacturer in a foreign target country and subsequently markets that product in the target country or elsewhere

2. Tender—is an offer or proposal to purchase a specified quantity of a commodity for a specified price.

3. Counter-trade—is an "umbrella" (general) term covering all forms of trade whereby a seller or an assignee is required to accept goods or services from the buyer as either full or partial payment. International counter-trade is a practice whereby a supplier commits contractually as a condition of sale to reciprocate and undertake certain specified commercial initiatives that compensate and benefit the buyer.

4. Compensation agreement—an agreement whereby an exporter will accept a specified amount of products from the importer as a full or partial payment in kind.

5. ITT—studies cover the economic relationship between a transferor and a transferee, as well as a whole series of related issues, such as the relevant national policies and legal framework of the nations in the world.

VI. Translate the following sentences into English.

(1) In the absence of exchange reserves or credit, or the possibility of negotiating another type of agreement, the only alternative is barter.

(2) In the event of unforeseen economic developments, parts of the agency contract may be changed by mutual agreement.

(3) After the Second World War, there emerged various forms of cross border business activities such as trade in goods and services, foreign direct investment and technology transfer, etc.

(4) Before entering into a licensing agreement, the licensor should have a thorough knowledge of the laws and regulations concerning the intellectual property rights in the licensee's country.

(5) If one part of the contract has been breached, it does not necessarily mean a termination of the entire contract.

(6) The representative will be assigned a specific territory. He will have to limit his activities to this area.

VII. Translate the following passage into Chinese.

技术转让有很多特点。第一,商业性的技术转让有很高的垄断性。目前的专利制度又进一步加强了这种垄断。技术的所有者为了维护其技术和产品的优势,通常不会转让技术,除非一些特殊的情况。比如当转让是占领市场的必要手段时,或转让对其垄断不构成威胁时。另外,科技发展不平衡的结果是发达国家为了维护其统治地位总是对先进技术的转让施加很多限制。

VIII. Speaking activities.

Omitted.

Chapter 3

I. **Answer the following questions.**

Omitted.

II. **Match the questions with their corresponding actions required.**

1. c   2. a   3. d   4. f   5. e   6. b

III. **Decide whether the following statements are true or false by writing "T" for true and "F" for false in the bracket besides each statement.**

1. T   2. T   3. F   4. F
5. F   6. F   7. F   8. F

IV. **Fill in the blanks below with the most appropriate terms from the box.**

1. adhere to   2. at the heart of   3. made strides in
4. in breach of   5. at stake, in terms of 6. access to
7. left out   8. come to   9. lead to

V. **Explain the following terms in English.**

1. Exporting—is the process of earning money by providing the right product at the right price at the right time in the right place beyond your home boundary.

2. License agreement—a business arrangement in which the manufacturer (the licensor) of a product (or a firm with proprietary rights over certain technology trademarks, etc,) grants permission to some other group or individual to manufacture that product (or make use of that proprietary material, trademark, manufacturing process, patent, etc,) in return for specified royalties or other payment for the firm granting the license.

3. Franchising agreement—which is a legal and commercial relationship between the owner of a trademark or trade name (the franchisor) and individual or group who wants to use that identification in business (the franchisee). The franchisor generally provides business expertise and the franchisee provides a way for the overall business to grow.

4. Joint venture—which is a type of partial structural integration in which one or more separate organizations combine resources to achieve a stated objective. The participating companies share ownership of the venture and responsibility for its operations, but usually maintain separate ownership and control over their operations outside of the joint venture.

VI. **Translate the following sentences into English.**

(1) This contract is signed by the authorized representatives of both parties on Dec. 9, 1999. After signing the contract, both parties shall apply to their respective Government Authorities for ratification. The date of ratification last obtained shall be taken

as the effective date of the Contract. Both parties shall exert their utmost efforts to obtain the ratification within 60 days and shall advise the other party by telex and thereafter send a registered letter for confirmation.

(2) We are willing to enter into business relationship with your company on the basis of equality and mutual benefit.

(3) We have been working on expanding our scope of cooperation with China.

(4) If you agree to our proposal of a barter trade, we'll give you paper in exchange for your timber.

(5) We may agree to do processing trade with you.

(6) Success means increasing the total amount of exports. It also means diversifying those exports—not only in terms of products, but also in terms of products, but also in terms of export markets.

(7) This extension of the trader's domain is highly important, since it enables the vendee to make a choice between alternative goods in satisfying his needs.

VII. Translate the following passage into Chinese.

　　一个国家必须从其擅于生产的产品的出口中获得盈余，以便它可以进口那些没有比较优势的产品。猎人将自己的剩余物和农民进行交换，而这种交易是建立在物物交换基础之上的。现在，无论在国内，还是在国际上，大多数贸易都用货币交换。

　　在从事出口贸易方面，尤其是在国家的层面上，许多目标被提了出来。然而，从事出口贸易的终极目标就是盈利。如果不能盈利，那么，其他的目标也就无从谈起。成本支出必须低于销售收入。如果不能的话，公司的资源就会流失，公司就会枯竭甚至消亡。从长远来看，为了使公司长久存在下去，收入必须超过成本。出口会产生巨额利润，但它也会涉及很大的风险。总之，不管是国家、公司或是个人都会在出口中得到很多好处。这个看似简单的问题不一定人人都明白。

VIII. Speaking activities.

　　Omitted.

Chapter 4

I.　Answer the following questions.
　　Omitted.

II.　Choose the best correct answers.

　　1. A　　2. B　　3. A　　4. B　　5. A
　　6. C　　7. C　　8. D　　9. C　　10. C

III.　Decide whether the following statements are true or false by writing "T" for true and "F" for false in the bracket besides each statement.

　　1. T　　2. F　　3. F　　4. F'　　5. F
　　6. F　　7. F　　8. F　　9. T　　10. F

Keys

IV. **Complete the following diagram according to what you have read in the text.**

INCOTERMS 2000

Categories of Terms	Name of Specific Terms
Group E	Ex Works(EXW)
Group F	1. Free Carrier(FCA) 2. Free Alongside Ship (FAS) 3. Free On Board (FOB)
Group C	1. Cost and Freight (CFR) 2. Cost, Insurance and Freight (CFR) 3. Carriage paid to (CPT) 4. Carriage and Insurance Paid to(CIP)
Group D	1. Delivered At Frontier(FAS) 2. Delivered Ex Ship (DES) 3. Delivered Ex Quay (DEQ) 4. Delivered Duty Unpaid (DDU) 5. Delivered Duty Paid (DDP)

V. **Translate the following sentences into English.**

(1) The buyer will assume all costs and risks and make arrangements associated with the transport of the goods, and must make payment according to the contract terms

(2) If other modes of transport are involved, these terms do not apply, even if one of the legs of the journey is by ship.

(3) In a CFR contract, the seller has the usual FOB obligations, and after the vessel is loaded the seller is absolved from liability for damage to the cargo.

(4) The seller's responsibility for costs and risk of loss will end when the rail car or truck trailer is loaded, or in the case of sea or air transport, when the goods are delivered to the carrier for loading.

(5) Normally the buyer will make arrangements for further transportation, though the contract might specify that the seller will make such arrangement.

VI. **Translate the following passage into Chinese.**

那些只在国内做生意的人避免了许多困扰国际贸易上任的问题。那些完全从事国内贸易的人避免了文化冲突之外，还免除了由法律、语言和商业管理不同引起的麻烦。国际商务法庭是一个通过诉讼解决大量误解合同的纠纷而且代价颇高的地方。

VII. **Speaking activities.**

Omitted.

Chapter 5

I. Check the following letter of credit with the given contract terms.

1. "at 90 days after sight" should read "at 60 days after sight".
2. "CFR Shanghai" should read "FOB Shanghai".
3. Contract number should be "97/51" instead of "97/54".
4. Delete insurance clause
5. "Freight Prepaid" should be "Freight to Collect"

II. Fill in the Blanks below with the most appropriate terms from the box.

1. guilty of   2. comply with   3. has no intention of   4. turned down
5. In the event of   6. take place   7. in question   8. associated with
9. broken down into   10. In principle

III. Look at the terms in the left-hand column and find the correct definitions in the right-hand column. Write the corresponding letters in the blanks.

1. d   2. f   3. p   4. j   5. h   6. g   7. a   8. c
9. e   10. i   11. b   12. k   13. n   14. o   15. l

IV. Decide whether the following statements are true or false by writing "T" for true and "F" for false in the bracket besides each statement.

1. F   2. F   3. F   4. T   5. T   6. T   7. T

V. Complete the following diagram according to what you have read in the text.

Works that Needs to be Done Before and After Making Offers
(From the Perspective of the Exporter)

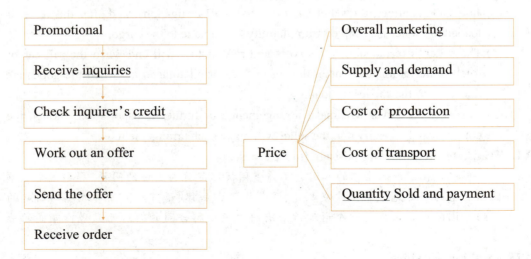

VI. Translate the following sentences into English.

(1) The company may prefer to submit quotes in the form of a pro-forma invoice for ease of administration as the pro-forma details can be simply transferred to a commercial invoice when the order is placed.

(2) Once the quotation has been submitted to the buyer, the exporter is committed to fulfilling all the terms contained within the document should an order be placed on the strength of it.

(3) The buyer, understandably, pointed out that the contract had been agreed and that the exporter was bound to its terms.

(4) Difficulties may arise when the purchasing company also includes its standard terms and conditions and tries to gain the upper hand.

(5) The exporter is advised to prepare some standard terms and conditions of sale that can be incorporated into the documentation in addition to the specific terms of the contract.

VII. Translate the following passage into Chinese.

运用出口成本计算以帮助出口商在考虑了所有的附加费用之后明确他们公司产品在目标市场上的竞争力。出口成本也叫"着陆成本",他们提供给出口商商品的总成本的目录分类,这样他们可以找出可以节省成本的地方来提高竞争力。出口成本应该被看作是这个公司财务计划活动的一个主要部分,尤其是在现金流预测方面,因为一个准确的成本计算会使公司考虑与打入市场相关的所有成本。

VIII. Speaking activities.

Omitted.

Chapter 6

I. Answer the following questions.

Omitted.

II. Translate the following terms into Chinese.

毛重	净重	公量	理论重量
公制单位	唛头/运输标志	货物	按规格销售
按样品销售	按说明销售	指示性标志	警告标志

III. Translate the following indicative handling terms into Chinese.

1. 重心居中   2. 勿摔   3. 最多堆数   4. 易碎品
5. 小心轻放   6. 勿近热源   7. 保持冷冻   8. 远离冷气
9. 保持干燥/防潮 10. 勿使用吊钩 11. 在此处吊钩 12. 此面向上

IV. Fill in the following blanks with an appropriate word (the begining letters of some words are given).

with   table   professional   around   cost-effective   Further   maintaining   serves   by   including

V. Translate the following Chinese sentences into English.

1. The green beans can be supplied in bulk or in gunny bags.
2. As you know, a large number of the bedspreads we ordered from you last year were found soiled when they reached us. I hope you will take necessary precautions in

packing this consignment.

3. We asked the factory to use stronger cartons and double straps.

4. Buyers see the package and its contents as a whole.

5. Your packing must be seaworthy and can stand rough handling during transit.

VI. Translate the following into Chinese.

1. 事实上,所有制造或加工出来的货物在它们的生产和经销阶段都需要包装。

2. 公司应该做出既满足客户和公司的目标,又不违背社会利益的决策。

3. 那些有意或无意泄露公司机密的人都会受到严惩。

4. 随函附上我们的产品清单一份,相信贵方会对其中某些商品感兴趣。

5. 取消价格管制以后,几乎所有商品和服务的成本都剧增了。

VII. Complete the following diagram according to what you have read from the text.

KE- The abbreviated name of importer

47- The code of the type of merchandise

001-The contract number

CF- The abbreviation of the country of export.

Chapter 7

I. Answer the following questions.

Omitted.

II. Look at the terms in the left-hand column and find the correct definitions in the right-hand column. Write the corresponding letters in the blanks.

1. d   2. f   3. b   4. a   5. h   6. g   7. e   8. c

III. Read the following pairs of sentences carefully and discuss with partner the different meanings of the words in each pair.

1. (A) 制度   (B) 海关

2. (A) 晚会   (B) 参与方,当事人

3. (A) 可商量的   (B) 可流通 / 转让的

4. (A) 句子   (B) 条款

5. (A) 成熟   (B) 到期

6. (A) 名称   (B) 所有权

7. (A) 草稿   (B) 汇票

8. (A) (得到)接受   (B) (得到)承兑

IV. Read the following passage and fill in the brackets with appropriate words, the first letter of some of them has been given.

movement   documentation   international   required   exceptions

authorities   merchandise   exporter   freight   License

certificate   customs

Keys

V. Decide whether the following statements are true or false by writing "T" for true and "F" for false in the bracket besides each statement.

1. F 2. F 3. T 4. T 5. T 6. T 7. T 8. F

VI. Translate the following sentences into English.

1. The draft is simply an instrument that requests payment.
2. As a financial instrument, the letter of credit benefits both importers and exporters.
3. Sight drafts as the name implies, require the bank to pay on demand.
4. As a document of title, a bill of lading can be used by the exporter as a means of obtaining payment.
5. The inspection principally covers such aspect as quality, quantity and packing of the products.
6. The quality of your goods shall be strictly up to the sample. Any goods inferior to the sample shall be rejected.
7. Inspection can be conducted either in export country or in import country.
8. Please work on our order without delay and advise US a few days prior to its completion, so that we may send you our shipping instructions in good time.

VII. Translate the following into Chinese.

为了保证及时得到支付，出口商在提示单据之前应该仔细核查所有的单据。总的来说，重要的是要保持与同一交易有关的所有单据之间的一致性。例如，对货物的描述，货物的价值以及不同单据中的其它条款都应该相同。如果是用跟单信用证，那么所有的单据都应该根据信用证的条款制备。当逐个讨论单据时，应给出更多的细节。

Chapter 8

I. Answer the following questions.

Omitted.

II. Please define the following terms in English, if necessary, please refer to the text.

1. general cargo vessel is built to carry various types of cargoes.
2. OBO (ore/bulk/oil) carrier is a multipurpose vessel for large volume of bulk cargoes.
3. oil tanker is specially designed to carry crude oil or fuel oil.
4. refrigerated ship is built with refrigerating facilities inside the ship for carrying perishable cargoes.
5. timber ship has spacious holds and heavy lifts for carrying timber or wood logs.

III. Translate the following sentences into Chinese.

1. 运输就是通过陆路、铁路、空路和水路承载乘客和货物。良好的运输对贸易来说至关重要，因为食物、原材料及其他商品必须尽可能既快捷又便宜地从生产商运到批发商和消费者手中。

2. 航空运输业支持的业务范围广泛。
3. 许多不同国家的运输公司组成了一个协会叫"航运工会",它有许多成员国,装运量占世界总额的 50% 以上。航运工会的宗旨是保护自己和发货人的利益。
4. 出口商必须考虑各种不同的影响运输条件的因素,例如费用、安全、速度和便利条件等。
5. 海运至今仍然是最普遍的运输方式之一,从能源来讲也是最有效的形式。对于长途运大批量货物来说,作为一种廉价的运输方式,它还是具有吸引力的。

IV. Fill in each blank of the following sentences with one of the words or phrases in the list given below and make changes if necessary.

1. raw   2. reliable   3. cycle   4. convenience   5. In terms of
6. isolation 7. as well as   8. advantage   9. obstacle   10. trying up

V. Read the following passage and fill in the blanks with appropriate words (some words are given the first letter or first several letters).

1. risk   2. containerization   3. consignment   4. utilization   5. stacked

Chapter 9

I. Answer the following questions.
    Omitted.

II. Look at the terms in the left-hand column and find the correct definitions in the right-hand column. Write the corresponding letters in the blanks.

1. d   2. e   3. a   4. j   5. h
6. b   7. i   8. g   9. f   10. c

III. Complete the following sentences by translating the parts given in Chinese.

1. automobile insurance is of more recent origin
2. Should the claim occur
3. that risk management has to overcome
4. more health insurance than other insurances
5. To purchase insurance
6. only slightly more than 30% insurance companies.

IV. Fill in the blanks(1)—(8) with the most suitable information about Marine Cargo Transport Insurance given in the text.

(1) Expenses   (2) Extraneous risks   (3) Partial loss
(4) Additional coverage   (5) Natural calamity   (6) Actual total loss
(7) Free From Particular Average   (8) All Risks

V. Fill in each blank of the following sentences with one of the words or phrases in the list given below and make changes if necessary.

loss   accident   reduce   admit   insurance

VI. Decide whether the following statements are true or false by writing "T" for true and "F" for false in the bracket besides each statement.

1. T 2. F 3. F 4. F 5. F
6. F 7. F 8. T 9. F 10. F

VII. Complete the following charts according to what you have learned from the text.

Insurance Value   Coverage   Rates   an insurance policy   claim

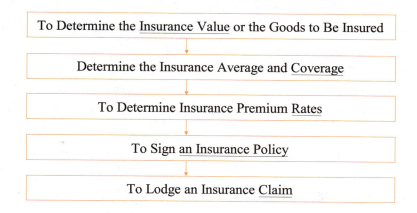

Chapter 10

I. Answer the following questions.
Omitted.

II. Choose the correct answers.

1. C 2. A 3. A 4. A 5. B
6. A 7. B 8. D 9. B 10. B

III. Decide whether the following statements are true or false by writing "T" for true and "F" for false in the bracket besides each statement.

1. T 2. F 3. F 4. T 5. T
6. F 7. F 8. T 9. F 10. F

IV. The following is a list of special terms. After reading it, you should find the items equivalent to those given in Chinese in the table below.

1. E 2. O 3. B 4. D 5. J
6. L 7. F 8. N 9. G 10. C

V. Translating the following sentences into Chinese.

1. 在提示汇票时,受票人通过在汇票正面标注"承兑"字样,他的签名以及承兑日期而由此承担了在汇票到期日付款的义务。
2. 支票的抬头可以是"凭指定",持票人,或者划两道平行线仅用于帐户的转存,或者由付款行保兑。

3. 通过在信用证中指定一家付款行,开征行授权该银行在信用证规定的或者可以计算出来的日期付款并且承诺在到期日偿付那家银行。
4. 由于这笔订购数量相当大,我们希望90%的信用证金额凭单据即付,其余部分试车证明令人满意后再付款。
5. 如届时我们仍未收到你方信用证,我公司将撤消该售货确认书并要求你公司偿还我们为你公司代付的仓储费用。

VI. Translating the following sentences into English.
1. We require full payment within 45 days with a 15% discount for cash payment in advance.
2. We shall open a letter of credit in your favour, to be settled in US dollars.
3. If after-sale service would be provided, we agree to make payment in full.
4. The terms of payment we wish to adopt are confirmed and irrevocable letter of credit.
5. You can refuse payment in case the documents are not in conformity with the contract.

Chapter 11

I. Answer the following questions.
Omitted.

II. Term Translation.

claim	force majeure	arbitration clause	chief arbitrator
hear a case	apply for arbitration	International Chamber of Commerce(ICC).	tribunal
award	Veterinary Inspection Certificate	Sanitary Inspection Certificate	the port of shipping
penalty clause	landed quality and weight	inspection agency	

III. Decide whether the following statements are true of false according to the text. If it is true, please write "T" in the blanks beside each statement, otherwise "F".
1. F 2. F 3. T 4. T 5. F 6. F 7. F 8. F

IV. Read the following passage and fill the blank with one word, some of which the first letter has been given.
dispute   final   parties   cooperation   obtained   awards   subject
recognition   signed   Convention   contracting   proceedings   arbitrators

V. Translate the following sentences into Chinese.
1. 一般说来,双方的分歧可通过友好磋商解决。
2. 以北京商检局的检验报告为依据,兹向你方提出索赔。
3. 本证明所列商品,其品质经我们检验,结果如下:特此证明。
4. 买方就这批货物的短装问题,向卖方提出索赔2500美元。
5. 这种产品与样品之间的偏差是在正常的允许范围内,因此,索赔不予受理。

VI. Translate the following sentences into English.
1. If the importer finds through inspection that the quality of the goods does not coincide

with that stipulated in the contract, he/ she may refuse to accept the goods.

2. They inspected the goods for any possible shortage.
3. Shipping quality is to be certified by and subject to thew Inspection Certificate issued by GCIB.
4. Your products are of poor quality, which is far below the standard that can be sold in this market.
5. We duly received the 30 cases of instant coffee you dispatched us, but regret to say that on inspection, four of them were found to be badly damaged, apparently attributable to faulty packing.

VII. **Complete the following chart according to the text.**
arbitrators   a case   an award

Chapter 12

I. **Answer the following questions.**
Omitted.

II. **Look at the terms in the left-hand column and find the correct definitions in the right-hand column. Write the corresponding letters in the blanks.**
1. d   2. a   3. e   4. b   5. c   6. h   7. i   8. f

III. **Decide whether the following statements are true or false by writing "T" for true and "F" for false in the bracket besides each statement.**
1. T   2. F   3. T   4. T   5. F

IV. **Translate the following sentences into English.**
(1) Party A agrees to appoint Party B to act as its sole agent in Hanoi, Vietnam for the sale of the under-mentioned commodity.
(2) I regret to say that, at this get-acquainted stage, such an arrangement would be rather premature.
(3) Party A agree to offer Party B a commission of 3% on the basis of FOB value of orders.
(4) This agreement is to remain in force for a period of one year, i.e. commencing on November1, 2006 and terminating on November 1, 2007.
(5) After serious consideration, we can't grant you the general agency.
(6) We have built up a lot of well-established business net workers for the sale of your products in our country.

V. **Translate the following passage into Chinese.**
出口商与商业代理之间的合作，应当通过一个正式协议来制约。这一协议应清楚地注明双方之间的责任与权利，如可能，协议中还应有拟定和批准的推销计划。代理商了解当地市场，并能提供有价值的信息。另外，国外市场激烈的竞争环境要求代理商能够为顾客提供及时的服务，比如在出现问题时提供技术援助。再者，代理商在当地市场上建立了多年的私人关系,这对向该市场介绍新产品极为重要。大多数代理商向委托商收取佣金,在某些情况下,佣金还要加上固定的费用。这一制度是用于代理商负责执行某些特定的任务,如制定推销计划、制作广告材料或安排货物仓储等。

VI. Speaking activities.

Omitted.

Chapter 13

I. Answer the following questions.

Omitted.

II. Look at the terms in the left-hand column and find the correct definitions in the right-hand column. Write the corresponding letters in the blanks.

1. e   2. h   3. i   4. g   5. d
6. c   7. b   8. a   9. j   10. f

III. Translate the following technique terms into Chinese.

1. 数字机制   2. 美国在线公司
3. 电子数据交换   4. 在线目录
5. 电子钱包   6. 网络营销
7. 宽带网络   8. 办公软件
9. 信息检索   10. 商业网络

IV. Fill in the blanks with the words or expressions given below, change their forms where necessary.

1. explosive   2. apply   3. faith   4. feedback   5. will respond
6. plunges   7. revenue   8. alliance   9. betting on   10. get into

V. Translate the following sentences into Chinese.

(1) 编一个程序让世界各地的学术机构都能在网上某一固定场所分享信息。

(2) 人和计算机总是各有所长,但是共有的长处却很少。

(3) 计算机还不能把不同信号源的接触点储存起来。万维网的梦想就是建立一个我们能够分享信息进行交流的共同空间。

(4) 万维网的价值就在于它使用一种通用的计算机语言,为人们相互之间的沟通和信息共享提供了便利条件。

(5) 网上浏览器和搜索引擎等新装置被开发出来。

VI. Translate the following passage into Chinese.

　　企业间的电子商务就是企业在网上彼此间进行的买卖。但不仅只是购买。企业间的电子商务已经发展到对供应链的管理阶段,因我更多的企业都把自己的部分供应链提供给贸易伙伴。

　　一个 B2B 项目将涉及哪些商业部门?与做生意相关的部门无疑都会涉及。特别是当你的公司是一个以老式方式处理订单的公司时,B2B 电子商务会彻底改变顾客的行为方式。销售和顾客服务部门与影响你从顾客那里接受和处理订单方式的项目有联系。不要忘记管理你库存的人。也可能与其他相关部门有联系,这取决于你所建立系统的功能。

Chapter 14

I. **Answer the following questions.**
   Omitted.

II. **Look at the terms in the left-hand column and find the correct definitions in the right-hand column. Copy the corresponding letters in the blanks.**
   1. b   2. d   3. e   4. f   5. c   6. g   7. a

III. **Decide whether the following statements are true or false by writing "T" for true and "F" for false in the bracket besides each statement.**
   1. T   2. T   3. T   4. F   5. T   6. F   7. T   8. F

IV. **Fill in the blanks below with the most appropriate terms from the box.**
   1. issue   2. agreement   3. disputes   4. negotiations   5. population
   6. accession   7. negative   8. domestic   9. bilateral

V. **Translate the following sentences into English.**
   (1) Environmentalists argue that if issues such as global warning and protection of the rain forests are not brought into the equation, commercial goals will win out and the environment will suffer.
   (2) Unconditional MFN status came in 2000, paying the way for WTO membership.
   (3) To the dismay of the US, the panel decided that Japan's market structure has nothing to do with its government behavior.
   (4) All countries enjoy a recognized right to safeguard national interests, but this principle, as well as the interpretation of WTO rules themselves, is subject to considerable latitude in interpretation.
   (5) A country found to be in breach of trade rules by a panel may appeal to the Appellate Body.

VI. **Translate the following passage into Chinese.**
   虽然世界贸易组织像关贸总协定一样代表了贸易自由化的多边解决办法,但是地区贸易协议的重要性在战后变得越来越显著。在更广泛的地理区域中,例如欧洲和北美大陆,国家间达成了地区贸易协议。他们的目的是在成员国之间减少贸易壁垒,以便向国内生产者开放地区市场。但是,他们的影响要深远得多,因为强大的地区市场能够对世界贸易格局产生重大影响。政治成分也起着关键作用,因为任何地区内的经济融合都是与政治力量的平衡不可分的。而且地区贸易障碍对全球的政治也产生影响。

VI. **Speaking activities.**
   Omitted.

Appendix

Appendix 1-1

销售确认书
Sales Contract

卖方 **SELLER:**　　　　　　　　　　　　　　　编号 **NO.:**
　　　　　　　　　　　　　　　　　　　　　　　日期 **DATE:**
　　　　　　　　　　　　　　　　　　　　　　　地点 **SIGNED IN:**

买方
BUYER:

买卖双方同意以下条款达成交易：
This contract is made by and agreed between the BUYER and SELLER, in accordance with the terms and conditions stipulated below.

1. 商品号 Art No.	2. 品名及规格 Commodity & Specification	3. 数量 Quantity	4. 单价及价格条款 Unit Price & Trade Terms	5. 金额 Amount

允许　　　　　　溢短装，由卖方决定
With　　　　　　More or less of shipment allowed at the sellers' option

6. 总值
   Total Value
7. 包装
   Packing
8. 唛头
   Shipping Marks
9. 装运期及运输方式
   Time of Shipment & means of Transportation
10. 装运港及目的地
    Port of Loading & Destination
11. 保险
    Insurance
12. 付款方式
    Terms of Payment
13. 备注
    Remarks

　　　　　　The Buyer　　　　　　　　　　　　　　　　　　**The Seller**

Appendix 1-2

货物进口合同
Purchase Contract

编号(No.): _____
签约地(Signed at): _____
日期(Date): _____
卖方(Seller): _____
地址(Address): _____
电话(Tel): _____ 传真(Fax): _____
电子邮箱(E-mail): _____
买方(Buyer): _____
地址(Address): _____
电话(Tel): _____ 传真(Fax): _____
电子邮箱(E-mail): _____

  买卖双方经协商同意按下列条款成交:
  The undersigned Seller and Buyer have agreed to close the following transactions according to the terms and conditions set forth as below:

1. 货物名称、规格和质量(Name, Specifications and Quality of Commodity)
2. 数量(Quantity)
3. 单价及价格条款(Unit Price and Terms of Delivery)

除非另有规定,"CFR"和"CIF"均应依照国际商会制定的《2000 年国际贸易术语解释通则》(INCOTERMS 2000)办理)。

The terms CFR or CIF shall be subject to the International Rules for the Interpretation of Trade Terms (INCOTERMS 2000) provided by International Chamber of Commerce (ICC) unless otherwise stipulated herein.

4. 总价(Total Amount)
5. 允许溢短装(More or Less) _____ %
6. 装运期限(Time of Shipment)

收到可以转船及分批装运之信用证_____天内装运。
Within _____ days after receipt of L/C allowing transshipment and partial shipment.

7. 付款条件(Terms of Payment)

买方须于_____前将保兑的、不可撤销的、可转让的、可分割的即期付款信用证开到卖方,该信用证的有效期延至装运期后—天在中国到期,并必须注明允许分批装运和转船。

By Confirmed, Irrevocable, Transferable and Divisible L/C to be available by sight draft to reach the Seller before _____ and to remain valid for negotiation in China until _____ after the Time of Shipment. The L/C must specify that transshipment and partial shipments are allowed.

买方未在规定的时间内开出信用证,卖方有权发出通知取消本合同,或接受买方对本合同未执行的全部或部分,或对因此遭受的损失提出索赔。

The Buyer shall establish a Letter of Credit before the above-stipulated time. failing which, the Seller shall have the right to rescind this Contract upon the arrival of the notice or to accept whole or part of this Contract non-fulfilled by the Buyer, or to lodge a claim for the direct losses sustained,if any:

8. 包装(Packing)
9. 保险(Insurance)

    按发票金额的_____%投保_____险,由_____负责投保。

    Covering_____Risks for_____110%of Invoice Value to be effected by the_____.

10. 品质/数量异议(Quality/Quantity Discrepancy)

    如买方提出索赔,凡属品质异议须于货到目的口岸之日起 30 天内提出,凡属数量异议须于货到目的口岸之日起 15 天内提出,对所装货物所提出的任何异议于保险公司、轮船公司、其他有关运输机构或邮递机构所负责者,卖方不负任何责任。

    In case of quality discrepancy, claim should be filed by the Buyer within 30 days after the arrival of the goods at port of destination, while for quantity discrepancy, claim should be filed by the Buyer within 15 days after the arrival-of the goods at port of destination. It is understood that the Seller shall not be liable for any discrepancy of the goods shipped due to causes for which the Insurance Company, Shipping Company, other Transportation Organization/or Post Office are liable.

11. 由于发生人力不可抗拒的原因,致使本合约不能履行,部分或全部商品延误交货,卖方概不负责。本合同所指的不可抗力系指不可干预、不能避免且不能克服的客观情况。

    The Seller shall not be held responsible for failure or delay in delivery of the entire lot or a portion of the goods under this Sales Contract in consequence of any Force Majeure incidents which might occur. Force Majeure as referred to in this contract means unforeseeable, unavoidable and insurmountable objective conditions.

12. 仲裁(Arbitration)

    因凡本合同引起的或与本合同有关的任何争议应通过友好协商解决,如果协商不能解决,应提交中国国际经济贸易仲裁委员会xxx分会。按照申请仲裁时该会当时施行的仲裁规则进行仲裁。仲裁裁决是终局的,对双方均有约束力。

    Any dispute arising from or in connection with the Sales Contract shall be settled through friendly negotiation. In case no settlement can be reached, the dispute shall then be submitted to China International Economic and Trade Arbitration Commission(CIETAC), XXX Commission for arbitration in accordance with its rules in effect at the time of applying for arbitration. The arbitral award is final and binding upon both parties.

13. 通知(Notices)

    所有通知用_____文写成,并按照如下地址用传真/电子邮件/快件送达给各方。如果地址有变更,一方应在变更后——日内书面通知另一方。

    All notices shall be written in _____ and served to both parties by fax/e. mail/courier according to the following addresses. If any changes of the addresses occur, one party shall inform the other party, of the change of address within _____ days after the change.

14. 本合同为中英文两种文本,两种文本具有同等效力。本合同一式_____份。自双方签字（盖章）之日起生效。

This Contract is executed in two counterparts each in Chinese and English, each of which shall be deemed equally authentic. This Contract is in _____ copies effective since being signed/sealed by both parties.

The Seller：   The Buyer：

卖方签字：   买方签字：

Shifeng Double-Star Tire CO., LTD.

NO.1 HUIXINROAD, GAOTANG COUNTY, SHADONG, CHINA
TEL 0635-3992377   FAX 0635-3992377

COMMERCIAL INVOICE

THE SELLER: SHIFENG DOUBLE-STAR TIRE CO.,LTD. INVOICE NO :TP050710-1
THE BUYER: QINGDAO NAMA INDUSTRIAL CO.,LTD. DATE: JUN.12, 2005
S/C NO.:TP050710-1

FROM QINGDAO, CHINA TO SAUDI ARABIA

NO. OF 40'HC	DESCRIPTION	QUANTITY (SETS)	UNIT PRICE (US$/SETS) FOB LIAOCHENG	AMOUNT (US$)
	750-16-8/17.27KG	7020	17.3000	121,446.00
	TOTAL	7020		121,446.00

AMOUNT IN WORDS: SAY U.S.DOLLAR ONE HUNDRED TWENTY ONE THOUSAND FOUR HUNDRED AND FORTY SIX ONLY.

Appendix 2-2

Commercial Invoice

TO:

INVOICE NO.:
INVOICE DATE:
S/C NO.:
S/C DATE:

FROM: _____ TO: _____
Letter of Credit No.: _____ Issued By: _____

Marks and Numbers	Number and kind of package / Description of goods	Quantity	Unit Price	Amount
SAY TOTAL:	**Total:**			

Appendix 3

Proforma Invoice

TO:

INVOICE NO.: _____
INVOICE DATE: _____
S/C NO.: _____
S/C DATE: _____

TERM OF PAYMENT: _____
PORT TO LOADING: _____
PORT OF DESTINATION: _____
TIME OF DELIVERY: _____
INSURANCE: _____
VALIDITY: _____

Marks and Numbers	Number and kind of package Description of goods	Quantity	Unit Price	Amount

SAY TOTAL: **Total Amount:**

BENEFICIARY:
ADVISING BANK:
NEGOTIATING BANK:

Appendix 4

Shipper	BILL OF LADING B/L No.:
Consignee	**COSCO**
Notify Party	中 国 远 洋 运 输 公 司
	CHINA OCEAN SHIPPING COMPANY

*Pre carriage by	*Place of Receipt	
Ocean Vessel Voy. No.	Port of Loading	ORIGINAL
Port of discharge	*Final destination	Freight payable at	Number original Bs/L

Marks and Numbers	Number and kind of packages; Description	Gross weight	Measurement m3

TOTAL PACKAGES(IN WORDS)

Freight and charges

Place and date of issue
Signed for the Carrier

*Applicable only when document used as a through Bill of Loading

Letter of Credit

凭
Drawn under ....

信用证
L/C NO ....

日期
Dated .... 支取 Payable with interest @.......%....... 按...... 息....... 付款

号码 汇票金额 宁波
NO...........................Exchange for Ningbo,............................20...................

见票..日后(本汇票之副本未付)付交

AT...........................sight of this FIRST of Exchange (Second of Exchange being unpaid)

Pay to the order of   the sum of

款已收讫
Value received ....
....

此致
TO: ....
....

Bibliography

曹菱主编,《外贸英语实务》,北京:外语教学与研究出版社,2000年。
程达军、李延玉,《国际贸易实务》,北京:高等教育出版社,2006年。
顾乾毅,《商贸英语》,广州:华南理工大学出版社,2003年。
国际商会中国国家委员会,《2000年国际贸易术语解释通则》,上海:中信出版社,2000年。
何泽荣编,《国际金融原理》,成都:西南财经大学出版社,2004年。
胡涵钧,《国际经贸实务》,上海:复旦大学出版社,2002年。
江春,《商务谈判英语》,北京:首都经济贸易大学出版社,2002年。
黎孝先,《国际贸易实务》,北京:对外经济贸易大学出版社,2003年。
梁树新、张宏,《国际贸易实务案例评析》,济南:山东大学出版社,2000年。
廖力平、廖庆薪,《进出口业务与报关》,广州:中山大学出版社,2000年。
廖瑛,《国际商务英语—商务理论》《语言与实务》,长沙:中南大学出版社,2004年。
刘法公,《国际贸易实务英语》,杭州:浙江大学出版社,2002年。
刘园、李志群,《国际商务谈判》,北京:中国对外贸易出版社,2001年。
马克态,《商务谈判:理论与实务》,北京:中国国际广播出版社,2003年。
孟祥年,《国际贸易实务操作教程》,北京:对外经济贸易大学出版社,2002年。
潘丽等,《国际贸易专业英语》,哈尔滨:哈尔滨工业大学出版社,2005年。
裘国芬,《国际商务英语洽谈》,上海:上海交通大学出版社,2000年。
屈韬,《外贸单证处理技巧》,广州:广东经济出版社,2000年。
帅建林、刘攀,《国际金融(英文版)》,成都:西南财经大学出版社,2005年。
帅建林,《国际结算教程(英文版)》,成都:西南财经大学出版社,2004年。
帅建林,《国际贸易惯例案例解析(中英文)》,北京:对外经济贸易大学出版社,2006年。
孙湘生、易浥,《国际贸易实务》,北京:清华大学出版社,北京交通大学出版社,2005年。
檀文茹,《国际贸易专业英语》,北京:对外经济贸易大学出版社,2005年。
田翠欣、张付先,《轻松学习外贸英语》,天津:天津科技翻译出版公司,2000年。
王沅沅,《国际贸易实务》,北京:高等教育出版社,2005年。
邬性宏,《国际商务英语教程》,上海:复旦大学出版社,2001年。
武义海,《粮油食品外贸实务英语》,北京:中国纺织出版社,2004年。
熊伟,《国际贸易实务英语》,武汉:武汉大学出版社,2001年。
熊伟,《国际贸易实务英语》,武汉:武汉大学出版社,2004年。
徐进亮,《国际商务惯例与案例》,南宁:广西科学技术出版社,2000年。
许葵花,《国际贸易英语教程》,西安:西安交通大学出版社,2003年。
杨国俊、邱革加,《现代商务关系英语》,北京:中国国际广播出版社,2003年。
杨丽华、董俊英,《贸易实务英语》,北京:首都经济贸易大学出版社,2000年。
叶乃沂,《新编经济管理专业英语》,成都:西南交通大学出版社,2002年。
尹翔硕,《国际贸易教程(第二版)》,上海:复旦大学出版社,2002年。

袁永友,《国际商务经典案例》,北京:经济日报出版社,2001年。

赵薇,《国际结算:国际贸易融资支付方法》,南京:东南大学出版社,2003年。

周玮、朱明,《国际贸易结算单据》,广州:广东经济出版社,2002.年。

周耀宗、庄学艺,《进出口业务概要》,上海:上海外语教育出版社,2000年。

Charles W L H. *International Business*. The McGraw-Hill Companies, 2000 2th Edition, Pearson Education, Inc., 2002

A. E. Branch. *Dictionary of Shipping International Business Trade Terms and Abbreviations*. London: Witherby & Co. Ltd, 1995.

A. E. Branch. *Elements of Shipping*. London: Chapman & Hall, 1996.

A. E. Branch. *Export Practice and Management*. Florence: Thomson Learning, 4th edition, 2000.

A. E. Branch. *International Purchasing*. Florence: Thomson Learning, 2001.

Ali M. EI-Agraa, *International Trade*. New York: St. Martins Press, Inc., 1983

Brenton Paul, *International Trade*. Oxford University Press, 1 997

William G Nickels, James M. McHugh, and Susan M. McHugh, *Understanding Business*, 6th Edition, McGraw-Hill, 2002

Dr. Carl A. Nelson, Import/Export, How to Get Started in International Trade, Liberty House, 1990

Paul R. Krugman and Maurice Obstfeld, *International Economics—Theory and Policy*. 5th Edition, Addison Wesley Longman, Inc. & 清华大学出版社,2002

Ralph H. Folsom, Michael Wallace Gordon, Hohn A Spanogle, Jr., International *Business Transactions in a Nutshell (5th Edition)*, West Publishing Co., 1 996

Edward G Hinkelman, *Dictionary of International Trade*, 4th Edition, California: World Trade Press, 2000

Goldsmith, Howard R., Import/Export, Prentice Hall, 1 989

Hervey Dunn, Kaye Christopher. *International Trade Practice*. London: Sweet & Maxwell Ltd, 2nd edition, 1997.

John H Jackson. *The Role and Effectiveness of the WTO Dispute Settlement Mechanism*. Brookings Trade Forum 2000,179-219

Joseph CKYam. *The WTO: China's Future and Hong Kong's Opportumty*. Cato Journal, 2001, 21(1)

Steven Suranovic. *Evaluating the Controversy Between Free Trade and Protectionism*. http://internafionalecon. com/v1. 0/chl20/120c010. html

Steven Suranovic. *Fairness in International Trade*. CHALLENGE, September 1997